CU00921865

# AN APARTMENT CALLED FREEDOM

# AN APARTMENT CALLED FREEDOM

## A NOVEL

# Ghazi A. Algosaibi

**KEGAN PAUL INTERNATIONAL**
London and New York

First published in Arabic as
*Shakait Al Horaia* (Apartment of Freedom)
in 1994

First published in English in 1996 by
Kegan Paul International
UK: P.O. Box 256, London WC1B 3SW, England
Tel: (0171) 580 5511 Fax: (0171) 436 0899
E-mail: books@keganpau.demon.co.uk
Internet: http://www.demon.co.uk/keganpaul/
USA: 562 West 113th Street, New York, NY 10025, USA
Tel: (212) 666 1000 Fax: (212) 316 3100

Translated by Leslie McLoughlin and edited by the publishers.

Distributed by

John Wiley & Sons Ltd
Southern Cross Trading Estate
1 Oldlands Way, Bognor Regis
West Sussex, PO22 9SA, England
Tel: (01243) 779 777 Fax: (01234) 820 250

Columbia University Press
562 West 113th Street
New York, NY 10025, USA
Tel: (212) 666 1000 Fax: (212) 316 3100

© Ghazi Algosaibi 1994

This translation © Ghazi Algosaibi 1996

Phototypeset in Garamond
by Intype London Ltd
Printed in Great Britain by TJ Press, Padstow, Cornwall

All rights reserved. No part of this book may be reprinted or
reproduced or utilized in any form or by any electronic, mechanical
or other means, now known or hereafter invented, including photocopying
and recording, or in any information storage or retrieval
system, without permission in writing from the publishers.

ISBN 0–7103–0550–8

British Library Cataloguing in Publication Data

Qusaybi, Ghazi 'Abd al-Rahman
An apartment called freedom
1. Arabic fiction – 20th century – Translations into English
2. English fiction – 20th century – Translations from Arabic
I. Title
892.7′36[F]
ISBN 0710305508

Library of Congress Cataloging in Publication Data

Qusaybī, Ghazī 'Abd al-Rahmān.
[Shaqqat al-hurryīyah. English]
An apartment called freedom / Ghazi Algosaibi; translated from
the Arabic by Leslie McLoughlin
p.   cm.
ISBN 0–7103–0550–8
I. McLoughlin, Leslie, 1935– .  II. Title.
PJ7858.U72S513  1996
892′.736–dc20    96–669   CIP

To

Ibrahim Khalil Almoayyed

# Contents

# AUTHOR'S NOTE

The writer was in Cairo in the period with which the novel deals. None the less, all the characters and all the events are the product of his imagination. Furthermore incidents portraying real personalities mentioned in the novel are also fictional. Any attempt to seek out the actuality in this fiction will be a waste of time for the reader.

# CHAPTER ONE

## August 1956

---

His mind was full of questions but he could find no answers. Now the captain of the aircraft was troubling him with another one. Maybe this was the thinking behind the competition, to keep the passengers occupied with one simple question so that they would not be bothered with more questions which could be in their minds. Still, it seemed a bit odd: 'How much fuel is this aircraft carrying?'

Passengers were told that the one who got the correct answer or the nearest to it would receive a prize. The steward passed along, each passenger took a form.

Fuad concentrated. 'How many gallons of fuel does this aircraft carry?' It had never crossed his mind before to wonder. Would it be possible to make an analogy with a car? He knew a car could easily have 20 gallons in the tank but an aircraft was carrying over 100 passengers with all their luggage, some of it very heavy like his own. He smiled as he remembered his baggage: four heavy suitcases apart from his considerable hand baggage. His brother Khalil had said 'Are you going on a trip to the moon? To the North Pole? Why all this luggage?'

But his mother had insisted that he should take with him everything he might need in 'the land of strangers'. Hence the bathroom towels, packets of tea, blocks of toilet paper, tins of biscuits and chocolate, a tiny radio. He smiled as he remembered all these things but then frowned as he imagined himself standing before Customs at Cairo Airport.

He had heard about these Customs officials, how they opened all the luggage and turned everything out, and then they would not let you through until you had paid up. This payment was really perplexing. His brother Nasir had said to him, laughing, 'Just imagine – you're going to Cairo to study law and you'll start your life there with a bribe, something illegal! Can't you just see yourself in a police cell? Do you know what the punishment is for a bribe? A year in gaol, at least.' He laughed.

But it wasn't funny at all; it was really serious. Friends who were old hands in passing through Cairo Airport said that bribery was unavoidable and bribery was a crime. It was true that he had never heard of anyone being arrested at Cairo Airport on a charge but ... who knows? He remembered Nasir cackling on. 'I really don't know how you are going to make out in Cairo, if you drown in a little puddle like that! I just wish I could be there to watch you in action. Immigration. Customs. You'll really get in a mess!'

It seemed like a big joke to his two brothers, but Fuad couldn't see the funny side. After all he was still only sixteen, twenty years younger than Nasir and ten years younger than Khalil. They were used to going abroad but it was his first trip on his own. Up to now there had always been someone older with him to take charge of the arrangements, and to handle the red tape. Even when he had left Bahrain Airport everything had been arranged for him and Nasir had even taken him to the aircraft door. But now he was alone. He now had to rely on himself and to remember that a new phase in his life was beginning. He had become a man who had to face strangers and confront problems as men did.

Foreign parts? Strangers? But, he was going to Cairo: how could Cairo possibly be a place of strangers? Cairo was the capital of the Arabs and the centre of the civilization of Islam. Egypt was God's land. Cairo was the Mother of the Universe, as the Egyptians called it. (Funny, they also called Cairo 'Misr', the word for Egypt, too!) Cairo was Cairo of Gamal Abdul Nasser, of The Voice of the Arabs, of the struggle against Colonialism, it was the city of hope. Cairo represented the nationalization of the Suez Canal. When this came to him every fear disappeared, the worried inner voices were stilled. He felt warmth coursing through his veins. It was only a few weeks since the nationalization and the memory of that historic speech was engraved on his soul. He could still hear ringing in his ears that strong, vibrant voice.

'Decree from the President of the Republic for the nationalization of the Suez Canal Company, an Egyptian joint-stock company.'

The Suez Canal? No, it was The Canal For Getting Rid of Colonialism, The Canal Leading to a Sunlit Tomorrow, which is being made for all the Arabs by the Egyptian Revolution.

And now he was on his way to the Cairo of the Revolution, the Cairo of Gamal Abdul Nasser. His feelings were in turmoil. He would be in the same city as Gamal Abdul Nasser ... Who knows, perhaps he would even one day be on the same street as the President. He might even see him in the flesh, might even shake his hand, or talk to him. Why not!? Had not Gamal Abdul Nasser replied to all the letters which the students had sent him from the secondary school in Bahrain? Had he not sent them a picture of himself if they had asked? The signature was just a rubber stamp but it was the signature. He must have signed the original himself.

Fuad's smile became broader as he recalled Mr Headley, their English language teacher. He would fly into a rage every time Nasser was mentioned, so the students would happily infuriate him by evoking Nasser whenever they could. Mr Headley would come into the classroom and find written on the board 'Long live Gamal Abdul Nasser!' He would then turn to the class. 'I know it would be a waste of time to ask who did this. The writing is ugly, and 'Long live . . .' is not written like that. Then he would sigh and clean the board. But one day he came in and found a picture of Nasser on the wall. Calmly he walked over with the famous coolness of the English, took it off the wall and placed it on the table in front of him. 'The owner of this . . . thing . . . can collect it after I leave.'

One of the students raised his hand. 'Mr Headley, did you hear Gamal Abdul Nasser's speech yesterday? He was speaking for more than three hours!'

'I feel sorry for those who had to listen!'

Another schoolfriend said, 'Look, Mr Headley! A picture of Gamal Abdul Nasser! Would you like to see it?'

'No! No! I know what he looks like and I don't want to see his picture. I thought that sending out pictures was something that only actresses did!'

Then the whole class would enthusiastically debate Nasser and the students would have killed three birds with one stone: they would defend Arab Nationalism; they would annoy their colonialist teacher and the hour would pass.

However these pleasant memories could not make Fuad forget practical considerations. Would anyone meet him at the airport? Where would he meet his friends who had gone ahead of him to Cairo? He did not know their address.

His father had sent a cable the week before to Mr Shareef who would be looking after him in Cairo. Surely Mr Shareef would send someone to meet him if he did not come himself. Anyway Fuad had the address in Dokki. He could go directly there if he had to. As for a place to stay, Mr Shareef would be bound to have arranged something. His Bahraini friends would be in the apartment blocks run by the Islamic Conference, and it would be easy to get the address from Mr Shareef or the Islamic Conference itself. The whole thing would be a breeze.

But in his heart he knew that it was not going to be simple. He imagined himself alone in Cairo with its three million people. How many people did he know there? Ten, at the most. He could see himself wandering lost in quarters of the city that had such weird names. 'Al-Agooza.' What kind of a name was that? He wondered where the name had come from. Had there been an old, grey-haired lady living in that quarter as the translation suggested? Or was it that that was the oldest quarter of Cairo? What was the story behind 'Nawal Street' where Mr Shareef lived? Was there a woman called Nawal? And what about 'Garden City'? How could Gamal Abdul Nasser allow the English name when the colonial era was over?

He thought of how well he knew Cairo before he had even seen it. He had seen the city in films and newspapers and people had told him about it. His Egyptian teachers in the primary and secondary schools had loved talking about Cairo. He had acquired a mass of information. The Andalucia Gardens were the most beautiful in the Middle East. The Zoo was the second biggest in the world after London's. There was an astonishing clock made of flowers in Cairo, a clock that talked. In Helwan there was a Japanese garden the like of which did not exist even in Japan. And as for the capital of Bahrain, you could put it in any one of Cairo's streets. You could hide it in the middle of the Shubra quarter and not be able to find it.

And what about the girls? All as beautiful as film stars, like his favourite, Iman. And they were emancipated like all girls in films and in the stories of Ihsan Abdul-Quddus. In Bahrain a girl from a well-known family had refused to wear the abbaya and this had caused a great uproar. No girls went unveiled in Bahrain except a few Christians and Jews from Iraq. In Cairo they were all unveiled except girls from the country districts and old women. And who wanted *them* to be unveiled? He concentrated on this delicious theme. Would he have his own girlfriend? Would they go together to the Metro Cinema? To the Andalucia Gardens? To the Zoo? How would he find her? The university was co-ed so there should be no problem. But he had a year ahead of him in college before the university and the college was not co-ed. But he might get to know a girl in the residential block or nearby. He had heard that a number of friendships had grown from a smile which had been carried, like a butterfly, across the street, from one balcony to another.

But there was one thing he would never do, and that was to go with prostitutes, no matter how attractive. Some of them were young, nice girls and you could hardly tell them from ordinary girls. But he knew that he could never love a body that could be bought for just a few dirhams. He recalled 'Grandol', the red-light district in Bahrain, one of the most hateful gifts left behind by colonialism, the panic that had seized him a few months ago when one of his friends had suggested they visit one of the houses there. He would have a girlfriend in Cairo but he would never make a friend of a whore.

But he had to address again the problem of the visa. He had none but he hoped he could get an emergency one at the airport and later get his residence permit. Why worry? Mr Shareef would organize 'everything', he had assured his father a number of times. Fuad had known Mr Shareef for three years.

4

He had been headmaster of the secondary school. Everyone said he had been the most energetic headmaster the school had ever known. During his short time in Bahrain he had quickly established solid ties with many people and he had got to know Fuad's father and they had become friends and he had persuaded his father to send Fuad to school in Cairo. But Mr Shareef was very strict. Would he be able to enjoy his stay in Cairo with a supervisor such as he?

Fuad's thoughts were interrupted by the steward asking him if he had filled in his form. He had as he scribbled down '10,000 gallons'. Would he be the winner? And what would be his prize? He decided that he would make the competition the omen for the journey: if he won or was close this would be a sign that all would turn out well; but if he did not win ... then there would be a big hassle with the visa, Customs and where to stay.

'May God open it before your face, my son!' He recalled how his mother had called to God for him as she embraced him in tears before he set out. She repeated her prayer and embraced him again. And for the tenth time she asked him if he had written down that verse from the Holy Koran. 'Dearest one, have you written down the ayya?'

His mother would never let anyone travel unless they had written on the wall the verse from the Noble Koran. 'He who gave you the Holy Koran will return you to your abode.' His mother had an unshakeable faith that anyone who wrote this verse must return home safely from any journey, God willing. This time she had been more insistent than usual and would not be calmed until he had written it three times.

Fuad was astonished that he had been able to part from her: what would his life be like without her smile in the morning and her care throughout the day, the stories she would tell in the evening? The way she doted on him was bantered about at home even by his father who seldom went in for jokes. It seemed to Fuad that his mother's tendency to spoil him increased as he grew older: the favoured, stifled, youngest child. Sometimes he thought that his mother believed he was no more than five years old and never would be, that his height of six feet was no more than a disguise, behind which hid her young child, Fuado, as she would call him.

This journey had created tension between his parents. 'Abu Nasir, how can you let Fuad live by himself in Egypt?'

'Fuad has become a man.'

'A man? He is still a child of thirteen.'

'Woman, is your son getting younger or older? He'll soon be seventeen, or he may already be seventeen. Have you forgotten that I married you when I was younger than he is now?'

'But Abu Nasir ...'

'That's an end of it, he will travel by himself.'

'May God open it before your face, my son!'

Fuad felt reassured: what a beautiful expression that was of his mother's. But: open what? The world. Cairo. Studies. The gateway to the future?

He tried to read the book which had lain neglected at his side but it was impossible to concentrate. His brain buzzed with so much else. He had not slept all night, sleep had never come easily to him. He always had to spend some time on his bed turning restlessly and thinking: for half an hour, sometimes much more. He always envied people who could drop off to sleep as soon as their head touched the pillow: wasn't there anything that worried them? Didn't they have anything to think about?

The pilot was now announcing the result of the competition. The winning number was many times greater than the one he had written down. The prize for the winner was a set of luggage. At this Fuad smiled since the luggage he had was more than enough. Then he became apprehensive since he had decided that the result of the competition would be a kind of omen for the whole journey. He looked at his watch: a few minutes before eight. The plane was making a slow descent and he looked down. He saw the barren, fawn-coloured desert, as far as the eye could see. Where was the Nile? Where were the Pyramids? Where was Garden City. How could the aircraft descend to Cairo without the passengers being able to see the Nile?

The door was opened and an official came aboard, wearing a black uniform and carrying a 'Flit' gun. Before this there had not been a single fly on the aircraft. He strode down the aisle, spraying from his gun and causing sneezes with every squeeze of the Flit. Behind him swarmed clouds of flies which had entered the aircraft with him and which were apparently immune to Flit. The official then disembarked, followed by three more officers in smart uniforms and stern faces. Immediately Fuad began to feel guilty: he had brought a radio with him and there was that visa problem. Also he had concealed in his pocket fifty Egyptian pounds in contravention of currency regulations. He quickly put these thoughts out of his mind and recalled that he had come to a revolutionary country ruled by a revolutionary army. It was battling against dangers imposed by the colonialists. The aircraft bringing him to Egypt had the name of Cyprus on it but it was owned by a British company. These officers, for sure, were the guardians of the revolution against conspiracies being brought in aboard colonialists aircraft. They would not be concerned with his 'tiny' crime. At this thought he began to relax, as the officers moved amongst the passengers, peering into every face. As they came to him he smiled but no one returned his smile. After an interval of staring silently at their faces they allowed the passengers to disembark.

His heart began to race: so this was Cairo, and the start of the great adventure. The first impression that leaped to his mind was that he had never seen an airport as large as this. He had seen the airports at Dhahran, Kuwait,

Beirut and Damascus but none of them was as huge as this. And none had such swelling crowds of people as now engulfed him. Some wore uniforms, some wore ordinary clothes and all were talking at the same time.

He found himself in the queue formed before the passport window and was delighted to see that the officer was smiling and completing each passport within moments. As he found himself before the officer Fuad was planning to explain that he had arrived without a visa because there was no Egyptian Consulate in Bahrain and he wanted to get an emergency visa. Instead he found that he did not dare to speak, and so he handed over his passport to the officer who flicked through the pages twice coldly.

'Where's the visa?'

'I have come from Bahrain . . .'

The officer interrupted him. 'Go back to the end of the queue!'

He obeyed but now found that the line was longer. Half an hour later he found himself before the same officer who again flicked through the pages. This time Fuad burst out, 'There is no visa in the passport because I come from Bahrain and there is no Egyptian Consulate in Bahrain and I have already stood here but you sent me to the back of the queue. I would like an emergency visa. Please.'

It looked as if the officer was about to send him to the back of the queue again until 'Please!' was blurted out with more pleading than Fuad had intended. This had some affect on the officer who looked at him and said, 'Step aside into this room and wait till I have finished with the other passengers.'

The 'room' was no more than an opening with a desk and two chairs. Ten minutes went by, then another ten and another. Fuad began to feel worried. Had they forgotten about him? Would he be refused a visa? Would they send him back? He decided that if anything such as this happened he would send a strongly worded cable of protest to Gamal Abdul Nasser. For sure he would then come down heavily on those who had brought about this. Finally the officer came in, sat at the desk and took the passport from him. He took a stamp from a drawer, marked one of the pages, signing in green ink and handed back the passport, saying 'That's a visa for two weeks. Renew it at the Mugammaa and register at the nearest police station within three days.' He turned away leaving Fuad bewildered: the Mugammaa?! What was that? Where was it? And what's this about registering at the police station? And what exactly would he register? Then it occurred to him that it was impossible that Gamal Abdul Nasser could be aware of these complications which were awaiting his young Arab admirers when they reached Cairo Airport.

He left, was swallowed up by the throngs of people swirling around, and was accosted by someone who had an official air about him.

'Excuse me, where would I find my luggage?'

'At Customs.' Saying this he moved off. Fuad then stopped one of the hawkers.

'Excuse me, where would I find the Customs?'

The peddler looked at him in amazement as he pointed. 'Over there!'

When Fuad turned he was shamed and saw why the peddlar had been startled. At the end of the hall was a sign. CUSTOMS. He found huge wooden counters. Luggage was piled up in the middle of the hall. Passengers took their bags to the nearest counter and waited for an inspector to arrive. But how was Fuad going to carry his cases when he was already struggling with his hand baggage? He rolled and pushed things and assembled them in one place. He paused, breathless and wondered how he would get across to the counter.

He was saved by someone in a crumpled and grubby grey uniform who wore a complacent smile. 'A porter, sir?'

'Yes. Please!'

The porter took two cases and carried them to the counter then came back for the rest. He asked Fuad to follow him. Fuad's heart beat furiously. Please God, all will be well. Please God there will be no problem! The porter went up to one of the inspectors, then in a decisive voice he said, 'This distinguished gentleman is in a great hurry. It would be much appreciated if you could clear his effects quickly!'

With that, the inspector put chalk marks on the bags. It was clear that the porter was in command of the situation. He thanked the inspector, summoned another porter to help him carry the cases and led Fuad outside. Fuad was now bewildered. It must have been that his mother's prayers had been heeded and doors were beginning to open in his face. He realized that this porter was an inestimable treasure which he would have to keep. Stay with me, please, to help me to find the man who is going to meet me. His name is Mr Shareef Hussain. He's short and fat and wears regulation issue spectacles . . .

Rather than listening further the porter shot off into the crowd, calling out 'Mr Shareef Hussain?' The porter looked and enquired everywhere and recruited the services of three of the drink-sellers. He then informed Fuad of what had always been clear. 'There's no one here by the name of Mr Shareef Hussain.'

Fuad asked him to choose a cab for him as there were a score of taxi-drivers pressing around. The porter thereupon chose the oldest, a man who must have been over seventy years, and putting the bags in the boot, said, 'Mahgoob, you have to look after this gentleman. He is an honoured guest among us!'

Before getting in the taxi Fuad anxiously turned to the porter and asked him, 'Please . . . what do I owe you?'

'Five pounds. Two pounds for the work and the rest is baksheesh.'

Fuad put a five-pound note in his hand, generous, too, in his thanks. The porter smiled. 'Not at all, sir. You have honoured us. You are most welcome. You have brought illumination to our country, Egypt.'

In the taxi Fuad's mind was busy with two problems. The first was that he had committed the crime of giving a bribe even though it was true that everything had happened with such speed that there had been no time to think and furthermore, there had been no agreement beforehand. But the fact was that the bribe had been offered and received. Unless, that is, baksheesh was different from bribery. But how was it different? Would they teach him the difference in the Faculty of Law? The second problem was more urgent. Why had Mr Shareef not been there to meet him in the airport? What was he to do now? If he did not find Mr Shareef in his flat, what was he going to do then? He was shaken out of these thoughts by the voice of the taxi-driver, Mahgoob. 'Welcome, you have honoured us, sir. Where is your honour from?'

'From Bahrain.'

'A thousand welcomes. But, saving your presence, just where is Bahrain?'

'Near the Kingdom of Saudi Arabia, on its eastern coast.' The taxi-driver smiled.

'The Kingdom of Saudi Arabia? The Hijaz?! Pray upon the soul of The Prophet Muhammad! Mecca and Medina. O Lord above, promise us.'

Fuad cautiously tried to make some clarification. 'Bahrain is a long way from the Hijaz.'

Geography, however was not enough to destroy the dream which had delighted the ancient driver. 'O Lord above, promise us. Let us come to you, let us visit The Beloved One!'

Fuad fell silent. So did the driver, surrendered to the spiritual rapture which the mention of the Hijaz had aroused. A few minutes later Fuad was taken by surprise.

'Did you know, sir, that the President has nationalized the Suez Canal?'

'Of course, this was a great and historic action.'

The taxi-driver ignored this. 'There will be war you know.'

Fuad was thunderstruck. True the drums of war could be heard everywhere, there were threats being issued all the time and fleets were assembling but surely there would not be a war? The colonialists were too cowardly to go to war with a revolutionary Egypt supported by the entire Arab Nation. 'The English will go to war with us. And the French. But we are not afraid,' the driver went on. He spoke without excitement, as if he were talking about some film. 'And we are not afraid because the Russians are on our side.'

Fuad felt disappointed. He had hoped that this bravery would be rooted in the high morale which Gamal Abdul Nasser had aroused. The driver went on to explain the situation. 'The Russians have missiles, Khruschev said so ...'

Before he could finish Fuad cut in, 'What do you think of Gamal Abdul Nasser?'

'The President? He's as great as Saad. No, Saad Pasha was greater than the President!'

Fuad thought to himself: he's talking about Saad Zaghlul, he's clearly senile. Better change the subject. 'Have we reached Cairo yet?'

'No, sir, this is Heliopolis.' Before Fuad could gaze at the broad streets and magnificent villas he was interrupted. 'What will you be doing here, sir?'

'I'll be a student.'

'Which college?'

'Law.' Fuad felt a slight pricking of his conscience as he told this lie. He was afraid that Mahgoob the driver would have had a shock if he had learned that this passenger discussing international politics had not yet finished high school.

The scene outside changed very quickly, with Mahgoob explaining where they were: Abbasiyya, Bab Al Hadid, Tahrir Square. The Nile! And then the suburb of Dokki where he waited in vain for a long time at the apartment of Mr Shareef, ringing the bell. He asked Mahgoob to take him to a phone and they went to a nearby grocery. The two of them looked up the phone number of Mr Shareef. When Fuad dialled, though, no one replied.

Fuad, now alarmed asked Mahgoob to take him to the headquarters of the Islamic Conference where he hoped he might find the address of his friends. But Mahgoob did not know where the Conference was and they wasted more than an hour. Eventually they reached a beautiful villa with a luxuriant garden in Zamalek but found no one there except for a watchman who told them that work had finished for the day. Suddenly, Fuad felt hungry. It was past three o'clock but he did not want to eat until he knew where he could stay. He asked Mahgoob to take him back to Mr Shareef's apartment and he rang the bell again and waited. After a while a servant came out of the apartment opposite and told him that Shareef had left for Alexandria a month before, but she did not know his address there or when he would be returning.

Mahgoob had the answer. 'I know a boarding-house in Zamalek, really comfortable. It's "Horus House", all the boarders are good class people but it isn't expensive. What do you say, sir, shall I take you there?'

On the way there they stopped to have a bean sandwich. It was more delicious than any other sandwich he had ever had and Mahgoob insisted on paying. 'You are our guest, sir. And when God fulfils his promise and we visit the Hijaz we'll be your guest there.'

When he reached Horus House Fuad felt overwhelming gratitude towards Mahgoob, and paid him double the amount on the meter, asking him to pick him up the following morning. He was met by an elderly woman who spoke Arabic with a Greek accent. 'Which embassy are you from?'

Fuad stammered as he explained that he was not from an embassy at all but had come to study.

At this she said sharply, 'Well, who sent you here?'

'The taxi-driver brought me.'

'It's a pound a day for the room and meals. Oh, and a week's rent in advance, if you please.'

Fuad had the feeling that the woman had never had a student stay at her 'pension' before and that her principle of paying a week in advance had just been invented. The woman took him to his room, which was spacious and light, and while his luggage was being brought up she began to recite her rules as if she were reading them from a text.

'Dinner is from 6 to 8, and breakfast from 7 to 9. Lunch from 1 to 3. Sorry, no meals in rooms. Sorry, no leaving your room in pyjamas. Sorry, no smoking on the balcony. Sorry, guests only in the drawing room. Sorry . . .'

When Madame Tanya eventually left him in his room he felt deeply depressed. He felt crushed by loneliness. He began to feel that this vast and beautiful city was no more than a terrifying vacuum and longed for his mother and his home in Bahrain. Maybe he had made the biggest mistake in his life in abandoning his family and coming to Cairo? Surely there must be some alternative? He felt panic and wept. With embarrassment Fuad tried to wipe the tears away. He went to Madame Tanya and asked her to direct him to the nearest road leading to the Nile. She led him to the balcony and showed him the way: there were only two streets between him and the river. On the way there Fuad stopped to buy cigarettes: he had experimented with smoking once or twice in secondary school but unlike most of his friends had not become addicted. But now he felt that the situation had changed and called for smoking. He had become a man who would face the problems men faced in the masculine way. Have a cigarette and things would clear up . . .

He felt slightly dizzy as he took the first deep pull but this soon passed and he sat down on the stone seat, contemplating the eternal river, whose waters were a dull grey, quite different from pale clear green he had imagined. The fancy came to him that what had made the waters this dull grey colour was the accumulation of sadnesses in the heart of the Nile through the ages. The river was very much broader than he had thought and life on it was frenzied. All shapes and sizes of boats and ships constantly came and went. He felt that he had blended into history, as if he were sitting not near to a river but on the threshold of a civilization. And now, as the streaks of cloud at dusk took clear shape after the sun had set, the waters were transformed from grey to crimson. At this he felt a curious and profound reassurance overwhelm him, dispelling his loneliness. Nonetheless, he walked back with heavy steps to the pension that night.

At breakfast Fuad got to know his eight fellow-lodgers. There were two Americans from the Embassy, staying at the pension till they could find suitable housing. Three Afghans were in Cairo to supervise an exhibition which Afghanistan was staging. There were also two Swiss businessmen who were there to discuss a new hotel project with the Egyptian Government. An elderly Greek lived there permanently and had done so for the last 20 years. He addressed no word to anyone and no one spoke to him. Fuad had never met an Afghan before and doubted whether they had ever met anyone from Bahrain either. There were lots of questions exchanged and finally got to the question which had been puzzling him. 'What has Afghanistan to exhibit in Cairo?'

'Lots of things. There are Afghan rugs which are every bit as good as Persian carpets. Then there is dried fruit. Many kinds of textiles. Why don't you visit the exhibition, it's here in Zamalek, in the Afghan Embassy.' The leader of the delegation replied enthusiastically.

Then one of the Swiss began to complain. 'We've been two weeks here in Cairo and haven't found anyone to discuss the hotel with. They pass us on from one department to another, from one Ministry to another. Our company is asking us to go back home but how can we go home without talking to anyone at all?'

One of the Americans replied. 'That's Egyptian bureaucracy for you. Didn't you ever hear of it? The Egyptians are the ones who invented it. Good luck to you! Building your hotel will take longer than it took to build the Pyramids.' The American laughed at this but Fuad felt annoyed: if foreigners didn't like the situation in Egypt then why did they come? Why not build their hotels in Switzerland or America? They come to exploit us and then make fun of us.

After breakfast Mahgoob welcomed him warmly. 'The top of the morning to you, young Mister Fuad! Where are we going, if God wills?'

Fuad explained to him that he had to sign on at the nearest police station, which Mahgoob decided meant the one at Boulaq. As this was the first time Fuad had ever been in a police station he was amazed. There were people arguing furiously, and in floods of tears, women hanging on desperately to the necks of their husbands, small children who were under arrest: dozens of people in one narrow room, like a rabbit's bolt hole. When they eventually got to the policeman in charge and explained why they were there he told them that the pension was not in his area. Mahgoob then put in some concentrated thought and decided that the station they needed was in Al-Agouza. But there they went through the same performance again, as they did in a third station, then a fourth. Fuad became fed up and told Mahgoob to take him to the Islamic Conference head office. 'If you wouldn't mind I'd like the address of the Bahrain students who are studying on scholarships from the Islamic Conference.'

'I beg your pardon, sir?' The official had never heard of any such students, but made a number of phone calls, without success. 'You must be mistaken, sir!'

Fuad stressed that he was sure of his facts and was sure that the Islamic Conference rented a number of buildings in Cairo where it housed students from all over the world, including the Bahrain students. The official then made more calls and finally said. 'Enquire in the Eastern Students' section at the Ministry of Education.'

What's this?! Was he looking for students from China or Japan? Nonetheless Fuad went from office to office, enquiring politely. But everywhere he met the same astonished looks as no one had ever heard of his fellow-students until one of the officials volunteered that it might be a good idea to contact the educational missions section. This was miles away. Once again he was referred somewhere else, this time back to the Islamic Conference. The official in the enquiry office was cool as he received him again. But he made some more phone calls.

'You should go to the International Relations department in the Conference. It's not far but you'll have to see them tomorrow as work is finished for the day.'

Fuad was angry as he returned to the pension: he had wasted several hours and had been able neither to register nor to find his friends. He was explaining to the landlady what had happened when the annoying American cut in. 'Didn't I just tell you? That's Egyptian bureaucracy for you. Getting your passport registered will take longer than it took to build the Pyramids.'

This was clearly the only joke he knew. But it was one which got worse with repetition. Fuad looked over at him furiously but made no reply. The landlady then offered to solve the problem since she regularly sent her guests' passports to the police station as this was the responsibility of the hotel or guest house not the visitor. At this Fuad felt a great burden lifted from him: he did not want to begin his life in Cairo in breach of the law. But as evening came on the loneliness came back. He could see, though, that the best way to express his feelings was to write letters to his relatives and started by writing a long letter to his father. He then wrote a longer letter to his mother and separate letters to Nasir and Khalil so that by the time he had finished it was nearly midnight and some part of his homesickness had gone. Before he slept he decided that he must find his friends tomorrow.

He had got to know his friends from the age of six in the First Year Kindergarten. They had stayed together, year after year, right the way through to studies in Cairo. Abdul-Karim, Yacoub and Qasim. Abdul-Karim was from a very old and religious family and both his father and grandfather had been

religious sheikhs, as had their fathers before them for at least seven gener-
ations. In fact one of Abdul-Karim's ancestors had been regarded as a holy
man and there was a shrine to him in Bahrain which ordinary people visited.
It was especially favoured by women who wanted to have children and
Abdul-Karim would receive with a proud smile sarcastic comments about
how virile his ancestor was, even in death. Abdul-Karim was good natured,
to the point of naivety, was generous to the point of foolishness and extremely
loyal to his friends. On the other hand his moods were changeable so that
you could find him happy and laughing but then suddenly he would be
overtaken by a wave of depression that would last for days. Often his
depression would be linked to suspicion and misgivings as well as hypochon-
dria. Abdul-Karim would suffer from a new ailment and would have sleepless
nights filled with the fear of death. He would lose confidence in any doctor
who told him that he was perfectly fit. Abdul-Karim endured profound
conflict since his religious upbringing had inclined him to be calm and peace-
able but at the same time had given him a desire to reject authority. This
paradox would burst out from time to time, terrible in its fierceness. He had
begun his revolt when he had refused to study the religious sciences in Nejef,
as his father had wanted. He had persisted by deciding that he wanted to
study law in Cairo, in spite of the opposition of the sheikh who objected
to laws that were not based on God's law. But Abdul-Karim had insisted
stubbornly. His father eventually agreed.

Yacoub was a different personality and from a very poor family and who
in the beginning had had a very hard life. He had been born with an inexhaust-
ible capacity for anger, which would end in a raging revolt and a desire to
blow up society in its entirety. He would never tire of taking up issues and
never weary of changing them. He loved books and newspapers and was
easily influenced. He once read something about the Sufis and locked himself
away in the mosque. Epicurus, however, led him to savour culinary pleasures
whereas Descartes inclined him towards scepticism. Gamal Abdul Nasser
steered him into Arab nationalism so he would embrace every view with total
conviction. He would embrace some opposing view and defend that with the
same enthusiasm. His main objective remained one of revolt, that of uprooting
the old society and establishing the new one which would be as different
as the current theory. Yacoub had many gifts; he was very good at drawing,
singing, poetry and oratory.

Qasim was the opposite as his father came from a family of *nouveaux
riches*. He had begun life as a labourer in BAPCO, the oil company. But he
became a self-made millionaire. Qasim had imbibed the principles of capitalism
with his mother's milk, so, ironically he was the only one in his school, and
maybe in all Bahrain's schools, who actually hated the son of the postman.
Qasim could not agree that it was possible that the son of a postman could

lead a society in a way better than a king and the son of a king. Qasim thought socialist doctrines were nothing more than hatreds felt by suppressed and depressed lower-class people. The division of the world into rich and poor was a natural order. Qasim was a powerful debater who made no attempt to conceal his views. His friends were apprehensive about the fate that awaited this young reactionary in Egypt at the time. Qasim was the only one among them who spoke fluent English and tuned into the BBC, read *Time* and *Newsweek*. He had wanted to study in the USA but his father had rejected the idea and had decided to send him to Egypt. Qasim wanted to finish his Commerce studies so that he could begin his 'real' work in America.

Fuad often wondered how it was that such a deep friendship was possible between people who were so different. The only conclusion he could arrive at was that each one in the little group complemented the others. The revolutionary fervour of Yacoub was a complement to Qasim's reactionary spirit while Qasim's readiness to rush headlong was a counter to the relaxed spirit of Abdul-Karim. But what of himself? Fuad pictured himself as an amazing mixture of the personalities of his friends, concocted by a wicked pharmacist. He had taken from Yacoub a little of his revolutionary fervour and from Qasim he had snatched something of a staider spirit of conservatism, and Abdul-Karim had lent him some of his apprehension and hesitation.

He made his way to the International Relations section, expecting repetitions of the same boredom of yesterday. But the third official he spoke to gave him a list of all the students who were on scholarships from the Conference. Within minutes he had found the names of his friends and rushing out to the car he told Mahgoob to take him to their address, an apartment building at Bab Al Khalq square.

It was only two weeks since he had parted from his friends but he felt that he had not seen them for years. The first one he saw was Yacoub who told him that Abdul-Karim and Qasim would be back soon. Yacoub suggested they go along to the Kasr El Nil Casino for lunch to celebrate the reunion. An hour after lunch the four were together at a table almost lapped by the waters of the Nile. They never stopped talking for one single second and Fuad was particularly keen to hear the latest news of his friends, while each one of them was eager to tell his part of the story.

Qasim started it by criticizing Cairo in both general and detail: its streets were filthy and its citizens went around in their pyjamas. Its atmosphere was unbearable. (Qasim had forgotten that it was much hotter in Bahrain.) No one could speak English properly and *Newsweek* and *Time* were censored. The BBC could only be picked up with difficulty from Cyprus, Al-Sharq Al-Adna, could not be heard at all because of the same interference. As for Egyptian food, it was inedible. But it was the accommodation that caused Qasim to really boil over with rage: he could not stay any longer. How could three students live in one small room? What about the germs and infections? Finally Qasim proclaimed that at the earliest opportunity he would be moving into an apartment. Those who wanted to go with him should pack their bags and follow. As for the rest, good luck to them!

Yacoub spoke. The building in which they were living was only a few yards from the Egyptian National Library which contained over half a million books and Yacoub would spend many hours a day there and then much of the night. He had found a collection of Tolstoy, translated into Arabic. He had now arrived at his final intellectual resort and would become a devotee of Tolstoy for ever: he even proclaimed that if the only benefit he derived from Cairo was studying Tolstoy it would be sufficient. He suggested that Fuad should do the same. Fuad promised that he would think about it.

Abdul-Karim did not have anything new or sensational to report: he had spent most of his time since arriving in Cairo engaged on arranging his studies and accommodation. This meant being shuffled from one department to another. That was just like Abdul-Karim: while Qasim gave himself entirely up to criticism and Yacoub to Tolstoy. So Abdul-Karim was landed with all the tedious work. Abdul-Karim accepted the situation without a murmur and set out on his paper-chase, cajoling the officials and filling in the forms.

The friends talked until just before sunset and then walked by the Nile. Qasim suggested they had their supper at the Auberge. He was the only person to have heard of this restaurant, but no one agreed. Yacoub then proposed they spend the rest of the evening in their flat debating Tolstoy's thinking. This brought jeers and derision. Eventually they agreed to go to supper at 'Al-tabi' ee Al-Dumyati' which was the most famous restaurant in all Cairo for dishes of beans and taamiyya. As the sun set the friends were strolling along the Corniche, their laughter echoing from bank to bank.

A week after Fuad had reached Cairo Mr Shareef returned from Alexandria. He had not received the cable and had not expected that Fuad would arrive so soon. He was abject. Immediately they began to seek an accommodation and Fuad shyly put forward Qasim's suggestion of moving into an apartment. At first Mr Shareef rejected this idea giving all kinds of complicated reasons but Fuad believed the real reason was that he was afraid of anyone having freedom. Mr Shareef decided that the best solution would be for Fuad to stay with a family which would treat him as one of their own sons, deal with all the domestic chores such as cooking and laundry so that Fuad could be free to study. Qasim decided that he would join him so as to escape from the chicken coop. But Abdul-Karim and Yacoub decided that their chicken-coop afforded them a freedom not to be found with living with a family.

But finding a suitable family was more difficult than Mr Shareef had imagined and they spent whole weeks, going from one family to another.

With each family he found some fault: this one had too many children to allow of studying; that family was foreign and had different customs; there were adolescent daughters in some families; this family lived too far from the centre of town; that wife was a terrible flirt. Fuad was beginning to despair when Mr Shareef announced that he had found a suitable place to stay. It was run by a divorced lady who let four rooms to students and gave all her time to ensuring their comfort. Her charges for full board and all expenses were quite reasonable.

Fuad endured a long lecture from Mr Shareef on the value of money. Thus he was learning that Mr Shareef had done a deal with his father. He would have 25 pounds a month, which meant that he would have 10 pounds over each month. He explained that this was a huge sum for a student of his age, and he must beware of taking taxis ('Goodbye, old Mahgoob!') and frequenting restaurants. Fuad smiled to himself as he listened to the lecture since his mother had promised that she would send him secret sums of money from time to time, via someone travelling from Bahrain, but neither his father nor Mr Shareef would know a thing about this.

The next morning Fuad brought his luggage to Mrs Khairiyya's place on Masaha Street. Everyone called it Abdul-Moneim Street. The apartment was on the fourth floor with no lift, but Mr Shareef explained that this was a great advantage since it meant compulsory exercise every day. Mrs Khairiyya, a lady of fairly stout build, received him wreathed in smiles and gave him a great hug as if she had known him for years. Fuad was introduced to his two fellow-residents, Adnan a Jordanian student doing engineering and Majeed an Iraqi reading history, both of them at Cairo University. As soon as Qasim arrived he engaged in heated debate with Adnan who had criticized King Hussain. While the Bahrain student stood heroically to his defence, the others merely relaxed and enjoyed it.

# CHAPTER TWO

## October – November 1956

The friends were split up in their studies. They had been for accommodation, Abdul-Karim and Yacoub going to the Khedivial School, being known as trouble-makers. While Fuad and Qasim went to Mr Shareef, tired with a long discourse on the Saeediyya School which was, in his view, the best school in Egypt. He explained that in the era of the Monarchy most of the Ministers had studied at the Saeediyya School from whence they transferred to the nearby Faculty of Laws. From that Faculty they would graduate as lawyers and then almost certainly become Ministers. The head of the Saeediyya was a close friend of his, Mr Abdul-Aziz Shukry Bey, and he had entrusted Fuad to his special care . . . only he had not done that . . .

During one history lesson, Fuad's favourite class, a messenger knocked on the classroom door and roared, 'Fuad Tarif is wanted by the Headmaster.'

All the boys were plunged into alarm and the eyes of the teacher opened wide: the Headmaster had never asked to see a pupil like this before.

'On your feet, Fuad, and may God go with you.'

His heart beat furiously: what had he done so wrong that the Headmaster should summon him? Fuad chased the messenger, 'Do you know why the Headmaster has sent for me?'

'No.'

A few minutes later they reached a small room and the messenger indicated the door. 'That's the way into the secretary's office.'

Fuad went in and greeted the male secretary politely. He replied with concealed irritation and then indicated where Fuad should sit down until the Headmaster was ready. The long wait made Fuad increasingly anxious. Then he heard a bell ring and the secretary indicated a door. 'This way. The Headmaster is waiting for you.'

Fuad registered the enormity of the room. He had never seen an office so huge. Abdul-Aziz Shukry Bey was a man of slender build, with greying hair who was almost hidden in his huge chair. Piles of papers almost obscured him.

'Welcome, my son, welcome.'

The Headmaster rose and shook Fuad's hand. This baffled him since no teacher working here shook hands with pupils. The Headmaster went on, but Fuad was still startled by the head-teacher's behaviour.

'Shereef Bey has recommended you to me. If you need anything, you have only to ask. You are most welcome.'

It was now clear that the interview was over. Fuad managed to stammer 'Thank you Sir.' He made his way back to find the history class was over and that Mr Yusri's English lesson had begun. He tapped on the door and Mr Yusri's reply neatly expressed a mutual disdain. 'Why is your honour late? Is this the custom of the great men of Bahrain?'

Fuad replied with unconcealed pleasure, 'I was with the Headmaster.'

The teacher flung him a glance which suggested that he thought he was a fool or a liar. But all the other pupils asserted that what he was saying was true. Then Yusri allowed him to enter. Afterwards all the pupils bombarded Fuad with questions and comments.

'Did you really see the Headmaster?'

'What does he look like?'

'Just your luck! There's no one can touch you.'

'The Headmaster is losing his grip!'

'Were you frightened?'

Fuad explained that the interview was over in a few seconds. He realized that none of his schoolmates or teachers would forget that he was the only pupil to be sent for by the Headmaster.

This was his eighth week in the school and his tenth in Cairo. After the crushing homesickness he had suffered earlier things had begun to settle down and he now had a daily routine. He would wake at 6, have breakfast at 7 and would walk to school or take the bus. He would be back at 3 for lunch and then take a siesta and in the late afternoon he would read and do homework. He would talk politics with the other student boarders then they would have their evening meal and he would listen to the news, followed by 'The Voice of the Arabs' from Cairo. Normally he would be in bed by 11 p.m. But Thursdays were different.

Either Yacoub and Abdul-Karim would come to his place or they would all meet at the Islamic Conference apartment block. Then they would have dinner overlooking the Nile, usually at 'The Casino of the Tree' before seeing a movie and chattering afterwards. Cairo was now familiar, its streets and squares, buses, cafés seemed safe. He had begun to feel warm towards everyone and had concluded that no one in Cairo was without a good heart or a sense of humour, at least.

The Saeediyya School, with its huge buildings and 2,000 pupils, its teachers, was vast and initially fearsome. Fuad had early problems with Arabic. Mr Sarhan accused him of copying the subject of the essay. Fuad was furious and would not calm down while Mr Sarhan would not be convinced that Fuad was the real author of the essay. Eventually Fuad brought him cuttings from the Bahrain press which gave his credence as a writer: he had written four short stories and five articles. Then Sarhan gave him special attention so that he became in effect the teacher's assistant during the Arabic lesson.

Fuad truly admired Professor Murad, who taught Philosophy and Logic. Murad was able to illuminate and simplify complex matters for his students. He was also able to inspire and interest. But with the English teacher LORD Yusri, as the students secretly called him, Fuad's relationship was dreadful. The teacher always referred to Fuad as 'The lad from Bahrain' and would seize every chance to make fun of him. Fuad was at a loss to understand this until some of his friends pointed out that the reason was the way he pronounced English words which he had learned from Mr Headley and which was quite different from Lord Yusri's. His relationships with other teachers were neutral. Most had personalities which aroused neither hatred nor affection. But his favourite was Mr Rif'at. Fuad had chosen history as his speciality for the school leaving certificate and this had turned out delightfully well. When the history lesson ended the students would be as exhilarated as if they had been watching marvellous scenes from a play. The teacher had begun the syllabus with Louis XVI of France and had gone through the events of the Revolution, day by day, taking the students to Louis' bedchamber, to the boudoir of Marie Antoinette, to the bread riots and to the storming of the Bastille. The students would look forward to the next lesson as if they were waiting for a new episode of an adventure film.

The main problem facing Fuad when he met another student in school was that no one had heard of Bahrain. The boys would look curious but what made things even more amazing for them was learning of his father's occupation. Fuad would tell anyone who asked that his father sold jewellery. The look he got showed that his listener clearly imagined a store filled with great piles of diamond necklaces and heaps of emeralds. How could Fuad explain that his father's little store amongst the traders' stalls in Manama produced just enough to feed a family and did not yield millions? Not even tens of thousands. How could he convince his listeners that there was not a single diamond necklace or emerald and that his father's wares were mostly gold bracelets and cheap pearl rings, the sad remainders of the old pearling industry?

Abdul-Karim began to be aware for the first time that he was a Shia. In Bahrain half the people in his part of the town had been Sunni and half Shia, just as it was in school, in the souq and everywhere else. This was just part of the pattern of life: the Sunnis were Sunnis or Arabs and the Shia were Shia or Baharina. There would be occasional clashes between Sunni and Shia, especially at the processions of Ashoura, but things would soon get back to normal. Banter between friends would sometimes degenerate into a scrap but again this was a part of life. But now here in Cairo Abdul-Karim was beginning to face a problem he had never thought about before, that of minorities.

The story began in the Khedivial School with the Arabic teacher when, in talking about a poem he made a slighting reference to the Shia, whom he called the Rejectionists. Afterwards Abdul-Karim made a polite protest. Mr Hussain, whom everyone called Sheikh Hussain because he was an Al-Azhar graduate, was surprised to find that one of his students was a Shia. So surprised that he asked Abdul-Karim to come back when there was more time so that they could discuss the matter more fully. The 'discussion' took the form of a flood of questions.

'How can you believe that the Mahdi is still alive after more than 1,000 years?'

'Do you still wait for him at the Bab Al-Sardab in Samarra?'

'Do you have a Koran that is different from the Sunnis'?'

'What is the difference between a Mut'a marriage and a fornication?'

'Why do you not recognize the Traditions of the Sunna?'

'Why do you not pray with the Sunna?'

'Why do you hate the Sunna?'

Although Abdul-Karim had grown up in the house of one of the leading Shia sheikhs in Bahrain he had never been questioned like this in his life. The principles of religious law and thought as taught by his father were clear and simple. The Shia were the supporters of the claims of the Imam Ali and his sons and hated all who were hostile to him and to his sons. He could not recall that his father had ever said a harsh word about any of the first four Caliphs, although his mother loved to insult the Caliph Omar. The Mahdi was still alive because God was capable of all things. He had never heard about the Mahdi appearing from the Bab Al-Sardab in Samarra. Nor had he heard of the Shia having a different Koran from the Sunnis. As for the Mut'a marriage this was something known and acknowledged by all Muslims until it was forbidden by the second Caliph. The traditions of the Shia were taken from the Imams who were of the Prophet's household: if there was any problem it was with the traditions of the Sunnis. As for praying with the Sunnis this had never been suggested. In Bahrain the Shia prayed in Shia mosques and the Sunnis in theirs and that was all there was to it. He had no hatred for Sunnis – his closest friends were Sunnis.

The dialogue going on between Abdul-Karim and Sheikh Hussain caught the attention of other students who began to take a special interest in this fellow who belonged to a sect that most of them had never even heard of, apart from the famous insult, 'You son of a Rejectionist!' Things almost reached the point of interrogation until one day Yacoub burst out, 'Give up with these stupid questions Sunnis and Shia! It is just divisiveness encouraged by the imperialists, a plot to divide the Arab nation! We are all Arabs and all Muslims. The British in Bahrain tried to stir up trouble between us through this separatist talk but we managed to foil them.'

This mention of an imperialist plot just after the nationalization of the Canal, and in Cairo at that, found a ready welcome and the result was that the students' curiosity about the Shia lessened. Even Sheikh Hussain's questions dried up. But still Abdul-Karim found many irritating questions bothering him. 'Is a Shia then so different from a Sunni?' 'Do the Sunnis hate Shias?' And most seriously, 'Can a Shia live in safety among the Sunnis?'

As for Qasim, his views after he arrived in Cairo were just as hostile to the revolution and the revolutionaries as they had ever been. He began, in spite of himself, to feel a growing affection towards the Egyptians he had dealings with but his attitude to Gamal Abdul Nasser and his officers did not change. In his first week at the Saeediyya School he got to know a classmate, Nash'at and they immediately formed a very strong friendship. It did not take a genius to see why since Nash'at was from a well-known aristocratic family and his father had been Minister of the Interior in several governments under the Monarchy. In addition he had been a Pasha, before the order banning the use of such titles. Qasim regarded this as one of the many crimes of the revolution. There was a complete sympathy between the son of a rising aristocrat from Bahrain and the scion of a declining aristocratic family in Egypt.

What was happening in Egypt gradually became clear to Qasim, through his talks with Nash'at. Nash'at told him of the truth which was getting lost in propaganda, of the tens of thousands of citizens who were being tortured in detention camps, about the tentacles of the intelligence apparatus reaching everywhere; about the fictitious plot attributed to the Muslim Brotherhood and which gave the regime a pretext for eliminating the Brotherhood; about the officers who now formed a new 'royal family' whose privileges and authority far exceeded those of the old rulers. Nash'at made clear to him that corruption in the days of the monarchy was as nothing to the corruption prevailing now. This was ammunition to be stored in Qasim's arsenal, and important ammo since it came from the son of a man who was Interior Minister and knew the inside story.

It made Qasim enraged that none of his friends shared his views. When he spoke to Fuad about the detention camps and what went on in them Fuad said (in English, to annoy him) 'So what?'

Qasim, when he tried to appeal to his natural sense of justice, surprised Fuad by giving a lengthy and noisy explanation. 'Qasim, when will you ever understand? When will you learn? There's a revolution going on here, one regime has taken the place of another. It's a battle, political, social and economic. Do you expect this is going to happen without some violence? Without detention camps? Without intelligence people? And who are these people in detention? Reactionaries, traitors and spies. It does not matter if 1,000 or even 2,000 people are arrested so long as the fate and freedom of an entire people is at stake.'

When Qasim tried to find a more attentive ear with Abdul-Karim he failed. Abdul-Karim simply shrugged. 'There are prisons and intelligence departments everywhere.'

Qasim never stopped wondering at these friends of his, clever, well-educated people who had been so brainwashed by Ahmad Sa'id that he had made them believe anything.

A terrible wave of hatred and rancour seethed in Yacoub's breast. He felt that he, personally, was experiencing all the torments that the Arab nation was suffering because of the machinations of imperialism. Their attacks had never ceased, not since the days of the Crusaders. They had attacked the Arabs with armies and with conspiracies, with spies and hirelings. The imperialists had managed to infiltrate into every part of the Arab world and had divided the nation into statelets and provinces through the Sykes–Picot treaty, releasing the spoils to their lackeys. And this was not enough for them: they had brought Israel into being and planted it right in the heart of the Arab world so as to ensure its division for ever. It seemed as if their plot had succeeded and that the Arab nation would remain a preserve of the imperialists and their hirelings.

But suddenly there was an event which no one had anticipated. A swarthy figure, called Gamal Abdul Nasser foiled all their plans and destroyed all their neat equations. Suddenly there had appeared a man of nationalist aspirations who had not come to power by inheritance or by the force of British bayonets. A man had arrived and with him had come a new world. The hopes of Arabs everywhere were now centred on this knightly figure. There was a series of victories: the evacuation of British forces from Egypt, the breach of the arms supply monopoly, Positive Neutrality, the High Dam, and finally the nationalization of the Suez Canal. The Arab nation had revealed a tremendous capacity for struggle, a capacity which had been lying dormant, and now it was surging forward.

And suddenly Israel was attacking Egypt. And before anyone could realize the truth of what was happening and before the heroic Egyptian army could punish the Israelis, the British and French had issued their joint warning. But the heroic Nasser would not capitulate.

British and French aircraft began the bombing of Cairo and paratroopers landed at Port Said. The despicable Tripartite Aggression stood revealed. Yacoub's anger intensified. How could he get to Port Said and kill the first British or French paratrooper he saw? How could he perform his duty in this decisive hour in the history of the Arab struggle?

Yacoub decided to volunteer but he did not know how. He set out for the police station at Bab Al-Khalq where the policeman on duty listened in astonishment to this young man from Bahrain demanding immediate admission to the Egyptian Army. He explained to him that this matter was not one for the police and advised him to make for the Army barracks in Abbasiyya. Qasim leaped into the first taxi and set off for the barracks where he explained what he wanted to the guards at the gate. They too looked astonished and contacted the Orderly Officer, a man with highly-polished stars on his shoulders. After he had listened to Yacoub he said, 'Go home, son, that would be best.'

Yacoub left the barracks boiling with rage: go home while the battle was at its height? While The Voice of the Arabs was calling on Arabs everywhere to fight? While Gamal Abdul Nasser, from the Al-Azhar mosque, was proclaiming, 'We shall fight on! Fight on!'

Yacoub rushed off to the Islamic Conference building and asked for a personal interview with Anwar Sadat, the General Secretary. The official in the enquiry office was disturbed by his request. The official then referred him to another official, who did the same, until eventually Yacoub found himself with one of Sadat's aides. Now for the first time since the morning Yacoub had found an official who could understand revolutionary students.

'In the name of Anwar Sadat I thank you. And in the name of Egypt. But how old are you, son?'

'Nineteen.' Yacoub had only added one year...

'Have you ever had any experience with weapons?'

Yacoub was amazed at this basic question. 'No,' he admitted.

'Any previous military training?'

'No.'

The official tried to explain to him that the country was at war and there was not enough time to train volunteers. Eventually they agreed on a compromise: Yacoub should join the Popular Resistance in his neighbourhood. It needed a number of phone calls to arrange this but at last the official told him that the committee of the Popular Resistance in Bab Al-Khalq was waiting for him.

Here Yacoub found a large number of university students. He was the only non-Egyptian among the volunteers. His colleagues in the Resistance welcomed this volunteer coming from an Arab country they had never heard of. He put on his khaki uniform – they even pronounced 'khaki' differently here from Bahrain! – and agreed with the commander of the group that his patrol would begin after sunset. The instructions for the group were very simple: to warn everyone to conceal lights during air raids, to help any citizen who needed it and take note of any suspicious activities. These routine actions were not enough to sate Yacoub's raging thirst to kill but this was the most he could get. When he got back to the apartment block he was bursting with pride and strutted about as his colleagues eyed his uniform, both puzzled and envious.

Fuad experienced the period of the Suez fighting like a troubled but oddly exhilarating dream. The spirit of resistance and steadfastness could be clearly seen everywhere yet everyday life went on naturally, with scant attention paid to the bombardment. Patriotic songs gave explosive expression to the enthusiasm in people's hearts:

'God is Great! He rises above all the wiles of the aggressor!'

'Leave our sky alone because our skies are a place of burning!'

'O, my weapons! By God! It has been a long time!'

Unlike Yacoub who felt that he must personally take part in the fighting, Fuad felt that he had become an integral part of the battle going on, from the spirit of steadfastness, from everyday normal life and from the inflammatory broadcasts in public squares.

1 November 1956.

At 11.02 a.m. on that day, in Opera Square, Fuad saw Gamal Abdul Nasser. This was no cinema newsreel, no picture or magazine cover, this was Gamal Abdul Nasser in the flesh! He was standing up in an open car addressing the crowds, his broad smile lighting things like the sun. Fuad was seized by a shivering feeling, but one of happiness, because this was his hero standing in front of him, smiling just as the aircraft of the criminals were bombarding the broadcasting stations and the airports and maybe even Nasser's home in Manshiet El Bekri. He was smiling just when the Tripartite Aggression was at its height. He was standing there, smiling in an open car, unafraid of the bullets of assassins. Was this the behaviour of a dictator? In the whole of history had there ever existed a dictator who would mingle with his people in this way, without guards, at the very height of a battle? He was almost ready to hit Qasim who at the very climax of this historic moment could only ask 'Why is he riding in a Cadillac if he is one of the popular leaders?'

What a stupid creature he is, this Qasim. In this drama can he only have eyes for the make of the car that Gamal Abdul Nasser is using? Fuad kept his contempt to himself.

Qasim kept trying to spoil Fuad's dream of nationalist fervour with bits of information which he would bring in each day but which Fuad knew came from the son of the Pasha. Qasim insisted that the British and French aircraft had destroyed every one of the Egyptian aircraft and that news broadcast by Egyptian radio that they had only destroyed wooden decoys was rubbish. Qasim said that the British and French forces occupied Port Said within hours and that all the talk about heroic popular resistance was pure lies manufactured by the German experts employed by The Voice of the Arabs who had been trained by Goebbels. Every day Qasim would come along with more malicious rumours: an imminent military coup; the return of Nahas Pasha; the suicide of Gamal Abdul Nasser. When the cease-fire was announced Qasim said that Nasser was about to escape from Cairo and he had only been saved from death by President Eisenhower.

Fuad spent many long hours debating the fighting and its consequences with his flatmates, Adnan and Majeed, who held identical views. They all agreed that the confrontation had ended in a historic victory, and that the aims of the attack had been to bring down Nasser and regain possession of the Canal. The Tripartite Aggression had failed in both aims since Nasser had not fallen and the criminals had not regained the Canal. Quite the opposite: Gamal Abdul Nasser had emerged stronger than ever and the Egyptian character of the Canal had been re-asserted. But when Yacoub joined in the discussion a new element entered the debate.

'With the announcement of the Soviet warning there was an end to US domination of the world. When Khruschev threatened Britain and France with nuclear warheads, the threat was really directed at America.' But when Qasim tried to talk about Eisenhower's role in bringing the fighting to an end his colleagues had nothing but contempt: his reactionary views were not worth discussing.

Fuad did not know when the friendship between himself and Abdul-Ra'ouf began. Both of them were usually very shy and neither formed new friendships easily. He had met Abdul-Ra'ouf on his first day at the Saeediyya School and at first their love of literature was the only thing linking them. Fuad had already published his first short story while Abdul-Ra'ouf was hoping to do the same. They soon realized that, between them, they had read more books than the rest of the class put together and then gradually they became aware of other things they had in common: a wish to analyse everything, or 'philoso-phize', as Abdul-Ra'ouf called it; an unwillingness to take life just as it was, as others did; the ability to see the funny side of every situation, as well as the tragic side, since they both recognized that comedy was hardly different from tragedy. They shared a tendency to be over-sensitive to other people's reactions, criticisms or praise ... and women. During the break the two of them would go off together to talk school, the world and people, and always the talk would come round to women.

'What do you think of Aqqad's position on the subject of women?'

'Isn't it just the same as Hakim's?'

'Has either of them come up with anything new?'

'How can a bachelor possibly understand women?'

'Do women's feelings differ from men's?'

'Which one is the hunter and which one the hunted?'

'Which of them is the more predatory?'

'Which of the sexes is the more faithful?'

They had many more questions about women than they had answers.

As his friendship with Abdul-Ra'ouf became stronger Fuad came to understand something of a problem which he had never seriously thought about before: poverty. In Bahrain all his companions had been middle class, like himself, and there had been few differences between them. Usually in class there would be two or three sons of wealthy 'merchants' and two or three from poor families but the rest were all on one level. The question of wealth and class did not occupy much of his thinking. He assumed that life in his home was not very different from that in any other home in Bahrain, with all the children sleeping in one room, going to school on cycles, used to having new clothes only at Eid, and being unfamiliar with both hunger or luxury.

Before he got to know Abdul-Ra'ouf Fuad was never aware that he moved in a world which was separate from the majority of people. He had never felt privileged before. His father had bought a car some years before but seldom used it, it had made almost no difference to Fuad's life. But now he began to realize that he was, whether he liked it or not, one of the rich. Poor people did not own cars or have jewellery shops, eat meat regularly and did not send their sons to study abroad with 5 suits and a monthly allowance of 25 pounds.

The only thing Fuad knew about his allowance was that it was equal to about 200 Bahrain rupees, a reasonable sum by Bahrain standards, and as for his suits it was not he who had decided on the number, quality or colour but his brother, Nasir. Now these things which he had taken for granted took on a new dimension since Abdul-Ra'ouf had only four pounds a month from his father and only one suit, with no tie. It was clear to Fuad that most of the students in his class had only two suits and so he now only wore two of his suits for school.

He asked Abdul-Ra'ouf in astonishment, 'How can you live on four pounds? How do you do it?'

Abdul-Ra'ouf was astonished that he was astonished. 'It's enough. I pay one pound as my share of the rent for the room I share with a relative in town. The rest is for food. I don't need anything for transport as I walk to school.'

'What about restaurants and the cinema?'

A little smile appeared on Abdul-Ra'ouf's lips and Fuad realized what a stupid question that was. It reminded him of Marie-Antoinette who advised the hungry mob to eat cake when the bread had run out. When Fuad went back to his digs after this discussion and contemplated his lunch – soup, meat, two kinds of vegetable, salad, a huge plate of rice and muhallabiyya – he felt for the first time in his life a pricking of his conscience.

*The square is thronged with people, cars and animals, with all manner of smells and noises arising from it. Abdul-Baqi waits for his bus but his patience is running out. A schoolboy turns to him and asks for the time. Abdul-Baqi points with irritation to the huge clock in the centre of the square.*

*'Thank you very much, sir.'*

*Abdul-Baqi is well aware of what that will mean. He will get to the office late and the Chief Clerk will relish putting him through torture before telling him that this time he will not dock him anything. Dock anything? Abdul-Baqi laughs. The young boy looks over and backs away. Dock something? There's almost nothing left from his pay to dock. After paying for rent, food, transport, the children's clothes, what was left except for debts? Why doesn't the Chief Clerk dock something from his debts?*

*Abdul-Baqi gets on the bus at the 2nd class entrance. People getting off try to trample on those getting on. They in their turn are trying to get over them. Abdul-Baqi has hardly settled on a place, standing, before he is startled by an old woman pressing on his battered shoe with her sandal.*

*'By the Prophet, sir, what time is it?'*

*'How can I possibly get to have a look at my watch, madam?'*

*'I'm sorry to bother you, son.'*

*This congestion has two advantages. Firstly, it is likely that he will arrive at his stop before the ticket collector gets to him. The second advantage is that the problem of remaining upright, in spite of the pressures on him from all sides, is such that he forgets any other problem. He actually does get off before the ticket collector gets to him. He moves a couple of steps and is then stopped by a villager who looks as if he has just arrived from Upper Egypt. 'Your honour, what is the time?'*

*Abdul-Baqi does not even look, makes no reply and just walks on, leaving the villager to shake his head and mutter. 'Just amazing! God alone is great, I tell you people. What kind of a town is this?' That's just it, what kind of a town is this? Abdul-Baqi blinks back his tears. Has everyone been struck blind? Every one? Can no one see that he is not wearing a watch? Don't they know that he has never even possessed a watch?*

Abdul-Ra'ouf asked him, 'What do you think of the story of the watch?'

Fuad replied, laughing, 'You've overdone it a bit, Abdul-Ra'ouf: is there any official who doesn't have a watch? Is there anyone who doesn't?' But as he was still speaking, Fuad recalled that he had never seen a watch on Abdul-Ra'ouf's wrist, and he went silent, his face turning red with embarrassment. Abdul-Ra'ouf noticed this.

'Don't worry, it doesn't matter. Don't take it so seriously,' he said.

But Fuad could not overcome his curiosity. 'But how do you manage to live without a watch?'

'There are clocks all over the place.'

'But why don't you buy a watch?'

'Maybe they are cheap in Bahrain,' said Abdul-Ra'ouf.

The next day Fuad brought in his spare watch, a Medo, which was just like new, and presented it to Abdul-Ra'ouf, who took it without hesitation, smiling. 'What about all the other people who don't have watches? Are you planning to give them all one as well?'

# CHAPTER THREE

## November – December 1957

The previous September Fuad had become a genuine university student. A new phase had begun in his life. The whole 'gang' had now joined the university and their school leaving exam results had been better than expected: Fuad had got 70 per cent, Qasim 67 per cent, Abdul-Karim 66 per cent, Yacoub 73 per cent, Nash'at 75 per cent. Abdul-Ra'ouf was the outstanding one, getting 85 per cent. These results were good enough for admission to Cairo University without the need for anyone to make a special plea at the Coordination Office, which was celebrated for being the only institution in the Republic not susceptible to 'influence'. Fuad, Abdul-Karim and Nash'at joined the Faculty of Laws, Qasim joined the Faculty of Commerce and Abdul-Ra'ouf joined the Arabic Language department of the Faculty of Arts. Yacoub decided to study Sociology after originally planning to study Law. He had also thought of studying Economics or Literature (the most effective weapon for opposing tyranny), but he chose Sociology because society was so complex that it was impossible to study it from one angle only.

The summer which Fuad had spent in Bahrain held many surprises for him. He began to tire of the heat of Bahrain in August and longed for the cooling breezes of the Nile. After the joy of reunion with his family he had begun to feel bored with the usual routine: home, then the shop and back home again. He began to suffer from the fixed aridity of thinking in Bahrain. He missed the morning papers and the magazines which you could buy and read right away, the walls of the Azbakiya Gardens where you could buy second-hand books at very low prices, not to mention the cultural programmes on the radio. He found he missed the very smell of Cairo, the product of a thousand years and a thousand and one scents and odours. This time when he boarded the Cyprus Airways plane a little before dawn his eyes were damp, but the tears were now of not only the pain of parting from his mother but of joy that he was going back to Cairo.

The university routine was different from that of the secondary school. It was not now a matter of being present or absent, with the doors being opened and closed, and sick notes for being absent. No one noticed if anyone was there or not. The huge amphitheatre could take over 1,000 students and the lecturer had to use a microphone to be heard. The lecture hall was usually packed and many students had to stand. Smaller groups, called 'discussion', were taught by 'repetiteurs' and no one would dream of attending who was not either a genius or a fool. The timetable was very relaxed, half of the week morning lectures and the other half evening lectures. The academic year had two terms with five subjects in each term and the only thing which annoyed Fuad was the lack of textbooks, since every lecturer would produce his own material on stencils and the students would have to buy the work which came out in instalments, one section per week.

Fuad realized from his first day that the Faculty of Laws was not the ideal place to get to know girls. Fewer than 10 per cent of his fellow law students were female and of these most were not the stuff of sexual fantasy: thick regulation-issue spectacles; severe features, and a studied seriousness. As Fuad let his eye wander over them he imagined that he was looking at the faces of judges of the Criminal Courts of the future. It looked as if all the pretty young girls at university were studying in the Faculty of Arts. That was the good luck of Yacoub and Abdul-Ra'ouf. In the English department the number of girls exceeded that of the young men and in the other departments there were equal numbers. As for the Faculty of Ministers, well, there there were only Ministers. And what about the women Ministers? But fate, which had deprived the law students of the company of beautiful girls had given them, nonetheless, a gleam of hope. The cafeteria of the Faculty of Arts. It was there that the beauties of the Faculty gathered. This cafeteria was the favourite haunt of the gang and when they spoke simply of 'The Buffet' this was the place they meant. If they were speaking of some other place they would specify it: The Law Faculty Buffet, or the Commerce Buffet.

The pattern of life had changed as Abdul-Ra'ouf and Nash'at had become members of the gang and the weekly programme now included at least one visit a week to the Union of Bahrain Students in a side street off the Square in Doqqi. There the Bahrain students studying in Cairo would collect in a spacious villa, some 50 young men and a small number of young women, to chat and play chess, cards and board games. From time to time there would be a cultural evening when Fuad might read out one of his stories or Yacoub recite one of his poems. The Friday programme included also performing the Friday prayers with Abdul-Ra'ouf in the mosque of Al-Malik Al-Salih in Roda and then having lunch at Casino near the Abbasiyya bridge. Yacoub would sometimes come to these lunches and then the talk would be of philosophy and culture.

A major decision awaited Fuad and his companions: where to live. Life with Mrs Khairiyya was extremely comfortable but it was like being at boarding school. There were too many rules in the apartment. All visitors had to be accounted for and at reasonable times, with of course no female visitors allowed. It was impossible to invite anyone to eat with them since the number of chairs exactly matched the number of diners. Even taking a bath required co-ordination with Mrs Khairiyya who undertook the warming of the water with the primitive device called a 'daafour'. Fuad was beginning to be convinced that Qasim's idea of renting an apartment was sound and Yacoub and Abdul-Karim announced that they were ready to join them. The only stumbling block was Mr Shareef but here Qasim had promised them that he would devise a 'devilish' plan to get over this.

Fuad had gradually learned how to deal with Mr Shareef. He had under-taken to supervise Fuad but had also assumed supervision of Qasim and of all the Bahrain students with whom Fuad came in contact. He would visit Mrs Khairiyya's apartment twice a week, at precisely 10 a.m. on Fridays and the other occasion at any time and without appointment. It turned out that Mr Shareef had a network of friends which could resolve immediately any dilemma facing Fuad or any of his colleagues. If a health problem came up Mr Shareef knew all the most famous doctors of Cairo. If there was trouble connected with studies Mr Shareef, through his work in the Ministry of Education, where he was a senior official, had sufficient influence to make short work of the obstacle. If things became really complicated Mr Shareef's wife was the sister of Colonel Shawkat who worked in Army Intelligence. And is there in Egypt any problem which cannot be solved by a Colonel who works in Army Intelligence?

What disturbed Fuad about Mr Shareef was not his personality but his political views. When he had been in Bahrain everyone had believed that he was the most enthusiastic supporter of the Revolution and its leaders and principles. But now it turned out that his apparent enthusiasm concealed great coolness towards the Revolution, indeed hatred of it. With something like shock Fuad realized that Mr Shareef's real admiration was focused not on his hero, the guide and leader of Arab Nationalism but on Saad Zagloul (just like Mahgoob) and on Saad's successor, Nahas Pasha. This hostility to Nasser was not restricted to Mr Shareef, indeed Fuad sensed it in anyone over 40 years of age. These gentlemen were still living on the delusions of the previous era: the monarchy, the Pashas and titles. Gradually Fuad learned how to use them. In Bahrain people hardly used titles at all so that when he went with his father for the first time to visit the Ruler and asked his father how he should address him his father said, 'It is enough to say "O you of long life!" ' That was how Sheikh Salman himself addressed people. But here in Cairo it was very complicated. Your honour. Your excellency. Your presence. Efendim. Even his own name would change depending on whom he was talking to. Mrs Khairiyya would call him See Fuad while the man doing the ironing would call him Fuad Effendi. The porters in the Faculty would call him Fuad Bey but the concierge at the apartment would call him Mr Fuad. Nash'at told him about the days of the monarchy. The Prime Minister had a title by right but if he had the State's highest decoration this title was 'The Possessor of the Elevated Status'. An ordinary Minister would be called 'The Possessor of Lofty Qualities' while his Permanent Secretary would be called 'His Excellency'. Any officer in the police or army reaching Brigadier would automatically become a Pasha and thus 'His Excellency the Pasha'. But now, since the abolition of titles, the situation had become chaotic, the only one officially used being 'Siyadatak' ('Your Excellency'), which was bestowed on the President of the Republic and the bus-driver too.

A vague feeling was creeping up on Fuad that Nasser was not all that he appeared to be. He began to wonder about the real feelings of the huge crowds which gathered whenever Gamal Abdul Nasser appeared. Was it true that it was the Intelligence apparatus which gathered the workers from their factories, peasants from their farms and students from the schools and 'fixed' these gatherings as Qasim said? But how was it possible to bring together one million people, no matter how efficient the Intelligence people were? Fuad still believed that the feelings of the masses towards Gamal Abdul Nasser were ones of love and loyalty and not just a show. But were those people still loyal to Saad Zagloul just stuffed mummies whom history had passed by? Fuad knew that the popularity of Gamal Abdul Nasser in Egypt was greater than his popularity abroad. But that was natural.

*The train was in uproar. Inside was a combination of shouting weeping, laughing, bewailing, of separation and anticipation of reunion. Outside were the voices of hawkers and peddlers, inspectors, porters, whistles, the crash of heavy wheels on the rails. But all this noise could not overwhelm the thoughts clashing in Dr Muhammad's mind. Doctor?! He had got so used to this that it had become part of his name even though he was not qualified, still in his third-year, but the traditions of the Faculty gave any student the title of Doctor from the first year. Everyone called him 'Doctor', his relatives, the conductor on the bus, fellow-students, everyone but the real doctors who taught him.*

*His thoughts were getting ahead of him and of the train and were already in Tanta. They had leaped into the taxi and reached his father's new home which he had not yet seen. In his mind he was seeing his father's new wife, whom he had not yet met. He had had no contact with his father for the year, since he had married again. He had made the excuse of being too busy with his studies, so as to stay in Cairo. He had not discussed the matter of the marriage with his father. Their relationship was based on his total respect and blind obedience.*

*The strange thing was that his mother, who had been just as surprised by the wedding as he, had accepted the* fait accompli. *In fact she had tried to restore contact between himself and his father. She poured out advice during her visits to Cairo and in her letters. 'Blood is thicker than water . . .' 'Your fingernail cannot leave the flesh . . .' But Dr Muhammad could not forgive his father and could not understand what could make a man over 60 marry a woman no older than his children. He could not accept the situation even if everyone else did.*

*Why, then, was he rushing to see his father and the woman who had proved that blood was not thicker than water and shown that the fingernail could be removed from the flesh? God's curse on illness and on that telegraph 'Your father has a heart complaint. Come right away. Firdaws.'*

*There had been no choice, the cable had made him forget everything except the wish to see his father before he might die, to kiss his brow and his hands, as he used to do before. Where had she come from? All he knew was that she used to come every day to his father's grocery shop. And now she was killing him. What could an old man who married a young girl expect but to have a heart attack?*

*Events now seemed to collide. The train, the station, his father's brother and his own younger brother waiting for him, the new home and the new wife. She was much more beautiful than he had expected and not as young. She was wearing modest clothes and looked at him shyly, blushing if her eye caught his.*

*Right away Dr Muhammad got into a lengthy discussion with the doctor treating his father. It now appeared that the heart attack had not been as severe as had been feared: he thought that his father needed two weeks complete rest before getting back to his normal routine. His father could not conceal his joy to see him. He might have even been happy to have had this heart attack which had brought his eldest son back to him. He turned to his wife.*

*'Firdaws, get the room ready for Dr Muhammad.'*

*'But father . . .'*

*'Firdaws, get the room ready for Dr Muhammad.'*

*'Please, See Muhammad, we may need a doctor in the night,' said Firdaws.*

*Muhammad was unable to contradict his father. He went to the old house and spent some time with his mother and later went back to the new house and the guest room.*

*The train left Tanta station with Dr Muhammad laden with all kinds of*

*delicious foods, some from his mother but most from Firdaws, and he could not erase disturbing memories of the two nights he had spent in the new house.*
*'Good night, See Muhammad.'*
*'And a very good morning to you, See Muhammad.'*
*The glass of warm milk in the night. The cup of hot tea in the morning. The way she blushed. Dr Muhammad felt something like nausea coming on . . .*

Fuad asked Abdul-Ra'ouf what he thought of the story.
'Sensational. What will you call it?'
' "Nausea" '.
' "Nausea?" like Camus?'
'Why not? Didn't he write most of his stories about Tanta?'
'How old is Mrs Khairiyya?'
'What's that got to do with my story?'
'Just answer the question.'
'I've no idea. She says she's about 30 but I think she's older.'
'Is she pretty? What I mean is: do you think she's pretty?'
Fuad still looked puzzled.
'The story is about the two of you: Dr Muhammad is Fuad and Firdaws is Mrs Khairiyya.'
'Abdul-Ra'ouf. Really! Didn't we agree that writing that just conveyed reality was not literature?'
'Yes, but we also agreed that writing must have *some* connection with reality. But you are not just conveying reality: you have added a few spices and done a bit of touching-up. Why did you choose Tanta?'
'Since when did short stories need memoranda explaining them?'
'What I mean is: has anything happened between you and Mrs Khairiyya?'
'We aren't Roman Catholics and I'm no priest.'
'OK. Did anything happen between Firdaws and Dr Muhammad?'
'No. Unless you call the warm milk and the hot tea something.'
'Do you know why Dr Muhammad suffered from nausea? It's because the student living at Mrs Khairiyya's has discovered that the relationship between the two of them is no longer one of son and mother, and not one of son with the wife of his father.'
'God rot you!'

If a fortune teller had ever told Abdul-Karim that one day he would track a young woman through the streets of Cairo he would have laughed. If an astrologer had told him that he would one day become a spy trying to gather information about one of his fellow-students he would have smiled. But now here he was, a detective *and* a spy. He followed her on the bus. He got to know the names of her friends. He got to know the size of her skirts and shoes. He learned what time she left home and when she got back. And the strange thing was that he learned all this while she knew nothing about him. The pursuit was discreet and from a distance with the object of it quite oblivious.

Nash'at, who in addition to being good looking, was confident with women, said to him, 'Listen, Abdul-Karim, don't waste your time. Introduce yourself. Or I could introduce myself and then introduce you.'

'No, no, no!' said Abdul-Karim, knowing that Nash'at was all too capable of accomplishing this. 'That's very kind of you, but leave her alone.'

'OK, OK. Just let me know if you change your mind.'

How could he get to talk to her? Just one look at her from afar and Abdul-Karim felt an electric current flow through him. He would begin to tremble, his shoulders shaking. Yacoub murmured, 'As the bird was swooping down, it got drenched by a drop of rain,' and Fuad would laugh as he observed the symptoms. 'Here they come again!'

Nash'at would say something subtle, like, 'The girlfriend has arrived.'

If Farida just appeared at the door of the lecture-hall or in the Faculty buffet, Abdul-Karim was flustered. Abdul-Ra'ouf had some sympathy for Abdul-Karim: he was the only one who did not make fun of him. Perhaps he had at some time gone through a similar experience.

'Abdul-Ra'ouf, how can I explain it? Maybe it is like the feeling of man as he first enters the world, or as he dies. What I mean is . . . it's different from any feeling I've ever had before. I feel as if all my days had been wasted but in Farida they have found a goal, and now have taste and colour. Even the moon looks different because I can see her features carved there.'

Abdul-Ra'ouf listened in silence, moved, but unlike those other fools, did not suggest that he introduce himself to her.

Fuad had lost hope, one year after arriving in Cairo, of ever finding a girl-friend. It was clear to him that Egyptian society was every bit as conservative as Bahrain's and that all that talk he had read in the stories of Ihsan Abdul-Quddoos was rot. His entire emotional harvest after all these months was no more than signs and signals exchanged with the girls in the building opposite. These would stop the moment a relative of one of the girls came onto the balcony. There had been a few nuisance phone calls (this happened even in Bahrain) but apart from this there was nothing but talk, talk, without end about girls.

From the beginning Qasim had insisted that the only way was through cash, which was in accord with his general materialism. Qasim did not know why his fellow-students were wasting their time looking for girlfriends when they could get hold of a 'sweetie' through one phone call and spending a small sum. Qasim soon accumulated a tidy collection of phone numbers of

'Madams' along with their tariffs, ranging from 2 Egyptian pounds to the best available at five pounds. The only obstacle was the venue for the tryst and for this reason Qasim had redoubled his efforts to escape from the 'prison of modesty' in which they were living to an apartment.

But Fuad knew when he was on his own that his real problem was shyness, or to be more precise, cowardliness. There were girls everywhere, at the bus stop, on the bus, in the same apartment building, but the problem was his lack of boldness at the last moment. Making a signal to a girl on a balcony was one thing but talking to a girl face to face was something else. Fuad knew that if he did not get over this problem he would never have a girl-friend in Cairo. And yet the way in which he actually did get to know his first female fellow-student was easy and spontaneous. He was standing in a queue when he was asked by the girl standing behind him, 'Do you know how many sections came out today?'

'There was one on the Introduction, one on Roman Law and two on the Sharia,' said Fuad.

'Do you think we'll get the remainder before the end of term?'

'That's what they say, but personally I have my doubts.'

'Your accent is not Egyptian. Where are you from?'

'Bahrain.' There was not the usual puzzlement; it seemed that she had heard of Bahrain.

'What about you?'

'I am from Damascus. Suad Wazzan.'

'Fuad Tarif.'

He extended his hand and he looked into green eyes set in a round rosy face and was framed with blonde hair. Fuad said, 'I've never seen you in the lecture hall.'

'How could you see me? Blessings on Shaikh Abu Zahra.'

Shaikh Muhammad Abu Zahra was the head of the Sharia Department and Dean of the Faculty and a staunch opponent of co-education. He had put out a decree setting aside for women students a section to the left of the lecture theatre, from which they must not stray and which no male student could penetrate. Fuad laughed. 'What do you think of the Shaikh?'

'He's a first-class reactionary. Here we are in the twentieth century and Abu Zahra wants to put us back in the Middle Ages. How could a revolutionary government put a reactionary like him in the Faculty of Laws? The Faculty that is supposed to teach justice and equality.'

The ferocity of her reply surprised Fuad. He decided to wind her up a little. 'But how can there be equality between a man and a woman? There are basic differences. Can you deny that?'

Suad answered at once. 'That's the influence of Abu Zahra and the rest of the reverend gentlemen. There are differences, of course there are. A man doesn't get pregnant, or give birth or have periods. Is there a difference in intelligence? In ability? In feelings?'

This was the first time in his life that Fuad had heard the expression 'to have a period'. And this young woman was speaking without any embarrassment as if she were speaking about something such as reading or writing. He blushed.

'You're shocked. Do you know why? Because you've been brainwashed. Because you have been taught that women are something shameful and so is their menstrual cycle.'

They were still going at it an hour later. When Fuad invited her to the Faculty buffet and she accepted without hesitation. Before he went to sleep that night Fuad decided that he now had a girlfriend. The whole thing had happened without any planning or thinking, and he felt that he had known Suad for a long time. He had been talking with her the way he talked to Abdul-Ra'ouf and Qasim, freely and without any flutterings of the heart or coldness in his limbs! In this first meeting they had debated, had their differences, raised their voices, just like old friends and when they separated to go into the lecture – he with the men and she going into Abu Zahra's prison – they had agreed to meet the following day.

Now he met her every day, spending hours talking to her but there was nothing romantic about it, no literature or trivial matters: their conversation was of politics and the future of the Arab Nation. She told him that she was a committed Ba'athist and he asked, 'Why join a party?'

'Fuad! If there's no party in the vanguard, the Arab Nation will never fulfil its eternal mission. It's essential to have a party breaking new ground and infiltrating every part of the homeland, teaching the masses, organizing them, getting them moving and then at the right moment imposing Arab unity, merging all entities into the one pan-Arab state. How can all this be achieved without the party?'

'Gamal Abdul Nasser is achieving all this right now!'

'Nasser is a great political leader but he has no vision, no ideology. Without a party like the Arab Ba'ath Socialist party he will not achieve anything lasting. The emotions of the masses are not lasting.'

In the past Fuad had dreamed of a girlfriend who would take him to moonlit trysts on the banks of the Nile and to dreamy evenings in the shadow of the Pyramids. He had imagined himself with this girl-friend as they strolled, after midnight, hand in hand, talking of love. But now he found himself in a vortex of books, theories and intellectual clashes. What strange fate had made this lovely blonde girl from Damascus into a committed Ba'athist? And what even more curious fate had driven him to her.

Fuad had heard of the Ba'ath Party when he was at school: Mr Muhsin was one of the few Bahraini teachers and had studied at the American University of Beirut where he had taken his degree and imbibed Ba'athist principles. He had encouraged students to study Ba'athist ideas, Fuad amongst them. He had read Michel Aflaq's book *On the Path of the Ba'ath* but Fuad had hardly understood a thing in it. It had seemed to him that Gamal Abdul Nasser had the only worthwhile answers. Anything coming between the commander and his soldiers, whatever its name, could only be a waste of time.

Suad tried to change his mind. 'Fuad, don't you believe in unity? In freedom? Socialism? As long as you believe in them you're a Ba'athist, whether you've realized it or not.'

'I believe in unity because it means the emergence of a unified Arab state. And I believe in freedom because it means getting rid of imperialism, but I don't understand what socialism is. How can I believe in something I don't understand?' He was not to be so easily convinced.

'Be careful, Fuad. Don't let your class origins influence you. Thinkers who are men of honour can overcome their class and origins, just as Tolstoy did and The Teacher.'

'The Teacher?'

'Michel Aflaq, of course.'

'But what is Socialism? I've read his writings but I didn't find a clear definition of Socialism.'

'You'll have to re-read his books. We'll read them together, and debate them.'

Fuad put a question to Abdul-Ra'ouf. 'Rauf, what do you think of Socialism?'

'What makes you ask? Is it your girlfriend from Damascus?'

'Yes. What do you think of Socialism?'

'Which Socialism do you mean? There are several kinds.'

'What are they?'

'There's Marxist socialism, i.e. Communism. Then there is the socialism of the British Labour Party, or social democracy. And there is the socialism of the dreamers. Which one are you talking about?'

'I am talking about the socialism that does not deprive the citizen just because he was born poor. The socialism that means the triumph of life over death. Socialism that is destiny!'

'Is that Ba'ath Socialism?'

'Yes, it is.'

'All that is just empty slogans woolly mumbo jumbo which doesn't mean a thing. *That's* the socialism of dreamers.'

'But what about you, Ra'ouf? Which kind of socialism do you believe in?'

'I don't believe in socialism because I believe in Islam.'

'Why are the two incompatible? Islam is a religion and Socialism is an economic doctrine.'

'You're wrong. Islam is a vision that organizes everything, economic and political matters and personal conduct and the system of worship of God. You can't just choose a bit from here and a bit from there in the way of principles and theories. You can be either a Muslim or a Socialist.'

'Abdul-Ra'ouf, that is a reactionary doctrine. I had no idea that you embraced these ideas.'

'You hadn't asked me.'

'Just answer me one question: are you in sympathy with the Muslim Brotherhood?'

Abdul-Ra'ouf blushed but he made no reply and Fuad kept silent too as he realized that although he had known Abdul-Ra'ouf well, he'd thought, for more than a year he actually only knew him slightly.

Now new and knotty questions began to assail Fuad. Was Socialism the only method of treating poverty? Where did its ideas come from, from Islam or Marx or Michel Aflaq? Was Abdul-Ra'ouf right? Were all Socialists enemies of Islam? Was Gamal Abdul Nasser a Socialist?

As usual Qasim had all the answers. 'I tried to warn you off Fuad: I warned you about your little friend. Don't let this nonsense about Socialism fool you. It's just propaganda to lead the unwary astray. There's the communist system applied in the USSR and the capitalist system applied in the USA. And that's it! Those Ba'athists are just communists. And their leading light is Mr Muhsin in Bahrain!'

It was hopeless trying to reach an understanding with Qasim.

Abdul-Karim, too, thought that socialism was beneath contempt.

'Please, Fuad, just leave me alone with my sweet dreams: let me think of Farida. Be a Socialist if you want to but don't bother *me* with this rubbish!'

Once Fuad went with Suad to the Metro Cinema and another time went with her to have lunch at the Island of Tea. They went to the Garden Aquarium but each time a third person was with them – The Teacher, Michel Aflaq: his theories, his genius and his struggle. Fuad noticed that his love for Gamal Abdul Nasser was as nothing faced with the holy status which Suad conferred on The Teacher. He began to feel jealous. When he would take her hand as they walked to the bus that would take them from the Pyramids to Cairo their fingers would be interlaced but what they talked about was the concept of 'The readiness to overthrow the system' in the thought of Michel Aflaq.

But they were lifted by the exhilaration of their first kiss as they sat on a bench near the Nile, and her blonde hair blowing in his face. He breathed her perfume.

'Fuad, do you love me?'

'Yes, I do, Suad.'

'Say it.'

'I love you, Suad.'

'Will you join the party?'

'Yes, Suad!'

They then became lost in their second kiss.

Before he went to sleep that night Fuad realized that at the age of 18, he had kissed a girl for the first time and that he had told a girl that he loved her and that he had also decided for the first time to join a political party. All of this in one evening.

# CHAPTER FOUR

## February – March 1958

H
ow was it possible for all this to happen within a few weeks, in fact in a few days? It was just like a miracle, a miracle within a dream, a dream within a wish. There were huge crowds on the main squares, the Syrian President arrived in Cairo, there was an agreement in principle on union between Egypt and Syria. Then there was a referendum of the two peoples, the establishment of the United Arab Republic and the election of Gamal Abdul Nasser as President of the newly-born state. The Arab masses celebrated, while the imperialists, their lackeys and Israel were enraged. It now seemed that Arab unity was an objective within reach.

Fuad murmured, 'Suad, I just can't believe this has actually happened.'

'Why are you surprised, Fuad? This is the moment of birth, the moment of re-birth.'*

'How could it happen so quickly?'

'Three reasons. The party, the masses and Gamal Abdul Nasser. It was The Teacher who first launched the idea of union. It was a historic opportunity that there was a leader ready like Nasser.'

Fuad was also taken by surprise by the aggressive attitude of Mr Shareef to the union. 'What is this childishness? It's really stupid. Is the name of Egypt to be abolished? This historic name is to become The Southern Region? Are Communists in Damascus to be allowed to impose their views on us?'

'Mr Shareef, the communists are opposed to the union. This is the will of the masses.'

'What masses, Fuad? Have you noticed a single person celebrating here, apart from the government and its organizations? We'll have to spend all we have on that lot from Damascus. We'll have to take on all their problems. They'll compete with us in everything. Those Damascenes are the craftiest merchants in the world. You can kiss the Egyptian economy goodbye.'

*Translator's note: re-birth = 'ba'ath' in Arabic.

Qasim half-relished this reactionary view and was able to add new information from his rumour-mill. 'Do you know what actually happened? Ten Syrian Army officers said to Nasser, "Either you accept union or we leave Syria to the communists." Your friend gave his approval right away. And why not? More authority for him but God help Syria.'

Fuad said, 'Qasim, can't you see these millions with your own eyes? Didn't you see how the crowds in Syria carried Gamal Abdul Nasser's car on their shoulders? Don't you see what happens everywhere he goes? What ten officers could bring all this about?'

'You are a good-hearted fellow Fuad, but easily duped. These very same masses will turn against Nasser if they hear something different on the radio.'

'Half the broadcasting stations in the world are attacking Nasser and still the masses applaud him, in Damascus, in Beirut, Baghdad, Tunis, and Bahrain.'

'Fuad, that's just propaganda. If the Voice of the Arabs were to talk about me the way it talks about him the crowds would be applauding me, not Nasser!'

'That'll be the day!'

A few days after the historic kiss Fuad formally joined the Ba'ath party but he was surprised to find that, although he had joined the party for the sake of Suad's green eyes, she would not be in his group. She belonged to another, higher one. His group consisted of four people. The first meeting was held in the leader's apartment and began with introductions. 'I am Bassam Nuweilat from Jordan. The comrade here is Majid Zubair from the Kingdom of Saudi Arabia. The comrade here is Fuad Tarif from Bahrain and our other comrade is Muhammad Assaily from Lebanon. Our woman comrade here is Victoria Nassar from Iraq. You are all most welcome to the Party.' The word 'Comrade' fell like a hammer blow on Fuad's head. He had imagined that its use was confined to the communists. He shuffled in his chair and noticed that Majid Zubair was equally uneasy. The two of them exchanged glances as Bassam Nuweilat went on.

'Absolute secrecy is imperative. You all know that activity by the party is banned in Egypt. If the authorities knew that our meeting today was to do with the party we would be pursued and might even go to gaol. Always use extreme caution. You will have to learn to take care as all of you could be prosecuted when you return to your own countries.'

The whole of the first meeting was about organizational matters which seemed odd to Fuad. Pass words, code to be used on the phone, the convolutions necessary to arrange meetings: when the meeting broke up he was relieved.

After that there were meetings at least once a week and in the beginning the main topic was the constitution of the party and its principles.

*The Arab Nation was a spiritual and cultural unit and all existing factors for division among its sons would pass away as Arab consciousness became awakened.

*The Arab Nation was an integrated political and economic unit and none of the Arab countries could achieve completion of the conditions of its life in isolation from the others.

*The Arab homeland was for the Arabs. They alone had the right to manage its affairs and wealth and to direct its destiny.

There was a flood of questions. What exactly was the meaning of spiritual unity? What was the role of Islam in forming spiritual unity? How could political unity be achieved? What was the position of the party on military coups? How would the Arabs dispose of their wealth? Was nationalization the best method? What was Arab Socialism? And what about Nasser?

For Fuad the last question was most insistent in his mind. When the UAR was established the Ba'ath party in Syria dissolved itself, bowing to the wish of Gamal Abdul Nasser. Fuad expected that party meetings would be automatically terminated but their meetings were not affected by the decision to dissolve the party. He asked Suad, 'The party has dissolved itself so why do we carry on our meetings here?'

'That was just Syria. We are not in Syria and we are not carrying on any domestic political activity. We are acting for the the entire Arab nation. If we stopped it would betray all Arabs.'

'But how can our activity carry on here when the main activity has stopped in Damascus?'

'Dissolution of the party does not mean stalemate. The party is now an essential element in the government, it carries on its work, but as a partner.'

'Gamal Abdul Nasser has no partners in wielding authority, Suad, and he never will have. He will rule Syria the way he has ruled Egypt, with no parties, and relying on mass support.'

'The situation in Syria is different. Don't forget that it was the party which handed him power there. It was we who taught the masses the idea of union. We demanded union immediately. He will be the Head of State but we will have the intellectual and political leadership.'

'You seem pretty optimistic.'

'You don't know Syria the way I do. Our party will be the real ruler. And Gamal Abdul Nasser, will reign but not rule.'

Gamal Abdul Nasser will reign but not rule . . .

If February 1958 has gone down in the history of the Arabs as the month of union between Egypt and Syria it went down in the history of Abdul-Karim as the month of The Meeting. Ever since Nash'at had suggested that first he would get to know Farida and then introduce Abdul-Karim to her the idea had been buzzing in his brain. Every day his feelings for Farida grew: he knew that he could not go on for ever in the grip of trembling from afar. But even as this took root he realized that it was impossible for him to take the initiative.

When he began, shyly, to drop hints Nash'at cut him off abruptly: 'Just leave it to me!'

Two days later Nash'at came to him, smiling broadly.

'Problem solved. 10 a.m. tomorrow in the buffet.'

Abdul-Karim stared at Nash'at in astonishment. Finally he asked what had happened.

'Everything went very smoothly. I stopped her and introduced myself. Then I told her about you and she said she would like to meet you, especially as you are from Bahrain.'

'What do you mean?'

'Nothing. Maybe she is a Ba'athist like the girlfriend of Fuad.'

'Yes, but I need to know more. I want to know what you told her about me?'

'I said you were a nice young man, of a good family, a bit shy and you wanted to meet her. That's it. Tomorrow in the Arts Faculty Buffet. Shine your shoes. Wash your face and try to look handsome.'

That night Abdul-Karim did not sleep. How could he sleep when tomorrow he had his date with Farida? What would he say to her? What would she say to him? Look handsome. How? Could he ask his glasses to disappear? Could he grow a bit taller? How would he start? A thousand dialogues went through his mind as he tossed and turned. Then he heard the call to the dawn prayers, got up and spent nearly 2 hours in the bathroom. At 7 he was at the bus stop and at 7.30 he stood before the university. A few moments later he was at the Arts buffet waiting for its doors to open. He was the first to go in and Hassanain, the aged waiter, greeted him.

'You are most welcome Karim Bey. Why so early in the morning? Coffee?'

'Yes. With extra sugar. And sugared almonds.'

Abdul-Karim began to sip his coffee. He looked up to see how the buffet was slowly coming alive. A table would fill up here and immediately the sandwiches would arrive and the tea and then just as suddenly the tables would empty. The ping-pong table in the middle was as yet still. Abdul-Karim could see at one table, on the side of the buffet, a group of law students, but he ignored them. Over there a Ph.D. from the Arts Faculty was engaged in debate. The vast room filled up. Suddenly everyone left to make the 9 a.m. lecture. The seconds passed more slowly, than the creep of a cripple, but still they went by. Tables would again become congested, then empty. Cups of tea and coffee would be gulped. Old Hassanain hovered. 'Have some more Karim Bey, by the Prophet. Have some more.'

It was five past ten. Then the place froze and everything became bewitched and the sun exploded. River banks burst. Farida had entered with Nash'at. They were talking and laughing and were coming over.

'Mlle Farida, I present my friend Abdul-Karim Al-Shaikh,' said Nash'at.

'Welcome, we are honoured.'

How had Abdul-Karim managed to get these few words out? No champion weightlifter had ever made an effort to compare with this. But then he was struck dumb. The situation was saved by Nash'at. 'Do sit down, Mlle Farida. Have you had breakfast or are you on a diet like the people of Damietta? What do you say we all three breakfast here? The bean sandwiches here are fabulous. They'd put Groppi's to shame. Hassanain, three bean sandwiches and three teas, but look out, make sure it's clean.' He explained, 'Tea here very much depends on the mood Hassanain's in. One day it's tea, another day it's wood, and another day it'll be both. Bring us some of that tea that you keep for His Nibs, The Dean.'

The fancy came to Abdul-Karim that Nash'at carried on talking for months before the flood of words was interrupted by the sweet voice of the nightingale,

'Abdul-Karim, what's the matter, why are you so quiet? Hope you are not depressed or anything.'

Abdul-Karim realized that if he did not speak now he never would.

'What can I say? I'll just have to wait till "The Voice of Nash'at" broadcasting closes down.'

Her laugh was even more delicate than he had imagined. 'Just imagine, Mlle Farida, there was one time Nash'at began talking before The Voice of the Arabs came on the air, and he didn't stop until after close down.' She laughed again and at this point Nash'at intervened tactfully, 'I have had enough, I'll leave you two now, all the best!'

Somehow was he able to tell her the story of his life. How was he able to let go and not stammer at all, or get confused or hesitate? All that trembling and apprehension vanished and Farida listened, rapt.

Qasim could not have defined the moment when he was transformed from a revolutionary with no theory to one with a scientific doctrine. Everything started with his being introduced to Mr Sobhi Farhat, the Lector who taught him in the 'Discussion' seminar. Sohbi was not like the traditional Lector. He had been the top student in all Egypt in the leaving certificate exams and the first of his year on graduating in Sociology as well as Psychology. He had also been top graduate in Education. He was spending his last year in the Faculty before going to Paris for his Doctorate and no one – not his professors, his colleagues or his students – doubted that he would be the top student at the Sorbonne.

His involvement with Sobhi began with a mild argument when Sobhi was talking in class about primitive societies and their religions and was saying that most of these societies did not have religions of any kind. The categorical way in which the Lector was talking provoked Qasim so he cut in, 'But, sir, what about Adam? Wasn't he the first human being? Wasn't he also a Prophet? So how could there be primitive societies without religion?'

Sobhi Farhat quietly said, 'I'm sorry, I did not catch your name.'

'Yacoub Al-Haddy from Bahrain.'

'You are very welcome. Here, Yacoub, we are teaching Sociology, not Sharia. If you want to study Sharia, you'd better go to the Azhar.'

'But, sir, facts do not change if we change faculties. Adam actually existed.'

'Just let me finish the lesson for now. We can meet later and talk.'

And 'later' there were many meetings and at every one there would be a lengthy and heated debate. 'Yacoub, you were trying to provoke me. I doubt if you actually believe in Adam. In every religion, primitive or not, there is a myth about the father of mankind: everywhere in the world, on every continent, and in every tribe.'

'If you will permit me, sir, you are contradicting yourself. In class you were saying that most primitive societies do not have religion and now you say that they all believe in Adam.'

'Where's the contradiction? You can believe in Adam without believing in any religion and you can believe in a religion without believing in Adam. There are primitive societies who have a belief in their first father who is also the father of all mankind but in spite of that they do not have religious beliefs.'

'But how do you distinguish between religion and faith? Isn't religion synonymous with faith?'

'Sometimes, but not necessarily. I'll give you an example. I do not have any religious belief but I have faith in the doctrines of Marx and Freud.'

'So, sir, you worship Marx and Freud?'

At their next meeting their talk was of Marx.

'Mr Sobhi why all this enthusiasm for Marx? What has he produced?'

'Marx is the first person to have proved that history has movements which are regulated by fixed laws. He made clear that the economically dominant class in any society puts its imprint on all aspects of that society, from habits to laws to religion, and hence it is impossible to change that society without removing this class for good.'

'But what is so new about that, Mr Sobhi? Every revolution in history has been launched from the starting point of getting rid of the dominant class.'

'Every revolution has got rid of one class and put another in its place and nothing has really changed. Marx's doctrine gets rid of the economically dominant class it does not put any other class in its place but replaces it by the people which possesses the entire wealth.'

'That's only theory.'

'Theory? This is science and realism. And we can see it now being applied in the USSR, in China and in Eastern Europe.'

'But sir, in these places it is the Party, not the people who are ruling.'

'The Party is in a transitional phase, as Lenin has said. It is just a step on the way to true Communism which will come in the next historical phase.'

'And what about Stalin and his massacres? Khruschev is attacking Stalin now.'

'Individual excesses will always take place but a system based on the interests of the proletariat can always correct mistakes.'

They also discussed Freud.

'Why are you so impressed with old Sigmund?'

'Freud is the intellectual twin of Marx. He represents the other wing of the scientific understanding of man. Marx has made clear how societies move, while Freud has shown us what motivates man.'

'As I see it Freud has only said that sex is our basic moving force.'

'No. That is a fallacy put about by those who are only half-educated. Mankind didn't need Freud to realize the importance of sex. Freud's greatest discovery was that of the subconscious the actual motives and impulses which govern us and which the upper consciousness is unaware of. Before Freud no one recognized the unconscious nor of the forces which control it.'

'And do all these forces go back to sex and childhood and breast-feeding?'

'Most of them. If you were to look at your peers and you were completely conversant with Freud's theories you would not have any difficulty in understanding anything. Don't you think, for example, that the dictator who exercises the most cruel form of despotism is simply expressing complexes in his subconscious?'

'Mr Sobhi. Please don't start talking about Gamal Abdul Nasser!'

'He's just a petty bourgeois trying to become a member of the upper middle class.'

Gradually and one difficult book after another, Yacoub Al-Haddy changed from being a shambolic rebel into a Marxist–Freudian revolutionary. The mingling of the two doctrines was a key which enabled Yacoub to analyse all that surrounded him. Yacoub felt that he had been blind in the past. But still he was unable to follow Sobhi right to the end of the road: in spite of the Marxist–Freudian doctrine he refused to see in religion merely the opium of the people or a simple reflection of the power of the father in the subconscious of the child.

*He had known her from the time when they were together in the third grade and maybe even before that. All he knew was that from the time he got to know her he was never separated from her. They became something of a* byword in the village: Zainab (or Zoba) and Abdul-Sami'a (or Abdo). They would play together as when sun came up until sunset.

Years went by: Koranic school with Abdul-Sami'a a pupil and Zainab kept at home with her mother; the village school with Abdul-Sami'a a pupil and Zainab working with her mother in the fields. But when school was out there were still hours for the two of them to be together in the fields. They would start their games among the corn stalks and the sycamores or along the banks of the canal.

He did not remember those days between childhood and adolescence but imperceptibly they were growing up. Abdul-Sami'a was finishing at the village school and was preparing to travel to Al-Bandar where he would stay with his father's brother and study. A suitor arrived to ask for the hand of Zainab. Her father gave his approval and so preparations began for the wedding.

He remembered every moment of that day, how he and Zainab met shortly after the dawn call to prayer, the corn and the sycamores and the canal still in darkness. He recalled how she appeared with the first light, half a child and half a woman and how he approached her with a composure fitting for one who was half a child and half a man,

'I'm leaving for Al-Bandar, Zoba.'

'I know, Abdo. I will often think of you.'

'How could you marry Hajj Younus? He's the same age as your father.'

'That is my fate.'

'Do you love him, Zoba?'

'What's written on the forehead must be seen by the eye. And anyway you're going to Al-Bandar and leaving me behind.'

'You're the one who has left me. Aren't you getting married next Friday? Look at the henna'

The henna. Her hand. Her leg. Her lips. Her eyes. The corn. The sycamore. The canal. He had not intended to do anything. Nor had she. He was half a child and half a man, and she was half a girl and half a woman. The child began to play with the girl and without them being aware the man began to play with the woman. And then they found smears of blood on Zainab's dress. She went to the canal and washed her dress, weeping. He sat, looking on and also wept. They both knew that her husband, as soon as he learned that she was no longer a virgin, would divorce her and that her father would kill her that night.

The night came and Abdul-Sami'a was a witness but he could not join in the singing and dancing. Meanwhile Zainab, inside the house, awaited her fate. The hours dragged. The drums became silent and the songs were stilled. There were no more rounds of celebratory gunfire. Everyone held their breath waiting for the reddened handkerchief that would announce to the world that *the bride had been a virgin, and that the honour of the family had been preserved. Her father was waiting with the wedding guests.*

*Suddenly there came the sound of a woman's voice calling from far away. It was Zainab's mother and soon her father was contemplating the red handkerchief that the women were carrying aloft, a smile of pride on his lips. From all around voices rose.*

*'Congratulations to the headman!'*

*'A woman of virtue and the daughter of a man of excellent family!'*

*The gunfire rang out in celebration once again and Abdul-Sami'a fainted.*

Fuad looked over to Abdul-Ra'ouf slyly and said 'Ra'ouf, that's a very strange story.'

'In what way?'

'A young woman having her virginity restored!!'

'It's just a story.' ·

'What have you called it? The red handkerchief?'

'Don't be ridiculous! I'm going to call it "The canal".'

'The canal? What's a canal got to do with it? The point of the story is her virginity, surely?'

'The canal remains, always and forever, virgin. That's the whole point.'

'Abdul-Ra'ouf!! Have you become a Surrealist? What do you mean?'

'The canal in my village has been there since the days of Cleopatra. Nothing in it has changed. It is still virgin.'

'Ah! I see, "The Return of the Spirit" and all that . . . Now I understand.'

'You've not understood a thing.'

' "The Virgin Canal". It could make a great film. Let's have Hind Rustum as the heroine and Hassan Imam as producer. What about Zainab? Was there a real Zainab?'

'Of course, haven't you read Heykal's story?'

'I know who you mean. I am asking about your Zainab, Zoba.'

'There was a young girl, called Zoba.' He tried to laugh.

'And did you love her?'

· His friend nodded.

'Did she marry Hajj Yonous?'

'And what happened then?'

'She lived out there in the sticks and had lots of children.'

Qasim worked out his plan carefully. He looked around for the right apartment and consulted Nash'at, who in turn asked his friends. There was an apartment in Zamalek, another one in Minyal, and a third in Dokki. There was a fourth in Giza but none of them was right. This one was too small, that one too expensive, the doorkeeper of that one was vicious, this building did not accept bachelors, that street was much too noisy. But finally, 'Eureka'.

It was Qasim who said it and Nash'at echoed the cry. It was on Durry Street, in Al-Agouza, on the third floor of a building with no lift (which fitted in well with the inclination of Mr Shareef to encourage physical exercise). It was Apartment 6, in an ideal position, only twenty minutes by bus to the university. It was a dream of an apartment with four large bedrooms, and two bathrooms, a kitchen and a big entrance hall which could easily be changed into a sitting room, with room for dining. There was a small room for the help and the rent was only 18 Egyptian pounds.

Abdul-Karim proclaimed that the apartment was ideal and Yacoub agreed. Fuad said he was ready to move in right away, but there was still the matter of Mr Shareef and this was where the plan came in. Qasim asked to see Mr Shareef, who was astonished at this request since he would normally see Qasim once a week at least at Mme Khairiyya's. Qasim had only been once to Mr Shareef's, when he was invited to lunch with Fuad. At that time he had been introduced to his wife Fatima whom Mr Shareef called Batta. He had also met his son Muhammad (whom he called Meemo even though he was over ten) and his other son Arif (whom he called Foofoo even though he was eight years of age).

Mr Shareef made Qasim welcome and his wife greeted him and left. Then came Meemo and Foofoo who did the same. Coffee was served and Qasim began cautiously. 'Mr Shareef, I just had to come and see you here because I can't possibly talk in front of Fuad and Mme Khairiyya.'

'Why not, my son? I hope all's well . . .'

'I hope so. And I hope that our talk will remain confidential between us. Will you promise me, Mr Shareef?'

'Of course, my son, please proceed.'

'Mr Shareef, I'm afraid for Fuad.'

'Why, is he sick. Does he have a problem with his studies?'

'No, it's not that.'

'Then, what's the problem?'

'Mme Khairiyya.'

'Mme Khairiyya? Has she fallen out with him?'

'On the contrary, Mr Shareef, on the contrary. For some time there has been a "relationship" between them.'

'God forbid. A relationship!?'

'Mr Shareef, please spare me from going into the details. It's just enough if I tell you that she goes into his room at 10 at night, in front of us all, and doesn't emerge until morning in full view of us all.'

'God almighty. Mme Khairiyya. She's old enough to be his mother. How?'

'That's the part that's a mystery. Mr Shareef. A little while ago I saw a strange man in Fuad's room, muttering words I couldn't understand. He was wafting incense, too, and when I asked Mme Khairiyya about him she got all confused and started stammering.'

'Aha! He's put a spell on him. That explains everything!'

'And now Fuad is totally lost and his mind is wandering: he can't eat, he can't sleep and he can't study. If we stay in the apartment I'm afraid he will go mad. Mr Shareef, we've just got to get out of that place.'

'That's right, you'll have to move. I'll look for another apartment right away, and a lady who is respectable.'

'No, Mr Shareef, don't. Don't put yourself to any trouble. I've found just the right apartment and we can all stay there, the four of us: Fuad, Abdul-Karim, Yacoub and myself. And I can promise you, Mr Shareef, that we'll keep Fuad under close observation.'

'I had been worried about what would happen if you lived in an apartment and that's why I chose Mme Khairiyya. And now look what's happened. Qasim, there's just one thing that bothers me.'

'What's that, sir?'

'Is Mme Khairiyya, er, expecting a baby? Has she accused Fuad of anything?'

'No, I don't think Mme Khairiyya is pregnant and she hasn't accused Fuad of anything.'

'Thank God for that.'

'Mr Shareef, wouldn't you like to see the apartment? The doorkeeper, Zakariyya is waiting.'

When Qasim told the group that Mr Shareef had approved of the idea of their moving no one believed him until they saw the key in his hand. Fuad asked 'How did you manage to persuade Mr Shareef?'

'Easily, Fuad. I cast a spell.'

On the tenth of March 1958 the four musketeers moved to Apartment 6 on Floor 3 of the apartment building standing halfway along Durry Street. And their first decision was what to call it. There were lots of suggestions: Rafaa, Hadd, Urooba, but Qasim said bitterly 'Everything here in Egypt is called Victory so why don't you call it The Apartment of Victory and have done with it?'

The others were just about to agree, to spite Qasim but Yacoub put in an objection. 'No. Freedom. We've moved here to have some freedom, so we'll call it "APARTMENT FREEDOM".'

The next step was to draw up a constitution to regulate life there so Fuad and Nash'at were commissioned to formulate one. Para. 1 said, ' "APARTMENT FREEDOM" is an integral part of the Arab Nation whose original denizens are Abdul-Karim Al-Shaikh; Yacoub Al-Haddy; Qasim Sudfy; and Fuad Tarif. Associate members are Abdul-Ra'ouf Buhairy and

Nash'at Mahram. The apartment is endowed with sovereignty and independence and its nature is based on the principles of equality, justice and democracy. Decisions shall be taken by majority vote and any member may propose any topic for discussion, with the exception of the political situation in Bahrain . . .'

'Why this exception?'

'Nash'at, this is a very thorny subject. It's for the best. Every time we debate it we fall to screaming and falling out. Once or twice it nearly came to blows. Qasim takes the view that this movement was a communist conspiracy while Yacoub believes it to have been the greatest revolutionary movement in history. Abdul-Karim, on the other hand, thinks it was all a British plot. As for me – I just don't know.'

The constitution eventually ran to 70 clauses which regulated the budget; disbursement policy; the jurisdiction running of the apartment; the writ of the hired help, male or female; time allowed in the bathroom (this clause being inserted to protect the others from the tendency of Abdul-Karim to hog it); and protocol for receiving guests both male and female. Fuad insisted that the constitution must specify 'It is absolutely not allowed to have female guests in the apartment in the month of examinations, whether in the first or second terms.'

Nash'at, however, proposed an amendment reading 'Unless such female guest should be the mother, sister or grandmother of any of the residents.'

The principles were accepted and the final clause stipulated that no provision of the constitution could be changed except by unanimous vote of the original denizens and associate members.

# CHAPTER FIVE

## May 1958

Less than two months after moving in the furnishings and equipping of Apartment Freedom had been completed. Mr Shareef took charge of everything since it turned out that he knew a first-rate carpenter, the owner of a furniture showroom, and a plumber as well as an electrician. Qasim insisted there should be a heater in each bathroom since he had truly suffered bitterly in Mme Khairiyya's apartment where the water was heated only in dire necessity. He also insisted a proper fridge should be bought after suffering from the primitive gadget at the same apartment. It had worked on the basis of putting an ice mould in the upper half so as to refrigerate the bottom half. Qasim undertook to bear the additional expense himself. In the end the apartment was not as luxurious as Qasim had wished but, it was way beyond standards normally expected of bachelor students' places.

As soon as they had installed themselves Qasim insisted that they should exercise their newly-acquired freedom by arranging an evening's entertainment with 'little sweethearts'. He soon found out, though, that this was somewhat difficult. In the beginning his fellow-students refused to attend. Abdul-Karim insisting that his love for Farida stood between him and a session with the ladies of the night while Yacoub said that he could not go back to sex until he had reached a proper scientific understanding of the subject through his studies of Freud. Fuad said that he rejected on principle the idea of harlots. After a great deal of effort Qasim persuaded them to stay with him for the sake of celebrating their liberty, no more. He added that there was nothing compelling any one of them to take any action. The girls would be coming for the sake of the money which he would pay, and for them it was all the same whether anything happened or not.

Having persuaded his fellows Qasim fell to planning the details but here an unpleasant surprise awaited him. The phone numbers which he had been accumulating over the last few months were either out of order or there was no reply. In fact the only number which responded brought the voice of a man who roundly cursed him and made threats if he were to call again. Eventually Qasim realized that the Madams, under the threat of pursuit from the Vice Squad, had had to change their numbers. So he collected numbers from Bahraini tourists and experimented until he found the desired response from Madame Lola. She, once she had established his *bona fides* was reassured. Initially she insisted that she could send only three girls while Qasim sought four. After that came the question of price with Madame Lola asking for 5 pounds per girl and Qasim offering two. Final agreement was reached at three pounds. There then arose the questions of the girls access to the building and their leaving. Qasim told her that he had an understanding with the doorkeeper. Lola insisted Qasim come himself to her apartment and accompany her charges, later to return them safely to her. Yacoub offered to be his companion. Agreement was reached on timing: 7 p.m on Thursday and Qasim must see them safely back by 11 p.m.

From Thursday morning a state of emergency was proclaimed in Apartment Freedom. Qasim took over all the arrangements. Zaki, their cook, was given a holiday lasting from lunchtime for 24 hours. A contract was agreed with the restaurant 'Al-Haati' for delivery of a dinner to be served at 8 p.m. Qasim had the fridge filled with Stella Artois and appetizers: cheese, olives, cucumber, and carrot sticks. His nerves were frayed as if he were making preparations for a mass execution, not for a party.

Qasim set off with Yacoub for the Madame's apartment in Zamalek from where they duly returned with the girls. Old Zakariyya the doorkeeper turned a blind eye and to their great good fortune none of the residents in the building was encountered on the stairs. So when everyone had settled down in the living-room and glasses of beer had been handed round Qasim felt that the plan over which he had toiled so earnestly had been a success.

Qasim had no idea what the real names of the girls were since he had only heard their 'working' names, or, as might have been said in the Ba'ath party, their names 'in the movement'. They were Zeezi, Shooshoo, Reeri and Deedee. They were all about the same age as their clients. The prettiest was Zeezee who, Qasim had decided, was for him. She was fair, of full body, with almost no make-up. Shooshoo, who right away got into a heated discussion with Yacoub might have got a grade of 'Good' by university criteria although she had a distinctly brownish tint to her features while Deedee would have rivalled Zeezee if it had not been for her violently peroxided hair. Reeri sat alongside Abdul-Karim and the two of them exchanged wary glances. Fuad sat alongside Deedee attempting to discuss cinema.

Fuad had never drunk beer before. The rest were all familiar with it from their days in secondary school in Bahrain. Access to beer had been a dangerous adventure and drinking it even more so since the penalty for drunkenness in

Bahrain was 6 months in gaol. But it was generally agreed in school that manhood began only with beer to cigarettes: you were half way there and only the other half remained: women. Yacoub was the only one who had carnal knowledge which he had acquired at 'Grandol', the red-light district in Bahrain and various secret locations in Cairo. Fuad had never had any wish to touch beer either in Bahrain or in Cairo in spite of the mockery of his companions. Even Abdul-Karim had drunk it with the rest. God alone knows what would have happened if his father the Shaikh had discovered that his son, who claimed to be going to 'private lessons' was actually heading off to bars. Fuad decided that the ceremony of inaugurating Apartment Freedom deserved a glass of beer. What surprised him was how bitter it tasted since he had imagined that it was sweet like Pepsi or had a neutral taste like water. He had to spit out the sip he had taken and splashed his clothes to the amusement of his friends. They explained that beer was drunk not for its taste but for its effect.

The ashtrays filled and the bottles of Stella disappeared with astonishing speed. Laughter rose into the air and Fuad found himself launching forth in a way that he had never before experienced. He swore for the first time, and told questionable jokes. Yacoub was singing in his lovely voice one of Abdul-Halim Hafez's songs which he could imitate beautifully,

'Greet him, you lovely one, to go with the longing that is in his eyes . . .'

The girls sang along and then came the dinner, so the party was going swimmingly. Qasim whispered that it was getting near 9 p.m. and that it would be better not to waste any time.

Zeezee was with Qasim in his room, the smartest room in the apartment, with diverse pictures on the walls. His father's portrait, his mother's and his uncle's. There was a coloured picture of Elvis Presley, one of Brigitte Bardot and one of President Eisenhower taken from the cover of *Time*. Zeezee contemplated them and stood bewildered in front of Eisenhower. Qasim could not hold back his laughter.

'Wot's up with you, wotcha laughing at? Who is he, I mean?'
'Eisenhower.'
'But wotcha put his picture in your room for?'
'I am an admirer of his.'
'Admiring an ugly old guy like him?'
'It's not his face I like, Zeezee, its his politics.'
'Hey, wot's politics got to do with us?'
'All right, then, we'll forget about politics.'
'Yeah, much better, no headaches. Er . . . is there anything wrong with us?'

'No. Why.'

'Everything's OK but aren'tcha going to strip off?'

In a rapid movement, that did not seem to Qasim to last more than a second Zeezee had got rid of all her clothes and had sat down on the bed. Qasim blushed and could not speak.

'Aren'tcha going to strip off?'

Qasim felt a chill strike him reaching his limbs and paralysing him.

'Wot's up? Aren'tcha going to strip off and get into bed? Now, wot is it? Don'tcha like me?'

'No, no, it's not that, it's just that I'm . . .'

'You're wot?'

Qasim had imagined that the room would be darkened and that things would get started with delicate whispers and soft kisses. But for things to start in the glare of lights with a woman who expected him to undress like her in a second and then pounce on her like an animal – well, this was a real dirty trick. He tried to save the situation. 'May I put the light out?'

'Oh, yer can't get it up. Why didn't yer say so? Anything but that. But why make out you were a man?'

Qasim felt an overpowering rage. Why should he put up with these insults? Hadn't she come just for the money? And hadn't she been paid already? With a show of resolution he told her, 'I've changed my mind. I don't want to tonight. Get up and dressed. I'll wait outside.'

As soon as Abdul-Karim entered his room with Reeri he put the question to her.

'What's your name, I mean your real name.'

'What's my real name got to do with you? Are you from the public prosecutor's?'

'No, I'd just like to know.'

'No need. Reeri's nice.'

'Listen, Reeri, can we talk a bit?'

'What, again. You must be from the public prosecutor's!'

'For God's sake, no. But I'd like to get to know you better. How old are you?'

'18.'

'Did you go to school?'

'What's this, do you think I'm straight from the farm? I did Intermediate. But my dad died and mum was left with a little boy and three girls. I'm the oldest.'

'What did your dad do?'

'He was a soldier. He died in an accident.'

'Wasn't there a pension?'

'Eight pounds.'

'When did you, er . . . I mean . . .'

'You mean: when did I start work? Two years ago.'

'Does your mother know?'

'I give her money. She doesn't ask and I don't say.'

'But what do you say to her when you leave the house, like tonight?'

'Didn't I tell you? She doesn't ask.'

'How much do you give her a month?'

'Her due. What's all this pestering for?'

'Forty pounds, say?'

'Some hope. Sometimes twenty, at the most thirty.'

'And the Madame takes what?'

'Two for every one I take.'

'That's scandalous. Why don't you leave her?'

'Where would I go? On the streets? This is much better.'

'And where are your clients from?'

'From your part of the world. Kuwait, Saudi Arabia, Qatar.'

'But we are not from those places.'

'Where from, then?'

'Bahrain.'

'Ah, I thought you were Kuwaitis, you talk the way they do.'

'Can I ask you the way you feel. . . .'

'Listen, Mr Kuwaiti or Bahraini, whichever you are. That's enough. Don't you want to get on with it?'

'No, no, thanks. Talking is enough.' Abdul-Karim delved into his pocket and pulled out five pounds. 'Here, take this, Reeri. A little present. Let's go and finish our conversation in the living-room.'

As soon as Shooshoo entered the room with Yacoub her eyes fell on the pictures of Marx and Freud.

'Who's the old boy, then, the one like a Shaikh?'

'Karl Marx.'

'And who is His Excellency? An ambassador?'

'No, an economist.'

'Economist? You mean he's the owner of Chicorel?'

'No, no. He developed an economic doctrine taught at university.'

'And the other guy, who's he?'

'Sigmund Freud.'

'And who's he?'

'A great scholar. He discovered the science of the mind.'

'The mind. Is that a science? OK, then tell me a bit about myself.'

'Well, you are a human being who is oppressed, defeated and crushed.'

'Oppressed, defeated, OK. But crushed – rubbish!!'

'If you weren't crushed you wouldn't be doing a job like this, would you?'

'What's the job got to do with it? I'll soon be a film actress. Are they any better looking than me?'

'Shooshoo, who was it that treated you badly?'

'Lots of people. Hey, what's your name?'

'Yacoub.'

'That's a difficult name. Don't you have another? I'm going to call you "Bobby". I'm just teasing you. Tell me, Bobby, are you oppressed as well?'

'Of course. By society.'

'Huh, everyone's treated you badly, you poor thing!'

'Well, not everyone, but most people are oppressed.'

'So who treated you badly? The big shots?'

'Yeah.'

'Yes, but soon you'll be graduating and then you'll go back to your own country and then *you'll* be a big shot!'

'No, I won't, I'll always be on the side of those who are the weaker. Listen, Shooshoo, I'll explain. There are two types of people in society, a class that exploits and becomes rich and a class they exploit and that stays poor.'

'You're dead right.'

'And we have to change this situation.'

'Yeah, but how are we going to do that?'

'A socialist revolution.'

'Haven't we had that?'

'Not yet.'

'And when that comes, what will happen?'

'Exploitation will end.'

'We'll all be rich, then?'

'Yes.'

'But that'll be great, Bobby. But why didn't the President do all this?'

'Well, Nasser made a start.'

'Well, let's be patient a while, then.... Hey, Bobby, haven't you talked enough? I have. Why don't you sing to me a bit?'

'No, you sing!'

'But I've already sung "You alone are my darling!" twice.'

'Well, sing it a third time. We'll go and sing together in the living-room.'

Fuad goes into his room with Deedee and she ignores the pictures of his father, his mother, and Gamal Abdul Nasser and stops in front of a picture of Fuad with Suad in the Faculty garden. 'Who's the girl?'

'A fellow-student.'

'What's her name? Suad? Is she Egyptian?'

'No, she's from Syria.'

'From Syria. Haven't you heard the song "From Cairo's Bazaars to the Hamidiyya Souk"? Haven't we become just one country? So, she's an Egyptian.'

'A Damascene?'

'OK, a Damascene.'

'Is she pretty?'

'Her photo's in front of you.'

'Hmm . . . , not bad. Is she a lawyer?'

'No, she's a student in our class.'

'So later she'll be a lawyer and open an office here in Egypt, not in Syria.'

'Deedee, Syria is a rich country.'

'Rich? Well, then, why are we spending so much money on them? Everyone says so. Nasser, wasn't he working on union with Saudi Arabia, to bring us a bit of oil, instead of those hungry Syrians!!'

'The Kingdom of Saudi Arabia is a reactionary country.'

'Reactionary! But they've got oil. And the Hajj. By the Prophet, union with the Kingdom of Saudi Arabia would be better!'

'But the idea doesn't appeal to the rulers of the Kingdom.'

'They're pretty smart; they don't want to spend their money on anyone.'

'Deedee, it's not like that at all. It's all connected with Arab unity. It's a question of principle, not just one of interests.'

'So is the principle that we join up with a lot of no-hopers and forget those who are well-off? And which group is your girlfriend in?'

'I don't know.'

'Haven't you asked her?' He shifted his anger for a moment. 'Are you going to marry her?'

'I don't think so.'

'I wish I could marry someone from your country.'

'From Bahrain?'

'From anywhere there's oil. Isn't there oil in Bahrain? Some oil is better than none at all. Why don't we get married?'

'No thanks.'

'Oh, so I am not up to your standard, then? Maybe the girl from Damascus is nicer-looking?'

Fuad is afraid the situation is slipping out of his grasp and suggests that they carry on talking about marriage in the living-room. There they are surprised to find Abdul-Karim, Qasim and Yacoub together with the three other girls.

The next morning at breakfast Yacoub tittered.

'Listen, guys, I want you to know that last night I didn't do a thing.'

Fuad looked over to him sadly. 'Nor me!' Abdul-Karim abjectly admitted he had not got lucky either. Eventually Qasim hesitated and said he'd also failed. They all laughed. Then Yacoub said, 'That's fine, I have had some experience and so now I have scientific reasons for not having sex. But you are all virgins: why did you waste the opportunity? What about you, Abdul-Karim?'

'I was thinking about Farida.'

'And you, Fuad?'

'I was thinking about Suad.'

'And you Qasim? Were you thinking about Brigitte Bardot?'

'I wasn't thinking about anyone but the atmosphere wasn't right. The girl whipped off her clothes and expected me to do the same. I was expecting . . .'

'A bit of romance? Some affection? A little love? You remind me of what Al-Sayyab said in his verse.'

'What did he say?'

'O you, you drunkard
You who want from a whore what you wish from a virgin
Do you expect from this human debris used by all
The warmth of spring and the joy of the innocent lamb in the morning?'

Qasim looked over to him furiously and screamed, 'Shut Up!'

# CHAPTER SIX

## November 1958

The really happy surprise awaiting Fuad in the Faculty was how easy it was to study. Despite stories about how long the curriculum was and how arduous law studies were, he discovered that concentration together with intensive revision in the last weeks of each term was enough to guarantee success. His grades during the first two terms varied between 'Acceptable' and 'Very Good' and it was the same with his companions. On the whole they were average or a little better with the exception of Abdul-Ra'ouf who had consistently outstanding grades.

Nor did Fuad find that study in the Faculty was as dry as he had feared. In fact he delighted in studying law. He now began to use legal expressions in everyday speech. The subject he particularly liked was Sharia Law, because Professor Shaikh Muhammad Abu-Zahra inspired him. The role which Islam would play in the coming Arab national state, was something that increasingly preoccupied him. After lectures he would frequently visit the Shaikh where he would pose questions. The Shaikh would respond to his questions with warmth and frankness. When he lectured, the benches of the lecture hall would be packed and every lecture would be enlivened by laughter and barbed remarks. Every day he would launch a sally against the paper *Akhbar Al-Yawm*. The paper would then reply the following day but would repay him with interest.

So study was not a problem for Fuad even though it occupied the major part of his time. He now began to concentrate on two main subjects, Suad, and the other to do with his head, the Ba'ath party. His relationship with Suad was deteriorating day by day. Superficially there were no problems and everyone saw them as an item. But something was eating into the heart of their relationship, without any obvious symptoms. Two or three days would go by and they would not meet but neither would reproach the other. When it was time for their weekly meeting one or other of them would find themselves busy. Even when they met their kisses did not have the former warmth.

Then again, his relationship with the party began to have tricky periods and even though he still believed in the principles of the party and its doctrines its actual conduct of its affairs caused him more and more worry. After the first rapture the weekly meetings, they became a chore with the usual old topics being repeated. The party's activities now did not go beyond slogans. The party's instructions endlessly rode roughshod over his thoughts. He began to resent the need to treat every party member as a dear friend.

Fuad's first encounter with Michel Aflaq came as a shock. Every day for some time Suad had been talking about meeting him. When the day dawned she and Fuad went to the hotel on the Nile where Aflaq was staying and they found him, in a corner of one of the reception rooms surrounded by admirers, a short man with very ordinary features. He smoked incessantly as the questions flowed and he answered slowly and briefly. Every answer was received with what sounded exactly like the moans of lovers. Suad was transfixed.

'Comrade Fuad, Sir, is a writer of short stories. Just as you used to be.'

Aflaq looked at her as if he knew her well. He smiled. He then looked at Fuad, unsmiling. 'I abandoned the short story because it is futile romanticism.' Suad nodded agreement but Fuad was upset.

Fuad's meeting with Salahuddin Bitar was no happier than that with Aflaq. Again he was surrounded by sycophants, but some found their voices. Bitar seemed to Fuad more intelligent and lively than the rest. Suad told him that Fuad was a short story writer.

'What is your theme, Fuad? What do you deal with in your stories?'

'There isn't just one theme. Every story has a subject.'

'Fine. But there has to be one central idea in all the stories.'

'I write spontaneously, sir, without thinking like that.'

'Literature without an issue? That's just bourgeois amusement.'

Suad nodded.

Dearest Suad,

I know that this letter will not come as a surprise. Maybe the surprise is that I did not write it sooner. Our relationship has been so tepid these last few weeks. When I talk about our relationship I don't mean our friendship. I am confident that will endure as long as we live.

Remember how sad I was when we left the majlis classes of The Teacher? I told you then that I rejected the idea that my gift, humble as it might be, is worthless. And when we left the majlis of Salahuddin Bitar I told you that I considered my gift to be as important as The Great Issue. Both times you insisted that my gift, if it were not in the service of the party, was of no value. Suad, this is the big difference between us. You are a very rare person, the kind that puts their cause above all other things and persons. I am so sad that the cause which once brought us together should now divide us. I have to tell you, Suad, that I am no longer able to accept party discipline and demands whether personal, intellectual or political.

I have told Bassam that in future I shall not be able to attend. I fear that ending my contact with the party means you will end our relationship. Suad, I had really hoped that we should be able to have a private relationship, away from the 'Comrades', within which we could have our differences and our agreements. But now I know that you place every relationship beneath your principles.

My dear, I shall never forget our happy hours, remember your sweet features, your lovely smile, our noisy arguments. And I shall always share with you the faith in the destiny of our Arab nation, one and everlasting. I send you my true and sincere love, for ever and always.

Fuad.

My dear Fuad,

It had been my dearest and sweetest hope that we should stay together and make plans for the future of our Arab nation as well as for our own. I dreamed of the house we would share as well as dreaming of the one Arab state which would bring together all the scattered parts. But my hopes faded when I noticed that you were trying to separate personal issues from the general. They cannot be separated. Fuad, you believe that Arabs can reach the goals without a doctrine and without an intellectual leadership, without organization. You still believe in intangibles, a religion based on the unseen, an unseen leader, but I have realized that the dream cannot be realized except through the leadership of the Ba'ath party. It requires intellectual engagement which can only bring fruit if there is a discipline. You have preferred to let your sentiments rule your mind. This choice is your right. It is a choice I accept but I do so with pain and regret.

Yes – and this is a promise from me as well – our friendship will survive. Our memories will remain. But we have reached the parting of the ways: you will go to where your gift leads you – and you are doing yourself an injustice if you imagine that it is a modest gift – and I will go on to where the destiny of the nation leads me.

Suad.

*Zaghloul shivered on the cold paved floor. He tried to curl up and make himself as small as possible so as to get warm. He heard the footsteps of Corporal Mahrous pacing along the corridor and made a silent prayer to God that he would not halt at his cell. That meant only one thing: another bucket of freezing water flung at him. A little before dawn he closed his eyes but then awoke to say his prayers and make silent invocations. The small piece of burnt bread was brought to him and the cup of tepid tea. The warder grinned.*

*'Well now, boss, did we have a nice sleep?'*

*Zaghloul was taken off for interrogation and the officer began, 'Why don't you just confess – it'd be better for you?'*

*'Confess to what?'*

*'Terrorism.'*

*'Sir, I am just a poor man who minds his own business. From the mosque straight home, from home straight to the mosque. Ask people.'*

*'We did, and they confessed to the weapons you're all storing at home, you sons of bitches.'*

*'May God forgive you, sir!'*

*'May God destroy your house! Are you going to confess or do we get the electrician in?'*

*'But what can I confess to, sir?' The nightmare circle turned again.*

*The warder took him back to his cell. Before he went in he turned to the warder and asked, 'Corporal Mahrous, by the Prophet, could you please let me have a little water so I can wash? How am I to pray if I don't wash?'*

*'Listen, boss, you've said enough prayers: weren't you the Imam?'*

*'May God guide Corporal Mahrous!'*

*'May God ruin your house!'*

*Then it was time for the evening interrogation.*

*'Are you going to confess or not, Zaghloul?'*

*'Confess to what, sir?'*

*'OK, Mahrous, fetch the electrician.'*

*'Sir, just a moment . . .'*

*'You mean, you are going to confess?'*

*'What's the need for the electrician, sir?'*

*'Just a couple of shocks to get your brain working. And if that doesn't do the trick we'll send for the dogs.'*

*'Sir – there's no need for any electrician or any dogs.'*

*'You mean, you're confessing?'*

*'I'll confess.'*

*The officer smiled. 'Mahrous, send for the Prosecutor!'*

Fuad looked at Abdul-Ra'ouf, smiling. 'The confessional stool! Book, production and starring role by Yusuf Whabi! My God! What is all this?'

'It's no exaggeration.'

'Dogs and electricity and prisoners prevented from praying. Where does that happen?'

'Here. In Cairo. In the Military Prison.'

'You're joking.'

'Is this something to make jokes about?'

'OK, maybe I can accept a bit of poetic licence.'

'Look, Fuad, this is not just a story. This really happened.'

'You mean there is really a person called Zaghloul? And that he had treatment like this in the Military Prison?'

'Yes.'

'Why?'

'Because they, the police, the Army and the Intelligence people were looking for weapons belonging to what they call the terrorist group. In his house they found booklets written by Sheikh Hassan Al-Banna.'

'Was this his only crime? And was he a member of the terrorist group?'

'He wasn't even a member of the Muslim Brotherhood. He used to collect religious pamphlets and he happened to have some by Hassan Al-Banna. He made a confession.'

'And what was the sentence?'

'Three years' hard labour.'

'How do you know all this?'

'From Zaghloul. He's my brother.'

Abdul-Karim found all this happiness too much and could not believe that fate was not storing up some horror. Farida loved him: was this possible? Or had he lost his senses and started imagining things? Suppose it was a dream that had gone on so long he had begun confusing it with reality? And what would happen to him if he woke? And was he dreaming alone now, or was Farida dreaming with him? Was he a part of her dream too? How had all his fears been blown? How had he achieved this self-confidence anyway?

After that first meeting in the buffet there had been many more dates. The first real one had been the trip they made to the Nile Barrages. The Faculty organized the trip for scores of male and female students but for Abdul-Karim it was just for the two of them. The details of it were etched into his memory with her perfume: how they gathered at Rawd Al-Farag; the big boat that carried them all; the trip on the Nile; the jokes, songs and speeches. Seeing the Barrages themselves for the first time. Gardens stretching in every direction. Everywhere there was uproar and laughter. The students broke up into small groups and he went off alone with Farida. They talked and laughed and time raced by. On the way back Abdul-Karim felt that he was being borne on a magic carpet to the world of myths. Farida stood close to him, the Nile breezes playing with her hair. The setting sun stole in.

> This is the first time you've been in love, my heart
> And this is the first day that I have known true happiness. . . .'

The words of the song went directly from the boat's microphone to his heart as Farida beside him murmured the words of the song. The boat tied up and the dream-like day was over . . .

The days flew by and Farida seemed to him more beautiful and more desirable. The most marvellous part of each week was their date for the cinema matinee performance. In the cool auditorium their hands would touch. This was a meeting of day with night, of thirst with means to quench it. When they found themselves in the back row he would get a little closer to her and she would turn her face to him. They would look into each other's eyes in the darkness and then he would edge even closer. Their lips would touch. Then there would come a feeling from outer space. Or maybe it was from some region closer, from the stars. Or possibly from the area of the clouds. Her lips were rosy, sweet and luscious. When he went home he would have the trace of her perfume on his mouth and on his hands. He would drink in her perfume, intoxicated. Then sleep and dream of her.

When did the idea of marriage first come up? Was it in his mind or hers? Or was the idea born in both their minds at the same time? After their fifth date, or maybe their tenth, they began to talk cautiously about the future.

'After you graduate what are you going to do, Karim?'

'I don't know yet, maybe I'll go on to more study.'

'Aren't you going to open a lawyer's office?'

'I've thought about it. There's a shortage of good lawyers in Bahrain.'

'Here there are more lawyers than there are worries in the heart.' She continued, 'Is Bahrain nice, Karim?'

'To me it is.'

'Will I see it one day?'

'Why not?'

And then they fell to planning a future together. 'That's it, Farida. I've decided to open my law office in Bahrain. You shall work with me.'

'As an employee?'

'No, as a partner. My partner for life.'

'Just like that, all at once.'

'Well, will you be my partner for life?'

'Are you serious?'

'I'm not joking, by God!'

'OK, let me think about it.'

'No, without thinking.'

'I agree.'

'Seriously, seriously? Swear?'

'Seriously, seriously. I swear.'

When Abdul-Karim told his friends that he and Farida had spoken of marriage he was met with a silence which quickly changed to noisy objections. He had expected that his friends would be happy for him, so their reaction was like a slap in the face.

Qasim started it. 'Have you gone mad, have you lost your mind, Abdul-Karim? You are still a second-year student and you are thinking of getting married? You can't possibly afford it.'

'Getting married requires psychological and intellectual maturity and, with the greatest respect, Abdul-Karim, you are still an adolescent. You are not twenty yet! Wait ten years,' urged Yacoub.

Fuad added, 'How can you marry a Sunni woman? And will she agree to marry a Shia? And what about your father – will he agree to the idea?'

Abdul-Karim paid no attention to Qasim because two *could* live as cheaply as one and as for Yacoub with his talk of adolescence and maturity – this was just Freudian nonsense. But Fuad's question was like a dagger's thrust. He had already discussed the matter of community with Farida and they had decided that Sunni and Shia would not be obstacles to their marriage, but Fuad's remark rang warning bells. Would his father, the elder of the community of the Shia in Bahrain, agree to his son marrying a Sunni woman! And an Egyptian?

Qasim had convinced himself the shambles of the first evening's entertainment was simply the result of Zeezee's stupid behaviour, and that the second experiment would be better. Another girl, Muna, was sent by a Madame but exactly the same thing happened. They went into his room, her clothes were off in a flash, she asked him to get a move on and he could not oblige. The third experiment was with Nadia, sent by a Madame who asserted that she was the loveliest of her girls, nicely behaved and therefore the fee was five pounds. Qasim agreed and it turned out that Nadia was indeed a beauty and not in a hurry. All the preliminaries which he judged to be necessary were observed, but still he could not perform.

'I have got a complex, Nash'at. I think I must be ill. I ought to see a doctor. Three times! Three different girls! And I still couldn't do a thing. I must be impotent!'

'Where did you find the girls?'

'They were sent by a Madame.'

'You paid, you mean?'

'Oh, no ... I got them for free.' He shrugged and grinned, then frowned again. 'Of course I paid!'

'Qasim, what are you doing with whores? The world is full of girls.'

'So how do I meet them?'

'Just a bit of front. You are a nice-looking guy, and you've got plenty of money. All you need is a bit of front.'

'But suppose the little darling insults me or slaps my face?'

'She won't.'

'So, all I need is courage? Sounds so easy.'

Qasim tried to forget his problem by immersing himself in his studies, but they kept breaking in on him. Suppose he really was impotent should he go to the doctor? Wouldn't he just say it was all in his mind? Would it end there or would he be transferred to the psychiatric ward? Just because he couldn't go to bed with a whore was he going to finish up in the nuthouse?

He talked about it with Yacoub and received a predictable reply. 'You are failing because deep down you think that you are about to have sex with your mother.'

'Yacoub, what a filthy thing to say!'

'Let me explain. We grew up in the society of Bahrain where they taught us that sex was a guilty act, a sin. And the child, as Freud has taught us, gets its first experiences of sexual pleasure from contact with its mother and in particular from the breast. Then he grows up and feelings get confused. Feelings of pleasure from the breast and the feeling of guilt muddle, so that every sexual act seems like fornication with the mother. That's the origin of impotence.'

'I have never heard such rubbish. No child experiences sexual pleasure at his mother's breast.'

'All children do. But they forget it as they grow up.'

'And is all this weird stuff the thoughts of Freud? To hell with you! And him!'

Qasim had not paid any attention to her. He thought that in her blue smock and pony-tail she must a schoolgirl and he had no time for those. As he grew more disappointed with whores he began to notice her each day. She lived on the same street in an apartment building nearby. He saw her almost every day at the bus stop. She got off at the Urman Model Girls' School in Dokki. One day he realized that she was not a little girl. The school uniform hid a body which was womanly and mature while her pony-tail did not express the luxuriant tangle of her thick dark hair. Suddenly he could imagine her in a short skirt with her curls falling by her face.

He remembered Nash'at's advice and so one morning he summed up his courage as they waited at the bus-stop.

'Good morning, Mademoiselle!'

'Good morning,' she replied as if she had been expecting this.

'The bus is late.'

'Oh, dear! They may close the gate!!'

'You go to the Urman school, don't you? Which year?'

'I'm taking my leaving certificate.'

'Arts or Sciences?'

'Sciences.'

When the bus arrived they carried on talking in the crush. Before she got off he had learned her name was Shereen Badr Al-Sharqawi and that her father was Dr Badr Al-Sharqawi, Dean of the Faculty of Pharmacy at Cairo University, and that she too wanted to study pharmacy.

As soon as Qasim saw Nash'at he shouted aloud, 'You're not going to believe it, I found my nerve!'

'And who is the unfortunate young lady?'

'She's our neighbour. Imagine! I was on the same bus every day and never spoke to her.'

'I'll bet she's ugly.'

'Ugly? Wait till you see her!'

'Is she a university student?'

'No, she's finishing secondary. Do you know who her father is?'

'King Farouq?'

'The Dean of the Faculty of Pharmacy.'

'Pharmacy? Look out, she may turn out to be poisoned.'

During his Ba'athist period Fuad had not felt intellectually attuned to any of his peers except for Majid Zubair. Bassam Nuweilat had been unbearably conceited, talking as if he had founded the Ba'ath party and before that the Arab nation; Muhammad Asseily had been charged with hatred as he was a Shia from South Lebanon who felt he was persecuted and Fuad felt that he had joined the Ba'ath party only to struggle against the dominance of the Maronites and Sunnis in running Lebanon; Victoria Nassar was a Christian and to Fuad it seemed that she had joined the party only to escape from the mental prison imposed on all minorities.

Fuad's relationship with Majid Zubair developed into friendship. He was from a well-known family from Uneiza and one day Majid told him that they had, at the beginning of the century, been visited by Rihani who had called Uneiza the Paris of Nejd. As soon as he heard the name Fuad felt stung.

'Rihani! When did Najib Rihani visit Uneiza?'

'Amin Rihani, you idiot. The philosopher.'

'And he called Uneiza the Paris of Nejd?'

'Yes, and he put that in his book.'

'Either he was never in Uneiza or he never visited Paris.'

Like Fuad, Majid believed in Arab nationalism and Arab unity as well as the leadership of Nasser but, like Fuad also, he had an instinctive faith in

Islam and could not see how he could embrace a doctrine which was in conflict with it.

'You know, Majid, the Ba'ath party is for minorities. It was established by a Christian, and just look at our group.'

'Yes, have you noticed how Victoria insists at every meeting on the secular and lay character of the party? And did you see how Muhammad and Bassam agreed?'

'Their motives are well known. The lay character of Lebanon means the end of Maronite domination and in Iraq it means the end of Muslim domination.'

'And what about the rest of the Arab world where there are only Muslims? Can you imagine a secular state in the Kingdom of Saudi Arabia?'

'Or in Oman or Yemen?'

Without planning it and to their mutual surprise Majid and Fuad left the Ba'ath party in the same month. Now Majid found himself in the living-room of Apartment Freedom smoking and thinking aloud, 'If the Ba'ath won't do, there must be another way for pan-Arab activity, there must be some other organization which is closer to the Arab world, some organization which knows the nation better.'

Qasim interrupted him angrily. 'You and Fuad, you are really so naive. What's this nonsense you are talking? Parties, organizations, Arab nationalism, Arab unity. The whole thing is actually just a matter of vested interests. It is to the interest of Michel Aflaq to talk about Arab nationalism, so that's what he spouts about. Nasser is just the same. And you two just swallow everything.'

Majid was astonished. 'But Qasim, the Arabs are one nation.'

'For God's sake, Majid, I ask you – are the Saudis like the Egyptians? And are the Saudis like the Bahrainis? Do you know what we call the Kingdom of Saudi Arabia in Bahrain?'

'No. What?'

'The Place of Peril.'

'May God forgive you!'

Qasim had become angrier. 'And I'll tell you something else. Even in tiny Bahrain we have Sunni and Shia. We have the Sunnis of Manama and we have the Sunnis of Muharraq. Then we have the Shia of the towns and the Shia of the villages. We have Shaikhs who have pedigree and Shaikhs who don't.'

'Don't you have the slightest feeling for Arabism?'

'Arabism? Of course I do: we are all Arabs, but we are Arabs of different kinds who do not form an Arab nation. Do you understand Algerian Arabic? And your Nejdi Arabic, when you get into it, I only understand about half of what you're saying.'

'Well, that's because you are not a real Arab. You have no pride.'

'Yes, but you don't understand our speech, either. What do these words mean? "Tomasha; Ghashmara; Jakkiyya"?'

'Well, what about you? You're of Iranian origin, and have become Arabized. Do you know what these words mean? "Mataziz; Qursan; Najr"?'

'My point exactly. You don't understand me and I don't understand you. Let's have an end to all this rubbish about one Arab nation. Why don't you just remember the story of the Sudanese student who had been calling for the unity of the Nile Valley, then he had his pocket picked in Cairo so he changed his slogan to: "Egypt and the Sudan are twenty different places." That's the truth: we are twenty different places!'

'I knew you were a reactionary but now I've discovered that you are a regional isolationist!'

'To hell with you. And with your "Mataziz".'

# CHAPTER SEVEN

## April 1959

When the Revolution took place in Baghdad in July 1958 Fuad was in Bahrain and the whole island was in a state of celebration. Nuri Sa'eed the principal hireling had fallen. The traitorous regime and the Baghdad Pact had fallen. Within days Iraq would join the UAR. Fuad himself was beside himself but his father shook his head, pained.

'But why did they have to murder the King?'

His mother was on the verge of tears. 'That poor young King Feisal, just a boy.'

Qasim, distraught, roared back. 'They are just a gang of criminals. They rebelled against their masters and slaughtered their king. They plundered the palace. Traitors. Robbers.'

These were among very few discordant voices, faint and slight, amidst the noisy rejoicing all over Bahrain.

In Baghdad, something very strange was happening. Iraq did not join the UAR and as time passed the dispute grew between Abdul-Karim Qasim – regarded by all as the Muhammad Neguib of the Revolution – and Abdul-Salaam Arif who was regarded as the Gamal Abdul Nasser of the Revolution. Arif lost, was stripped of all his posts while the speeches and pronouncements of Qasim took on a much more isolationist tone. Stranger and stranger slogans could be heard on the streets of Iraq.

'A Republic not a Region!'

Graffiti appeared, too: 'Union not Unity!'

The communists now seemed to be ruling Iraq. Abdul-Karim Qasim's stance was queried. Was he insane? Was he a communist? Was he an agent of the imperialists? A terrible climax was reached with the uprising of Abdul-Wahhab Shawwaf in Mosul, and the massacres which followed the suppression of the movement. The communists waged mass slaughter, in hundreds, thousands or in tens of thousands.

In Apartment Freedom there were endless discussions of what was happening and as usual Fuad was keenest for answers. 'How did the Revolution suffer all these setbacks? How was Arif pushed aside? Where are the nationalist officers?'

As usual their Qasim had them. 'Abdul-Karim Qasim always was a plotter, just like Nasser! How could either of them have any trust in the other? And then each of them wants power for himself so how could they unite?'

Yacoub had an explanation which was so complex that no one understood it.

'You have to take account of Iraq's situation. In the days of the monarchy Iraq was a feudal country. Every force creates an equal counter force. The dominance of the feudalists generated a reaction from the proleteriat and hence the Iraqi Communist Party was born. It was born strong because it faced a powerful enemy. Moreover it was born with a clear vision but the nationalists got things confused since most of them, were feudalists and so when the monarchy fell there was no strong organization in the field apart from the communists.'

'But Yacoub,' Fuad interrupted, 'it wasn't the communists who carried out the Revolution, it was nationalist and Nasserite officers and then Qasim stole the Revolution from them.'

'Listen, Fuad, you are just looking at the surface. The roots of the Iraq Revolution were purely Marxist, an ideology based on opposing feudalism and it had no interest in Arab nationalism or unity. The Revolution in Iraq was logically consistent with its roots.'

'You and your roots. This was a Revolution based on Nasser and it was hi-jacked by Abdul-Karim Qasim.'

Here Abdul-Karim interjected. 'Don't forget, too, that Abdul-Karim Qasim is a Shia.'

'No, he's a Sunni,' Fuad maintained, only to be angrily refuted by Abdul-Karim.

Qasim interrupted them. 'I've no idea if he's a Sunni or a Shia. He's a common criminal, and that's that!!'

'No, he's not merely a criminal. This fellow has killed Arab unity by stabbing it in the back,' Fuad cried.

At this Qasim exploded. 'Haven't I told you a thousand times there's no such thing as an Arab nation? You can see it, but are Iraqis like Egyptians? Or like Syrians?'

'And we've told you a thousand times,' said Fuad, 'that the differences between them are trivial compared to the things they have in common.'

'What things in common? The Egyptians are so submissive and they are peaceful to their dying day but an Iraqi would kill you first and then ask what your name is!!' Qasim's voice became even higher.

'Revolutions always have their own unique backgrounds.'

'Bullshit! You didn't grieve when King Feisal was killed and now that Shawwaf has been killed you are making a martyr of him. They're all murderers and criminals, just fighting for power.'

'Don't just look at the personalities,' cut in Yacoub, 'its more complex than that. Shawwaf, just like Arif, represents a phenomenon with no political roots in Iraqi society. But Qasim saw how strongly the communists felt and made an alliance with them. That's the behaviour of someone who is shrewd, not a madman.'

Abdul-Karim said with a smile that failed to defuse the atmosphere 'I told you he was a Shia. All the Shia are smart.'

'He's just a professional killer,' Qasim interjected. 'He's no communist. If he had known that Nasser would guarantee him power in Iraq he would have made union with him right away. But he knew that Gamal Abdul Nasser would betray him just as he betrayed Muhammad Neguib.'

'Gamal Abdul Nasser didn't betray anyone. He led the greatest revolution ever without spilling a drop of blood.' Fuad's response was angry.

'Oh, come off it,' said Qasim, 'what about the workers he had hanged? And what about the Muslim Brotherhood?'

'Nasser is just a petty bourgeois and the bourgeoisie cannot coexist with a strong workers' movement. So the workers who went on strike were executed. Similarly they cannot coexist with a strong reactionary popular tide and so the Muslim Brothers were also executed,' answered Yacoub.

'So this is what it's come to, is it?' Qasim screamed. 'Executions, gallows, prisons, and dragging bodies through the streets. We said "Hang on to this madman of yours or else someone will come along who's even crazier!" May God have mercy on the soul of Nuri Saeed: during fifty years he did not kill one in a thousand of those killed by this lot in one day.'

Fuad was still enraged. 'Don't call for mercy for traitors. God's curse on Nuri Saeed! And on all reactionaries!'

Qasim glared at him with mounting anger and muttered, 'God's curse on these butchers and on all who have sympathy with them.'

Yacoub tried to calm things down with yet another obtuse analysis. 'Listen, fellows, don't look at things from the personal angle. Try to understand the movement of history, try to understand the movement of development of societies. If you knew the difference between Egyptian society and Iraqi society you know the difference between Qasim and Gamal Abdul Nasser!'

'The difference is that Qasim is a Shia,' said Abdul-Karim.

*Her voice came over the phone.*

*'Listen, I have to see you. Right now, Emad. I've made my decision.'*

*Emad smiled: at last. He laughed. After months of flirting yet being unat-*

*tainable Nadia was responding. God alone knew how much he had suffered from hearing her conventional, bland teasings.*

*'I'm very fond of you, Emad.'*

*'Fond! You mean I'm a nice, dear chap?' He asked her what was the difference between love and fondness, and she had said there was a big one. 'You're like a brother to me.'*

*Like her brother. God forgive her. Did her brother spend most of the night dreaming of her? Did her brother go every day to the hospital where she worked pretending he was ill? Did her brother take her home very night?*

*'Samia, you're a nurse. Don't you have any affection in your heart?'*

*'My heart overflows with it. But that's different from love.'*

*Emad had seen Samia for the first time when he had gone to 'The Hospital For Writers' to visit a friend. When he went in he found the young surgeon who had performed the operation, Dr Adil Bahgat, and with him the beautiful nurse, Samia. From that moment he had been in love. He saw her practically every day and brought her presents and flowers all the time. She would smile, neither rebuffing him nor encouraging him.*

*'Samia, we can't go on like this. You have no idea what torture I am going through.'*

*'You mean you're being tortured by friendship with me?'*

*'I am being tortured by love for you.'*

*'But I've told you, Emad, that I also am very fond of you. I regard you as my brother.'*

*'And who told you that I'm looking for a sister?'*

*His sense of his own dignity was finally and fiercely aroused. This relationship had become a prison which he had entered willingly, putting himself at the mercy of his gaoler. He'd become a pet belonging to Samia, a dog that followed her tirelessly. No more!*

*And now, right in the midst of this great eruption of feelings she had telephoned! They agreed on 'Groppi's' on Suleiman Pasha Street. She would come at 5 p.m. She came in, her smile illuminating the café. Emad's heart was beating like a machine out of control, but she was laughing. He was waiting for the moment of admission. At last it came.*

*'Emad, I want you to be the first to know. Dr Adil has asked to marry me and my father has given his approval.'*

Abdul-Ra'ouf smiled as he handed the sheets of paper back to Fuad, 'I see: *The Blue Angel . . .?'*

'Well, more or less . . .'

'Is it Shahenaz?'

'Of course.'

'Do you love her as much as the story describes?'

'Do you know, Abdul Ra'ouf: more that that!'

'What about her?'

'She's . . . "very fond" of me. I don't know what to do. What did the schoolmaster in *The Blue Angel* do?'

'He abandoned his work, his books, his students, his house and just wandered around, pursuing the singer, infatuated with her, until he finished up as her servant.'

'I might do the same thing, myself.'

Shahenaz Shakir. What a name! Even the letters of the words seemed to sing, just as she did. The Faculty party . . . The huge pavilion . . . the links in the programme . . . the star of the party . . . then the announcement from the MC about the gifted new young singing star . . . she sang a song of Nagat Al-Saghira,

'Where has your heart gone? I can't find it.
And we didn't even have two days of love.'

Fuad was immediately crazy for Shahenaz, just the way Abdul-Karim had been smitten. But he was bolder than Abdul-Karim and right after the party he went up to her and told her how much he admired her. She thanked him warmly. He said how astonished he was that he had not seen her in the Faculty till now but she explained that she was an external student and only attended for examinations or on occasions like this. She told him that she was studying law at the insistence of her father, himself a lawyer, but she knew that her future lay in the arts and she had become a full-time student in the Faculty of Music and an external student in the Faculty of Law.

How could other blondes compare with her? Or rather how come he had so much to do with blondes? First the one from Damascus and now Shahenaz. A rare bird, a blonde Egyptian girl. And green eyes, too again. But there the comparison ended since the second was far prettier than Suad, more delicate, slimmer and taller. Her lips were more alluring and luscious, her hair longer and more luxuriant, reaching half-way down her back. Her voice was exactly like that of Nagat Al-Saghira. No, it was more beautiful. How could all these gifts come together in one girl? She could sing, she could act and she was a beauty. And on top of that she was studying law! And her name, Shahenaz, carried overtones of aristocracy and nobility. The spontaneity there was about his relationship with Suad hung around his relationship to Shahenaz. They could talk easily for hours about everything. Shahenaz welcomed this admirer from a strange country but he could not give proper expression to his real feelings except in writing. His letters were many.

My dearest,

I haven't the slightest doubt that soon you will be the biggest star in Cairo, in the whole Arab world. Your picture will be on every magazine cover and your voice will be heard on every radio, your face appearing on every screen. But then . . . will you remember me?

My dearest,

When you stood up to sing that night which is so near and yet so far when we came together just a few moments ago (or was it centuries) I felt that you were singing for me alone. That pavilion became our nest and you became that wonderful bird that sang for me alone. You ask me where my heart went: here it is, placed at your feet, so take it into your hands or else trample it underfoot.

My dearest,

You have no need of any Institute of Music to teach you to sing. You were born with your gift just like those nightingales who sing as soon as they open their eyes. You only have to smile and the whole audience will move to your rhythm. If you frown the world will weep; if you say just one fond word the universe will dance with joy, and my heart will dance too.

My dearest,

Do you know the meaning of your name? My friend Yacoub knows Persian and tells me it means 'The flirting of kings'. Could anything be more beautiful than that? But it did not surprise me, since you are, really and truly, the Queen of my spirit, its Princess and its Sultana. In you are gathered together all the alluring qualities of women. My beloved, my favoured one!

Shahenaz received these alarmingly intense letters with a mixture of amazement, pleasure and discomfort. Fuad was sure that the artist in her would empathize with them. The soul of the musician, would speak to the soul of the writer. But apart from this fellow-feeling was there anything else? She didn't reply and he had no idea of her emotions. But she did not get angry and break off the relationship. So he retained hope. Fuad came in for some heavy sarcasm.

Qasim led the way, 'What's got into you? Have you lost your wits? First a Ba'athist and now a singer!!'

'You're a literary man. Why don't you write songs for her?' asked Abdul-Karim.

Yacoub aired his usual French views. 'Fuad – this is not love. This is physical, sexual deprivation. If you slept with her once your love would go out of the window.'

'Don't talk about Shahenaz like that!' said Fuad angrily. 'She has more honour than you!'

'There's no such thing as a singer with honour,' commented Qasim.

'Shut up!' screamed Fuad.

Suddenly Abdul-Karim became sympathetic. 'Oh, come on, you guys. The man's in love.'

'This is a madhouse,' rejoined Qasim. 'There's one in love with Farida, another madly in love with Shahenaz, one crazy about Freud. Why don't we just call this place "The Crazy House"?'

Fuad could only really discuss Shahenaz with Abdul-Ra'ouf. 'Abdul-Ra'ouf, what can I do? I feel that I have been robbed of my will. It's unbearable.'

'Well, why don't you just put an end to it so that you can have some peace? And so we can be spared any more of your poetic *pensés*?'

'Believe me, Abdul-Ra'ouf, I've tried. I've tried to forget and avoid her but I find myself staring at the telephone and I am talking with her about our next date.'

'So, what happens?'

'That's the problem. Nothing. I go to the Institute of Music and watch her practising and often I take her back to her home.'

'Have you told her that you love her?'

'Abdul-Ra'ouf, you saw my letters. After letters like that do I really need to say more?'

'How would you describe her feelings towards you?'

'She "feels fond of" me.'

'Is she in love with someone else?'

'No idea.'

'Listen, Fuad, I think she's just using you. I think it satisfies her vanity that a writer is an admirer.'

'Oh, come on, there's no need to be sarcastic.'

'I wasn't being sarcastic. Let me finish. She's an artist who's just starting out and it suits her to have admirers. Where will she find a better one than you? She's toying with you and your letters.' He paused. 'This is a sick relationship. It harms you both. It feeds her conceit and destroys your pride.'

'A sick relationship? Are you another Freudian?'

'No, but I do know a bit about unrequited love.'

'Tell me about it.'

'You may read the story one day.'

My dearest,

Yesterday I made a pact with myself that I would leave on a journey. I promised myself that I would take my bleeding heart, my papers stained with blood, and my stumbling footsteps and depart from your enchanted world. And today I decided that I could not live another day without you, even if this love was from my side only, even if it was insane. It is enough for me that you 'are fond of' me.

Mr Sobhi left for Paris and began to write to Yacoub from there, telling him in one of his letters that one evening he found himself face to face with Sartre, but he was so bewildered that he became tongue-tied. However this encounter brought him to read the works of Sartre and his existentialist philosophy. Yacoub seized on this and immediately set about reading every book about existentialism. The more he learned the more eager he became to read on. He now considered himself an existentialist Freudian Marxist.

Abdul-Ra'ouf asked him if he could give him just a brief explanation of existentialism.

'I've read everything Anis Mansour has written on the subject and I couldn't understand a thing.'

'It's difficult to explain in a few words, Abdul-Ra'ouf.'

'All right, then. Explain it at length!'

'I'll try. Firstly, existentialism is not a theory. There wasn't just one thinker who came up with the idea and defined it, as with Marx and Freud. Throughout history there have been existentialist thinkers and existentialist positions.'

'I haven't understood a thing.'

'I told you it was complicated. If you have to have a very brief definition then it is responsible freedom or free responsibility. What existentialism means is that you must face up to existence and your decisions. You have to decide, for example, whether you have faith or not. Are you going to serve humanity by struggle or by living in an ivory tower? Existentialism means being freed from inherited clichés, ready-made answers and from packaged formulas. You should live, with eagerness and persistence, to take things as far as possible so that you take your destiny into your own hands. That is what existentialism means.'

'Sorry. I still can't understand.'

'Abdul-Ra'ouf, you are just playing dumb. When I'm moving along with the flock, with the masses, I think just like the others, I dress like them and believe in what others believe in. Then I am not free, I am not an existentialist. But when I decide that I have the right to have personal beliefs regardless of the beliefs of others, and when I face the world by myself unafraid of the consequences, then I become an existentialist. Now do you understand?'

'No.'

'It is as clear as daylight to me, but someone said "Explaining what is quite clear is a very complex matter." Let me give you some examples. Take Abu Nuwas: here was a 100% existentialist. He rebelled against the values prevailing in his society and lived by his own values.'

'Abu Nuwas was only a licentious and irresponsible poet.'

'That's where you're wrong! He was just as much a philosopher as Sartre. But take another example, Al-Maari. When he cried out, "Awake, you deluded ones! Your religions are just a snare devised by the elders" do you know what he was doing? He was adopting an unusual existentialist position. He was confronting believers of all faiths all of them in their millions, maybe billions, and he was confronting them alone. The feeble blind old man was proclaiming that he was right and they were wrong. Existentialism in its purest form!'

'What Al-Maari was saying was nothing but atheist and I hope to God he repented before he died. So, is existentialism atheism?'

'If Al-Maari had lived in an atheistic society and had proclaimed this he would not have been an existentialist, he'd have been just like the rest.'

'That's even more peculiar. So is existentialism just like the proverb, "The way to get known is to be different"?'

'God no! Existentialism is "If you really know then you'll be different".'

As this logic penetrated Yacoub's behaviour began to take on a markedly peculiar aspect. Existentialism found expression through the model of Abu Nuwas who became a hero for Yacoub. He devoured his poetry. The new existentialist began to follow the programme of Abu Nuwas and now plunged into a round of pleasure in the same way that Abu Nuwas had. Sexual activity now became a tenor of existentialism, heroic and not at all depraved. Yacoub plunged into the depths of sexuality seizing every opportunity. He ignored the jeering of his friends as he found his prey in the maids working in the apartment building and with ugly whores picked up from the streets. He even announced on one occasion that he had had sex with a boy and that he had had no regret: he was simply exercising his right as a human being to know of all forms of human experience.

Qasim became indignant. 'Yacoub, you have shamed us in front of God: you are carrying on with maidservants all the time. But why?'

'You're a reactionary even when it comes to sex, Qasim. Don't those girls suffer enough from social persecution without having sexual persecution as well?'

'But you're the one who is persecuting them, financially and sexually. Ten piastres! Isn't that the ugliest form of exploitation? And yet you claim that you are a Marxist.'

'The amount of money is not the important thing. The main thing is the attitude. When I go to bed with the servant of one of the neighbours I have adopted an attitude by which I proclaim that it is my right to go to bed with anyone I want to, even maidservants. That is my decision and mine alone. And the girl also adopts – without being aware of it – an existentialist attitude.'

'You mean, the neighbour's maid reads Sartre?'

'I told you – she is unaware of it. She is getting her revenge on her master and mistress who humiliate her. She is exercising her freedom when she has sex with me.'

'Don't kid yourself. She does it for money, not for freedom. When you are in bed with the maid don't you feel that you are fornicating with your mother?'

'Oh go to hell!'

Yacoub, while plunging into sex, became increasingly infatuated with Abu Nuwas' other great interest. He discovered a number of bars in Cairo: the artists' bar in Emad El Din, the journalists' bar in Abdin, the lawyers' bar in Bab El Luq and the bar where there were tourists, male and female at Mina House. He then astonished his friends by telling them that the cigarette he was smoking contained hashish. When they deplored this he explained that repugnance at hash was no more than an inherited taboo which must be broken if one wished to be existentialist.

'In the buffet, any of the waiters will supply you if you ask.'

'In the Arts buffet?'

'Or the Law buffet. Or Commerce. Just ask any waiter if he's got a "piece" and he'll bring it right away. Only 25 piastres.'

'I don't believe it.'

'OK, just try. That's how bourgeois society survives, lying and their contradictions. They teach you in the lecture hall that the penalty for smuggling drugs is death or hard labour for life and a few steps away from the lecture hall you can buy drugs. See for yourself. Try tomorrow.'

Every evening Yacoub comes back with tall stories. Tonight he tells the group that in the bar of the Hilton he has met Salah Abdul-Sabbour and they have recited poetry to each other. He pulls a piece of paper from his pocket. The lines of verse, he claims, are by Salah Abdul-Sabbour and in his handwriting. Another night he claims to have met Kamil Shinawi at 'Roy's' on Suleiman Pasha Street and to have spent an hour listening to him tell the story of his love affair with Nagat Al-Saghira. Another night he tells of how he has been on a houseboat on the Nile with Farid Shawqi. The group began to see him as a Baron Munchausen and they call is stories 'Yacoubisms', stories that amuse but which no one believes.

One night, just before 11 p.m. the door opens and in comes Yacoub, with a smiling man whose complexion is white but slightly flushed. Yacoub takes in everyone with a glance. 'Hey, fellows, greet Mr Bairam Al-Tunisi!'

# CHAPTER EIGHT

## June 1959

The residents of Apartment Freedom took turns in running it, observing the constitution, but it became clear that when Abdul-Karim was in charge there was a drop in monthly expenditure. Their costs were both fixed and variable, the fixed ones being rent, baksheesh for the doorkeeper, plus the pay of old man Zaki. Other expenses such as food, laundry, phone and electricity varied. The total of fixed and variable costs was about 80 pounds a month but there was a drop of about one third when it was Abdul-Karim's turn. He was the only one who had the face to go over Zaki's accounts and then to go himself to the grocer, the laundry and the butcher to check prices. Eventually the residents of the apartment took two decisions, the first requiring an amendment to the constitution whereby administration of the apartment became the responsibility of Abdul-Karim alone. Next they dismissed Zaki, but as soon as he had left Yacoub introduced the new maid, Hanim, to Abdul-Karim who gave his approval on condition that Yacoub did not go in for any existentialist activities with her.

All the residents had scholarships from the Egyptian government – the Eastern Students' Section – worth ten pounds. Another twenty-five pounds a month came to Fuad, Abdul-Karim and Yacoub from their families, not to mention secret remittances from mothers so none of the boys was strapped for cash. But Qasim was the only one among them who spent money indiscriminately. His father sent him 500 pounds at a time whenever he ran out of money. Qasim thus became the lender of last resort for them all. However instances of need were quite rare except for Yacoub who was in a state of constant bankruptcy and whose existentialism led to additional profligate disbursements. Yacoub, for his part, accepted this penury with the greatest enthusiasm and regarded it also as an existentialist position which demonstrated great dash and style.

As examinations drew near a state of emergency was proclaimed. Almost no one went to the Faculty since going to lectures was a waste of precious time. Beards grew long, clothes became dirty and faces thin. Endless cups of coffee and tea were made from dawn to after midnight. Nerves were taut and would snap for no reason at all. Hanim was on the verge of collapse with the incessant demands for 'Tea' 'Lunch' 'Dinner' 'A sandwich' 'A packet of cigarettes from the grocer.'

Yacoub would look at the slight little thing with her innocent and lovely features as she dashed uncomplainingly with her tray from one room to another and he would be seized with anger at bourgeois society.

The Faculty of Law was transformed into something like a concentration camp. Huge pavilions covered the grounds. Thousands of students trembled and perspired like so many sheep being driven to the slaughter and inside the atmosphere was even worse. Tough supervisors shouted, their faces distorted with the hope of finding some wretched student cheating. Drinks sellers hurried between the tables. The lecturer responsible for each subject would come in accompanied by a steward carrying the exam papers for distribution. A scream might go up and some young woman would faint. Nurses would rush over. Or a male student would collapse without a sound. There might be sobbing somewhere else, or merely tears. No exam would go by without at least 10 victims, some recovering and able to carry on while others would be kept in the medical tent for observation.

In the feverish atmosphere of the exams social activities were abandoned and even Nash'at and Abdul-Ra'ouf were infrequent visitors. Revision at Apartment Freedom was a multi-faceted art: Yacoub could only study by walking up and down, preoccupied and learning his material aloud. Abdul-Karim on the other hand could only work flat on his stomach on the floor, which, he claimed, was the ideal way to concentrate; Qasim's style was to read quickly, then to re-read and read again, each time marking the text with a different colour so that finally the page would look like a surrealist picture. Fuad was a slow steady reader who memorized.

All were suffering from forms of hysteria. Fuad would walk fast twice a day for an hour until his nerves had calmed down; Yacoub doubled his consumption of Stella and cigarettes; Qasim suffered from sleeplessness but Abdul-Karim allowed his fears to seep into his unconscious and he suffered from nightmares. These were terrifying since he dreamed that a man with the face of a beast was crouched on his chest, gripping his neck and throttling him and the nightmare would end with a scream which seemed to shake the foundations of the building.

Exam time was vacation time for everything except emotions. Quarrels broke out over the question of the phone. Abdul-Karim would talk to Farida until the others made a commotion, sometimes talking to her for two or even three hours. Qasim on the other hand would call Shereen often but for very short conversations while Fuad would contact Shahenaz once every two days. Yacoub's phone calls, though, were stacatto like cables, each one lasting only seconds.

When exams were over the atmosphere in the apartment was transformed, Abdul-Karim celebrating by tearing up his notes and Yacoub hurling his out of the window. Fuad and Qasim took a more cautious attitude and simply put theirs away which in Yacoub's view was unworthy of existentialism. The residents now set about compensating for the days they had lost: visits were resumed and the apartment now became almost rowdy. There was carousing and laughter; beards were shaved; shoes were once more polished and Apartment Freedom was just like a field which had been revived by the Spring after the long sleep of winter.

It may have been this exultant madness which accounted for what happened to Abdul-Karim one evening. His companions were out and he was in his room going over the accounts with Hanim. He was seated behind his desk going over an account, Hanim standing behind him. Suddenly she put her hand on his shoulder and he felt a flame shooting through his shoulder and descending... He pretended not to notice and carried on reviewing the account but her other hand touched his other shoulder and the rest of his body took fire. It was as if he were observing what was happening without participating in it: he saw himself get up and close the window and saw Hanim move to shut the door, then he saw himself and Hanim on the bed exchanging kisses, intertwined. Within seconds Abdul-Karim had lost his virginity and had betrayed Farida.

That evening he summoned his companions to an extraordinary meeting in his room. He was frowning and it could be seen that he had been crying. The others were shocked.

'What's happened?' asked Qasim.

'I don't know what to say,' stammered Abdul-Karim. 'Something awful.'

'Come on, what is it?" insisted Qasim.

'I don't know how to begin. After you all went out Hanim came for me to go over the accounts with her. Then...'

'Then you went to bed with her,' shouted Yacoub. 'Congratulations.' Abdul-Karim looked at him resentfully without a word.

'Did this really happen, Abdul-Karim?' asked Fuad.

'Yes. It's horrible. I can never forgive myself. May God curse the Devil. We'll not be able to keep her on,' Abdul-Karim went on. 'Every time I see her I'll be reminded. I hope you will agree to our giving her notice and paying her twenty pounds...'

'Twenty pounds. What for? You go to bed with her and we pay? Is that right? Have all the principles of the constitution been abandoned?' Yacoub was outraged. Abdul-Karim remained silent.

'Oh, come on, Abdul-Karim,' said Fuad, 'There's no need for that. I agree and so do all the others: just pay Hanim off and look for another maid. But just make sure that the new one is over 40 so she doesn't seduce anyone!'

Yacoub thought. 'We're going home in a few days. Let her stay till we leave.'

Abdul-Karim looked into the faces of his friends with relief and whispered, 'Thank you, thank you. How can I live with myself after I've cheated on Farida? Today I found out that I'm an animal.'

'We knew that a long time ago,' laughed Yacoub. 'But Farida should be grateful that things have turned out so that she's not going to marry an animal who's a virgin and doesn't know what to do on his wedding night.'

Fuad met Shahenaz at the café 'Qasr El Nil' after emphasizing that he wanted to see her alone before leaving for the summer vacation in Bahrain. They agreed on a lunch date and settled down to hummus, pigeon and all the rest. Fuad stared into her lovely smiling face.

'Shahenaz, I want you to be frank with me: is there any hope?'

'What do you mean?'

'You know what I mean, our relationship: is there any hope for me?'

'Haven't we discussed that already?'

'Yes, but this is the last time. I have to know.'

'Do you want me to lie and tell you I hate you?'

'No.'

'Do you want me to lie and tell you I love you?'

'No. I want to know if there is any hope. If the answer's no then this is our last date.'

'Fuad, that's up to you. You're my closest friend, isn't that enough?'

'It would be if I felt the same but my feelings are different. Shahenaz, I feel you're the sun that gives me light, and hope and warmth. Shahenaz . . . I want to spend my life with you. But I feel I am just a parasite, a wearisome guest that the host is too embarrassed to throw out.'

'Fuad, do you want me to be frank?'

'I asked you to be.'

'OK. I cannot love: it is not you, or anyone else, I swear to God. Do you think you are my only admirer? I'm not exaggerating if I say that before you there were scores, maybe hundreds. Ever since I was 14 I have, without intending to, attracted men.'

'And what about you, don't you feel anything?'

'No. But if I could love a man it would be you. Believe me. But I am only in love with my future and my heart flutters only when I imagine it. I imagine myself as more famous than Nagat Al-Saghira, as famous as Umm Kalthoum, greater than Fatin Hamama. Isn't that madness?'

'No, it's ambition. But why should there not be in your heart some small place for love as well?'

'I wish it could be so but when I sing about love it is as if the words come out from a vacuum. I just wish I had someone I loved, someone I could sing for, sing for him alone. That is the reason why you can have no idea how happy your letters have made me.'

'I wish I were as lucky as my letters. But don't worry, Shahenaz! Some day soon you will attain all you wish for. But will you take some advice from a friend, from a brother?' She nodded and Fuad went on. 'Be very careful, Shahenaz. The way ahead is full of dangers because when anyone is as beautiful as you beauty becomes a curse. Do you know that every man in this café is looking at you?'

'That is my destiny, Fuad.'

'Yes, but don't let your ambition lead you to things you may regret.'

'Do you mean with producers and directors? Don't worry about that sort of thing.'

He sighed. 'Would you like me to bring you something back from Bahrain?'

'No, just write to me.'

As they left men were stripping her with their eyes and he could feel the whips of their envy across his back. Fuad now realized that the second love story of his life was over here, on this sunny day in June beside the Nile. If only the Nile could speak of all it had seen and heard over the centuries.

My dearest,

You asked me to write to you from Bahrain but I prefer to write my last letter to you from Cairo. Two words: 'Thanks' and 'Sorry'.

'Thanks' because you have given me the taste of bitterness and the taste of sweetness but I can't say which one has made me the happier. It was an experience that made me absorb the lessons of centuries. I got to know what it means to be an orphan, without being one and I learned the anguish of separation when not apart. Thanks to you, Shahenaz, I became a person who can appreciate the sufferings of others. That was the bitter side but the wonderful side was sweet. When you were singing the world was changed to butterflies, to festivals of light and colour. No voice has ever thrilled me the way yours did. Thank you, Shahenaz, for giving me the chance to be near the most beautiful creature I ever expect to see. Just being near you was the happiest experience of my life.

'Sorry', because I made myself a burden to you. I'm sure my letters – and they must have been more than 50 – must have annoyed you at times. And I'm sure my pestering you must have caused you some inconvenience.

Well, after 'Thanks!' and 'Sorry!' I have one request I'd like you – in fact I implore you – to grant me. When we meet some evening, with me in the audience and you on stage, with everyone's eyes devouring your beauty, and your glorious hair illuminates the moon, when your eyes light on me – please, I beg you, sing to me:

'Where has your heart gone? I can't find it.
And we didn't even have two days of love.'

Fuad.

Yacoub tried to ignore the problem and then tried to convince himself that he was just imagining things. When the exams came along he was totally preoccupied. But still the problem persisted. There was a burning sensation before, during and after peeing; small yellow stains on his underpants. And the pain became worse, there were more stains. He wondered if he had some form of VD. Would he go mad and then die like so many existentialist writers in Europe in the nineteenth century? He knew that if he broached the subject with his friends they would laugh. He resolved to keep it to himself.

The plaque on the surgery door proclaimed that the doctor inside was an Assistant Professor specializing in dermatology and veneral disease. Yacoub entered and paid the three pounds fee plus a pound as baksheesh. One hour later the receptionist called him, ignoring ten people who had arrived before him. He went into the surgery and described his symptoms. The doctor nodded then gave him a painful examination, both front and rear. He took a urine sample and asked him to go back to the waiting room. One hour later the receptionist called him again and as Yacoub went into the surgery he could see signs of worry on the doctor's face.

'It's OK. It's a serious illness but it can be treated, thank God.'

'Gonorrhoea?'

'No.'

'Syphilis?'

'No. It's a microbe from a rare strain, but it can be treated.'

'And what is the treatment?'

'Well, son, it is expensive and it takes time.'

'How much? How long will it take?'

'400 pounds, half in advance and the balance at the end. It will take twenty sessions of electro-treatment, massage of the prostate, in addition to injections and tablets.'

Yacoub was thunderstruck. 400 pounds? Where would he get it? Even Qasim didn't run to that sort of loan. And what about the electro-treatment. And massage of the prostate. 'But, Doctor, I'm a student on a limited budget. Can I pay in instalments over several months?'

'I'm sorry, only two instalments.'

'All right. Just give me time to arrange the money.'

Yacoub went back to Apartment Freedom in despair. He had never been ill before and had never given his health a moment's thought. And now a microbe of a rare strain was visiting him requiring long-term treatment that would cost a fortune. The friends noticed that something was troubling Yacoub but he refused to speak. Just before going to sleep Fuad knocked on his door.

'I could see that you didn't want to talk, but I know about the problem.'

'How did you know?'

'Your underpants.'

'Who noticed them?'

'That's not important. Just tell me what you have done.'

'I've seen a doctor and he has told me that I need treatments that will cost 400 pounds.'

'400 pounds? Are you sure he's a doctor? Seems to me he's a charlatan.'

'His plaque says he's an Assistant Professor at the university.'

Fuad thought. 'I've got it. We'll tell Mr Shareef. He's bound to know a doctor we can trust. Look, Yacoub,' Fuad noticed Yacoub's hesitation, 'if your health doesn't bother you it does bother me. I don't want us all to be infected.'

Mr Shareef received the news remarkably calmly. It was as if he had known that something like this was certain to happen sooner or later, that he realized that Apartment Freedom was bound to be used for purposes other than study. From the time they moved in he gave up his surprise visits and restricted himself to the fixed visit each Friday morning. He went with Yacoub and Fuad to see a specialist who only needed a few minutes to pronounce that it was ordinary gonorrhoea which would respond to ten injections of penicillin. As Yacoub left the surgery he felt as if he had been born again: nothing could be worse than for a man to die insane.

Farida was keen that Abdul-Karim come with her to meet her parents but he insisted that he must get his father's approval first and then could see her parents and formally ask for her hand. They agreed that Abdul-Karim would seek his father's permission during the vacation and come back with the engagement present. They would then make an announcement. As Abdul-Karims departure approached, he began to think about how he would broach the subject. The awe he felt towards his father, especially in his presence, made it difficult to speak to him on a subject as delicate as this. Suppose he slapped his face? Wouldn't it be better to speak to his mother first? But she would resist the idea of this marriage even more fiercely than his father and would insist on his marrying his cousin. Abdul-Karim had almost forgotten her and the ridiculous promise his mother had made to her sister that Abdul-Karim would marry her daughter. That was when he was only five years old and the girl was in her cradle. Was it really reasonable that he should now be held responsible for such a rash promise?

Eventually he thought that the best approach was to send a letter explaining so that his father should be completely in the picture before he reached Bahrain. Abdul-Karim realized that this was the most delicate letter he had ever written, that his future depended on it. He made one draft after another and then asked Fuad to help. They eventually agreed on a final version:

My revered elder, lord and father, may God keep you!

I kiss your noble hands and your pure forehead and I hope from God that you and your lady my mother and all members of the family are in the best of health.

I am pleased to tell you that I finished my exams this week and I expect to be successful if God wills and thanks to your prayers. I have made preparations to travel in ten days' time and I am longing to see you and to benefit from your wise advice.

My lord, I should like to advise you of something new which has happened and in which it is imperative that I receive your directions and have your acceptance. I have come to know a lady student in the Faculty of Law who has the highest degree of chastity, modesty and virtue, coming as she does from a family which is both religious and conservative. When I found that she has all the desired qualities in a worthy wife I placed my faith in God and decided that after obtaining your noble permission I would marry her.

I should like to make clear to you that I have explained to her traditions and she has shown every readiness to wear the veil and to abide by all our customs. I am also very pleased to inform my lord that she has already shown me an intense affection for the family of The Prophet Muhammad (Peace Be Upon Him) and I am sure that after our marriage she will embrace the beliefs of our community. But, my lord, I have found it difficult to ask her to do this before the marriage so as not to embarrass her with her family. I hope that you will find my decision acceptable. Please believe me that nothing shall take place – if God wills – which does not please you.

In conclusion I call on God to lengthen your life and to allow us to continue in the enjoyment of your presence among us and not be deprived of the blessings of your prayers to God.

Your obedient son,
Abdul-Karim.

Abdul-Karim took the receipt from the post office after registering the letter. This tiny piece of paper guaranteed that his letter would reach his father. But what would happen when the old man saw it?

Yacoub got a great surprise when he found that his companions wanted him to stand trial before them, there was no other way of describing the confrontation. He was herded before the court with little warning, no chance to study the charge sheet and no access to a lawyer.

Fuad began, 'We hesitated for a long time before resolving on this meeting but then we realized that being frank was the only way. We can't remain silent anymore.'

'Just a minute. Just because I've got gonorrhoea? That's my business alone.'

'I am not talking about gonorrhoea, I'm talking about the general way you've been carrying on recently.'

'What do you mean, carrying on? Aren't we in Apartment Freedom? Wasn't the basic idea behind our moving here that we should be free?'

Qasim interrupted him. 'That's true, but there are limits and you have gone beyond all bounds: hashish, all kinds of types from off the streets'.

'I didn't want to tell you about this,' said Abdul-Karim, 'but now I have to tell you that the manager has spoken to me a couple of times and told me that the neighbours have been complaining. He has warned me that if things don't improve we are all going to have to leave.'

'That's just one side of it,' added Fuad, 'but the more important side has to do with you and your own future. How long do you plan to carry on like this? Every night parties, drinking and women?

'And the hashish,' shouted Qasim.

Yacoub remained silent and then sadly replied, 'So what's all this beating about the bush? I can see you are all agreed to get rid of me. You've made your decision and that's that, right? When do you want me to leave? Right now? Or can I wait till morning?'

'Shame on you,' said Fuad. 'No one wants to get rid of you. In fact no one would let you go even if you wanted to. The only thing we want is for you to take it easy. To think about your future.'

'That's my business. If you want me to go I'll go. I'm not a prisoner here. I won't let you interfere in my private life.'

'But your private life has begun to affect us all,' said Fuad, 'and *your* freedom has begun to restrict our freedom. Will it make you happy if we are all thrown out? Aren't you the one who's always saying that the liberty of the individual ends where the freedom of others begins? Just think a bit. About your name. The name of your family.'

'The name of my family? That's a good one.'

'Anyway,' said Fuad, bringing things to an end, 'we leave for Bahrain next week and you'll have plenty of time for some quiet thinking.'

---

'In the meantime,' retorted Yacoub, 'you can be looking for a new tenant. Maybe a Sheikh from Al-Azhar.'

# CHAPTER NINE

## September 1959

---

The wound caused by Fuad's relationship with Shahenaz bled all summer. When he reached Bahrain the depression only deepened with the heat. His self-confidence was shaken completely. Up till now he had never worried about his appearance but now he would look in his mirror as if he were seeing himself for the first time. Those glasses. God curse them! Who ever saw a pretty girl in love with a young man wearing prescription glasses? Apart from that he wasn't particularly handsome nor especially ugly. He had a fairly big nose, and what about his moustache? Maybe he would look better if he shaved it off? And what about his body? God's curse on his being thin but he couldn't change that. He'd have to take exercise, maybe weights.

But he knew he was just fooling himself if he imagined that the problem with Shahenaz was caused by spectacles and a long, thin body. Such dignity as he still had left protested at the principle of changing his appearance just for the sake of a woman. Anyone who loved him could love him the way he was. Anyway was it possible to play around with the external appearance without damaging the essence? If he got rid of his moustache, threw away his specs, changed the way he parted his hair and became transformed into a body-builder would that not be just proclaiming that a new personality had taken the place of the original one? And who could guarantee that the new personality would be better than the old?

What was worrying him went beyond appearances: was there a problem in his subconscious? How was it that his experience with women over a period of three years was confined to a revolutionary who preferred the party to him and a singer who preferred her art? Did he have a sixth sense particularly tuned to choosing exactly the wrong woman? And what about his writing? What about the stories and novels he planned to write? Didn't great literature need inspiration? Didn't a literary man need a muse? A love that was requited

and passionate? When would such a love come along? When the most delightful years of his life had been wasted?

Fuad's father suggested that they should go and greet the Ruler of Bahrain,
Shaikh Salman, and so Fuad proposed the idea to Qasim. It was agreed that
they would both go, and with their fathers who were also old friends. They
all set off one evening before sunset to the palace at Rafaa', where they found
the Ruler sitting on a cement bench outside, surrounded by a few visitors.
He greeted them warmly and invited them to dinner the following night,
emphasizing that the dinner was in honour of the two guests from Cairo.
The following night they returned and the Ruler showed an unexpected
interest in the studies of his two young guests.

'What are you studying, Qasim?'

'Commerce, may God lengthen your life.'

'Commerce? Does commerce need to be studied? It's your father who can
teach you the most. How do they teach Commerce?' he asked. Everyone
laughed.

'We study Accounting, Statistics and Economics.'

'That can't make you a merchant. What do you think Abu Qasim?' he
said, addressing Qasim's father.

'You have spoken truly, may God lengthen your life. Being a trader is a
gift, and it is God who provides the livelihood.'

'And what are you studying, my son?' he asked, turning to Fuad.

'Law, may God lengthen your life!'

'Yes, now that is something that can be studied at university.'

The Ruler then spoke at length about the law and about the Pearling
Council which he had headed for many years. He explained the law which
controlled the pearl trade and the agricultural sector in Bahrain: the method of
allocating shared water resources between the various gardens, the relationship
between the landowner and the cultivator and the agricultural Waqfs.

'May God lengthen your life, as they teach us in the university, customary
law is a basic source of law in all countries of the world, no less important
than the legislative process,' Fuad said.

The Ruler replied, 'That's true, it is the inherited customs which are the
foundation and we walk along the same path trodden by our fathers and
grandfathers, training our children in their turn. We are lost if we change the
system.' Was the Ruler talking about law or was he really giving his listeners
a lesson in politics?

They moved into the palace for dinner, all squatting on the floor at a simple
spread. The Ruler's retainers had a separate one nearby. The Ruler carved and
distributed the meat, eating little himself. He chatted with the two fathers
about old times which they had shared but he did not forget the young
students. Turning to Qasim he asked, 'Do you like Cairo?'

'Bahrain is more beautiful, may God lengthen your life!' said Qasim with unaccustomed diplomacy.

The Ruler smiled. 'Bahrain is very small, but it is our country, the source of our pride and our glory!' Turning to Fuad he asked, 'And do they teach you the Sharia?'

'They do, may God lengthen your life!'

'It is the Sharia which is the foundation, my son. Every good thing is to be found in it. If religion goes then everything goes.'

The guests left, dazzled by the humility of the Ruler and the warmth of his reception, as well as his wide knowledge of the law. Looking at Fuad Qasim took a dig. 'And when do you think your Gamal Abdul Nasser would invite you to dinner?'

Fuad replied, exasperated, 'Gamal Abdul Nasser is too busy: he's the Head of State for 30 million people!'

Yacoub returned to Bahrain full of disgust with himself: it did not need gonorrhoea or the 'trial' by his friends to let him know that his bohemian life was a waste of time and comprehensively damaging. He knew that for him to quote the example of Abu Nuwas was inappropriate because Abu Nuwas's name had survived through the ages because of the poetry he had written not because of his life-style. The same thing went for Al-Maari: could Yacoub be the Abu Nuwas of the twentieth century or its Al-Maari? Yacoub realized that he had been born with gifts. None of particular would guarantee him immortality. He would never be a great singer or poet or artist. With the gifts he had he could just about amuse himself and entertain others with his small talents.

His only real gift was as a revolutionary. If he were to change the world for the better the only path open to him was the path of revolution. From his earliest childhood he had absorbed and studied doctrines. But now the time had come to move from theory to practice. If he did not begin his work now, at the age of 21, when would he? Yacoub felt that the only true revolution was the Marxist one, the Communist one. He still admired Sartre but Sartre could talk for ever about the liberty and the responsibility of the individual and not change anything. He still had faith in Freud but Freud could write books for ever about dreams and the subconscious and his books would not bring the proletariat to power. The revolution led by the Communist Party was the only hope.

The period Yacoub had spent in Egypt had taught him that all the resounding Nasserite slogans had not changed dreadful social oppression. Little had changed since the days of the monarchy apart from expropriation of some agricultural land for political reasons which had been aimed at clipping the wings of the old feudal class. A new ruling class of military officers had arisen worse than the old. The companies which had been taken from the English and the French had simply been handed over to the officers along with the apartment buildings which had been sequestrated. Had anything changed in the situation of the fellaheen toiling in their fields? No. The old owner had gone and a new one had taken his place, the Co-operative Society, which in effect was a government organization which treated the fellah worse than the Pasha had. Had there been any change in the situation of the worker slaving in the factory? No. The factories were still owned by Abboud or Abu-Ragaila or the brother of one of the officers.

What was the use of Arab nationalism if it was simply a mask for the practice of capitalism with all its obscene oppression? Look what happened to Syria after Union. It was handed over to Abdul-Hamid Sarraj, who was nothing but a bourgeois executioner. The real link was between one oppressed person and another, between one hungry man and another, just like the link between one oppressor and another and between one bloated capitalist and another. What use was there in resisting imperialism if the economy remained capitalist linked. Wasn't the conflict between Gamal Abdul Nasser and the West just an illusion, a sleight of hand? Egypt was simply one of the bastions of world capitalism, and thanks to Gamal Abdul Nasser Syria was another now. Union had come about for one reason only, the abortion of the true revolution and the stamping out of the Syrian Communist Party. The Ba'ath party was feudalist with stolen slogans. What could a reasonable man expect from a party owned by Akram Hourani, a feudalist?

How had he come to applaud the Union when it had simply enthroned capitalism? Yacoub now looked out on the world with the scales fallen from his eyes. There was no difference between Arab and non-Arab, despite what the advocates of Arab nationalism said: the only difference was between those who were the champions of exploitation and its victims. There was no real freedom except in the shade of the communist system and as for Western democracy, well it was just a piece of skilful play-acting to fool the gullible. Capital decided everything: who should be President, who would become a Deputy, and all the voters had to do was to give their agreement. It was only when there were no more needy, suffering the humiliation that accompanied need, and when all were equal, that it would be possible to talk about freedom.

They talked about freedom of speech but the hungry man didn't want it; he wanted freedom to get some food. They talked about freedom of ideas but the naked man did not want it; he wanted freedom to get clothing. They talked about freedom of belief but this was not what the sick man was missing: what he wanted was the freedom to get medicine. In the end this was the difference between capitalism and communism: capitalism granted you freedom of speech, freedom of ideas and freedom of religion but communism gave you food, clothing and medicine. In this decisive summer Yacoub discovered his mission.

After his third week in Bahrain Qasim felt an overwhelming desire to return to Cairo. Where was that old spirit of bitter criticism he used to have for Egypt and for everything and everyone in it? Had he been struck by some strange infection, like Yacoub's rare microbe? He was missing Shereen and her gentle voice, her sweet face as she waited at the bus-stop. He was missing Nash'at and their talks on the foul-ups of the revolution. He was missing Apartment Freedom and the open windows facing the Nile, catching the gentle breezes. He remembered the wonderful nights of Ramadan: the bright lights, the children, the lovely fruit salads, the fried doughnuts, the nuts and raisins and the Punch and Judy shows going on till dawn. He romanticized the Eid in Cario, with its plates of cookies, the children's nursery rhymes and the firecrackers.

He kept himself busy with driving lessons and passed his test but where could he go by car? In less than an hour it was possible to cross Bahrain from one end to the other from Al-Hadd to Ras Al-Barr. It seemed much smaller to him now and in fact it now seemed to him to be a prison. Where could he go? The BAPCO restaurant, the BAPCO cinema, the BAPCO beach ... and then what? There was nothing else.

A shock was waiting for Abdul-Karim. As soon as he saw his father's face he knew that his old fears had been realized. As he kissed his father's hand and his forehead the old man was scowling and silent. Abdul-Karim realized that if he tried to talk to his father now it would only make matters worse. He waited until he was alone with his mother and then spoke to her.

'What did father say when he received the message?'

'He said that he would wash his hands of you if you married the Egyptian girl.'

'But why?'

'A Sunni girl? And an Egyptian? And you ask me why?'

'But she's a Muslim.'

'She's an enemy of our community. You are for your cousin and that's all there is to be said.'

'That's unjust.'

No, it was far more than an injustice, it was brutality, despotism and dictatorship! What right had his father to take a decision like that? How could he prevent him marrying the woman he loved when he had himself four wives, apart from the temporary ones he had in Iran when he travelled there? He would never give in and would never accept this. He would not allow his father to confiscate his right to freedom and happiness, even though he was one of the elders. Let him wash his hands of him. Let him cut off his allowances but he would not give in. He would go back to Cairo and marry Farida and prove to the world and to his father in particular that true love could destroy all obstacles. But he would have to move carefully and to do some planning. This was the time to practise dissimulation and he would eat humble pie to get his will in the end.

Something else that was preoccupying Adbul-Karim. He had written often to Farida every day of his longing but with no word of his father's attitude. Farida wrote once, twice, a third time and then her letters stopped. He tried to phone her but he was told by the Cairo exchange that the number did not reply. He then wrote to Nash'at asking him to make contact with Farida and find out why she was not writing. Nash'at replied that he had tried but failed to make contact. Abdul-Karim was now besieged with the darkest fears. Was she ill? Had she been in an accident? What a vacation this had been – a disaster.

Abdul-Ra'ouf waved the magazine in Fuad's face. 'Congratulations, Fuad! Your story got fourth prize and has been published in the magazine.'

'How about you?'

'I got second prize.'

'Congratulations, Abdul-Ra'ouf, a thousand congratulations!'

His hand was shaking as Fuad took hold of the magazine of the Writers' Club: was this really his story? 'Nausea'? And was this Abdul-Ra'ouf's story, 'The Watch'? Both of them had won prizes! This really was a turning point. Abdul-Ra'ouf had never had a story published before and his own stories had only been published in a Bahrain newspaper which might have published them just for politeness. But now the Egyptian Writers' Club was acknowledging his talent. His prize was a year's subscription to the magazine.

'Listen – when I went to the Club to pick up my prize – thirty pounds all in one go – the Editor, Ahmad Abdul-Bari, told me that he could introduce me to Mahfouz but I preferred to wait till you came back so that we could go and see him together.'

'Naguib Mahfouz?'

'Yes, what do you say?'

'When? When?'

'I'll have a word with Ahmad Abdul-Bari and tell you.'

In the simple café Naguib Mahfouz sat surrounded by a group of writers, old-established ones and others just starting out. But what a contrast between this majlis and that of Michel Aflaq! Aflaq who had behaved as if he were a prophet surrounded by his disciples, but Naguib Mahfouz was just one of a crowd, 'one of the boys'. Here there were no glances of adoration and no words of wisdom from on high but a group of friends exchanging jokes and comments and smoking hubble-bubbles.

They were presented by Ahmad Abdul-Bari to Mahfouz, who gave them a big welcome and congratulated them on their prizes. He then went back to his friends but Fuad, gathering courage, spoke.

'Sir, could I possibly have some advice?'

'Advice! I don't give advice, my son. If it's advice you want, better write to Amina Saeed!'

While everyone was still laughing Fuad went on.

'Well, then, can I ask you a question? Do you think a short-story writer can write a novel? I mean, are they two different forms?'

'Stories, basically, are just one form, whether the story is long or short. But there is a difference. A novel needs perseverance and persistence over years. But a short story can be written in just one day. Or in an hour.'

'So the novelist can write a short story?'

'Yes, if he wants to but a short-story writer can write a novel only if he has the patience of the novelist.'

'And you, sir: how do you write your novels?'

'With a pen!'

Everyone laughed and Fuad blushed as Naguib Mahfouz went on. 'Every Sheikh has his own religious doctrine. If you have talent you'll find your own style. Take your time.'

'But I'd like to know . . .'

'One of Naguib Mahfouz's novels took more than five years in the writing,' said Ahmad.

'That's true,' said Naguib Mahfouz, 'But the time is not the point. Many a day I sat at my desk and did not write a word. But other times in one hour I would write pages.'

Shyly, Abdul-Ra'ouf added, 'Is there such a thing as inspiration in writing stories, sir, as there is in poetry?'

'I don't know about poetry. Ask the poets. In story writing there isn't. There are no devils of poetry. There is the outside world, people and things. These are the raw materials for a story and then there is the interior world of the writer, his talent, his sensitivity, his level of culture, his experience – and it is from these two worlds that the story springs.'

'Can you tell us, sir, what is your opinion of women?' asks Abdul-Ra'ouf.

'Women! What have I got to do with them?'

Everyone laughed and Abdul-Ra'ouf felt embarrassed but stumbled on.

'No, what I mean, sir, is: does the writer need a great love to be able to create?'

'I don't know.'

Fuad hardly believe his ears: an elementary question like this and Naguib

Mahfouz claimed he didn't know the answer. 'Well if Naguib Mahfouz doesn't know, then who can know?'

'Listen, no one has done a census of the world's writers and their love affairs for us to know who were in love and who weren't. So how can I give you an answer?'

Fuad decided to risk an impertinent question. 'All right then, sir, have you ever loved?'

'Of course.'

'How many times?'

'Three times a day. Before eating.'

This time Fuad joined in the laughter.

When Yacoub decided during the summer to join the Communist Party, he realized that he was risking his liberty and maybe his life. If he made one rash move he would to to gaol and for this reason he must be careful where he was going to step before he made any move. He concealed his plan even from his friends after they had persuaded him to abandon his idea of leaving Apartment Freedom. He also decided to carry on wearing the guise of a bohemian to mislead people. His biggest problem was how actually to join the Party. How could he find someone to show him the way?

Yacoub was sure that Mr Sobhi was in some way connected to the Party so he decided to write to him. But he knew that letters reaching him in Cairo were opened by the censor. The authorities shamelessly stamped letters 'OPENED WITH THE KNOWLEDGE OF THE CENSOR', so he decided to write guardedly from Bahrain, hoping that Sobhi would be able to read between the lines.

To the noble brother, Mr Sobhi,

I preferred to write to you from Bahrain for reasons which would not be hard for you to guess. This letter relates to a subject of great importance. I would ask you to send to me the name of someone you can trust so that I can discuss the subject with him. But would you please address the letter to me c/o my father who will send the letter on to me via his own channels. With my best wishes,

Your devoted brother
Yacoub.

His father recommended that the letter coming from Paris should not be sent by mail but by the hand of someone he knew who was travelling from Paris. After a few days the reply came from Sobhi Farhat in Paris by way of Bahrain.

My dear brother, Yacoub,

I have received your letter and you can be completely at ease in discussing anything with a very dear friend who works as a journalist on *Al-Ahram* in the Economy section. His name is Ezzat Mukhtar and you can contact him at the newspaper.

With my very best wishes,

Yours sincerely
Sobhi Farhat.

As soon as he received the letter Yacoub contacted Ezzat. They met at Ezzat's little apartment in Abbasiyya and after brief preliminaries Yacoub got right to the point.

'It is about two years since I embraced Marxist doctrines thanks largely to Sobhi Farhat. I have formed a deeper and deeper faith in Marxism but now I think that embracing the theory is not enough and I must actually do something. In a word, sir, I have decided to join the Communist Party. Can you help me?' Finding Ezzat silent Yacoub went on, 'You can trust me, don't be afraid.'

'It's not a question of being afraid,' said Ezzat, weighing every word. 'This is a surprise. Why do you think that I have any connection with the Party?'

'Sobhi Farhat advised me to contact you.'

'Yacoub! Don't you know the situation the Communists are in in Egypt these days? Gamal Abdul Nasser is attacking Khruschev and he is hitting right back at Gamal Abdul Nasser! Relations with the USSR are as bad as they could be. Every known Communist is in gaol under the worst form of torture.'

'I know all that. And I am ready to face anything.'

'The matter is not as easy as all that. I can't make promises. I need time before I give you an answer. I'll be in touch.'

'When?'

'I don't know, in a month, maybe more. There's no hurry. The detention camps won't go away!'

Yacoub left the apartment with his pulse racing and his heart pounding. He had begun the way to glory or to gaol or to death and had an overwhelming longing to embrace one of these options or maybe all three.

When the friends arrived back in Cairo from Bahrain they found Nash'at waiting for them with two surprises, a locally-made car, a Nasr, and an import, a Swiss blonde. Qasim drove back to town with him in the car while the others took a taxi.

'Congratulations on the car and on the little sweetie!'

'Hilde, this is my friend, Qasim. Careful: she understands Arabic.'

'Let's start with the car, then.'

'It was only just now that my father became convinced that having a car would not distract me from my studies. I would have preferred something bigger but this was what there was available. It's a counterfeit Fiat, a Nasr.'

'And your little girlfriend? How did you get to meet her?'

'She's Swiss. Her father works in the Embassy here.' Then Nash'at turned to her and said in English, 'Tell him how we met.'

'Our hobby brought us together, horses,' she said. 'I saw him a number of times at the Equestrian Club at the Pyramids and one day I raced him and beat him and that's how we met.'

Nash'at added that she was studying at AUC, had been over two years in Cairo and had an excellent knowledge of Arabic. Qasim could see that he was very keen on Hilde and Nash'at confirmed his observation.

'Look, Qasim, the really good things are the imported ones! Not those peasant girls we have in the Faculty!'

In Nash'at's view anyone not belonging to the old aristocracy was a peasant but Qasim just laughed. 'Who can tell, maybe she is a peasant from Switzerland!'

'I'm no peasant!' retorted Hilde.

Suddenly Nash'at's features clouded over.

'Listen, Qasim, I asked you to get in with me so that we could talk on the way home. It's about Farida: I don't know how I am going to break the news to Abdul-Karim.'

'What's happened to her? He was complaining that she had stopped writing. Is she ill?'

'No, she's in excellent health, and as happy as could be. The problem is not Farida, it's Abdul-Karim. To cut a long story short, someone came along to ask for her hand during the summer, an Army officer. She agreed, her family approved and they have got married. It seems they regarded him as a bit of a find. Officers are the new kings in Egypt.'

'And how come you know all this?'

'When her letters stopped he contacted me and asked me to find out what was going on and put his mind at rest. I spoke to her and we met and she told me she was going to get married. She begged me to explain to Abdul-Karim that she could not let an opportunity like this pass. She swore she had never expected that something like this would happen but it was just fate. All she wants from Abdul-Karim is that he shouldn't hate her and should forget her.'

'Forget her?'

'I know that's out of the question and that's why I wanted to talk it over with you before I talk to Abdul-Karim. Shall I try to hide the facts, break it to him in instalments or bring it all out in one go?'

'Where is Farida now?'

'She's in Alexandria on honeymoon.'

'It's going to be a terrible shock no matter how we handle it. And the shock will be all the more cruel coming after his father rejected the idea of the marriage. He had been wanting to show that love would conquer all. I think you should push off now and hold the matter till tomorrow. We'll be with you when you break it to him and we'll do our best to soften the blow.'

As soon as Abdul-Karim saw the concerned faces around him his heart missed a beat: Farida!

Nash'at began 'Abdul-Karim, you are a person who has faith in God and in destiny . . .'

'Oh, come on, please: tell me, is she dead?'

'Oh, no, God forbid, set your mind at rest, her health is fine.'

'All right, then, so what is this blow from fate?'

'During the summer an Army officer asked to marry her, and as you know, these days in Egypt the girls prefer officers to doctors and engineers.'

'And did she agree?' cuts in Abdul-Karim.

'They are married. Right now they are on honeymoon. Farida asked me to send you her best wishes and to ask you to forget her.'

Before anyone could make any comment Abdul-Karim got up, his face as pale as death, went to his room and turned the key. A few seconds later the sound of sobbing arose, coming as if from a wounded animal. Gradually the noise grew louder and changed into a howling. The new maid, Aisha, the 40-year-old who had taken Hanim's place, wondered in astonishment, 'What's happened? Why is he going on like that, poor man?'

The whole of the following day was taken up with registration procedures and collecting study materials at the Faculty for the beginning of the third year, by common consent the most difficult and unpleasant one. It included Labour Law which was taught by Dr Gamal Zaki, famous throughout the Law Faculties of all Egypt and even abroad for his belief that the grade of 'Excellent' indicated perfection and since perfection was God's alone it was impossible for any member of the entire human race to obtain it. He believed, moreover that the grade of 'Very Good' was the grade which he himself would get if he took the exam and the most that any student could aspire to was 'Good' and then only if he were a genius. As for the serious student doing his best 'Acceptable' was the best he could hope for. The rest of the students would vary from 'Weak' to 'Very Weak'. The result of this philosophy as applied by Dr Gamal Zaki was that only one quarter of the students passed in his subject. It was in vain that the students grumbled or complained that many of them passed in all their subjects of the third year or all subjects of the diploma but, failed time after time to get their degree because they had been failed on Labour Law. Such was the terror of the students that many of them on reaching the third year had transferred to the Law faculties of Ain Shams or Alexandria. Some students handed in a petition of complaint to the President of the Republic. The reply from the Presidential Palace was that academic matters were the province of the universities alone. But when Dr Gamal Zaki heard of this he is said to have begun his next lecture as follows: 'It has reached my ears that a small group of you has been to the Presidential Palace to demand my dismissal and I should like you to know that I shall remain here so long as these walls remain standing. If they were to fall I should still remain to teach Labour Law in the open air.'

In addition the third year syllabus contained a number of complex subjects, such as the laws of status for non-Muslims and the laws on procedures which, as well as being complicated, were boring. To cap it all the special subject in Sharia was inheritances, the most arduous. This was taught by someone who lacked Abu-Zahra's knowledge, experience, skill in exposition and humour. A fourth problem was that Civil Law was taught partly, in the second semester, in French and this constituted one-half of the grade, while none of the group of friends had any French except for Nash'at. Thus Fuad faced his third year with foreboding.

No one noticed that Abdu-Karim was not with his friends in the Faculty and no one thought to wonder where he had gone or to make a connection between his absence and the news he had had from Nash'at. When they got back to the apartment it was empty and when evening came and he still had not appeared they began to worry. Fuad went to Abdul-Karim's room and on his bed found a one-line note. 'Farewell. Tomorrow you'll find my body in the Nile.'

Yacoub took charge of the situation.

'We've got to keep calm and think this through. What are the places on the Nile we go to and that Abdul-Karim used to go to with Farida?'

'Casinoor,' replied Qasim. 'Then there's "Qasr El-Nil" and "El-Shagara" and that's it.'

'I think he'll be in one of them,' said Yacoub. 'I'd go to a bar and get drunk before throwing myself in the river.'

'I'll go to Casinnor, Qasim can go to the Qasr El-Nil and Yacoub can go to El-Shagara,' said Fuad.

Yacoub found him near the river's edge at a table by himself and as soon as he sat down he realized that Abdul-Karim had drunk a huge amount of beer. Adbul-Karim stared at him in astonishment and slurred his words, 'Yacoub! How did you know I was here? Don't try to change my mind!'

'I won't. Mind if I have a beer with you?'

'Go ahead.'

A Stella was brought and Abdul-Karim carried on, wandering in his speech and talking disconnectedly. 'I'll not change my mind. I'm going to throw myself in the river. I'll drown. Then I can relax for a change. Get a rest from this filthy world. Get a rest from my father. I mean the Sheikh. And from Farida. And from you lot – don't try to change my mind. I've made up my mind and that's that. I'm going to jump in right now, in front of you. Don't try to stop me.'

'I won't. Drink up! Cheers!'

'I'm going to commit suicide right now. Here in front of you. In front of everyone. What's life worth? To hell with life! To hell with Farida! To hell with officers! To hell with the Sheikh! And you can all go to hell as well!'

'To hell with you!! Drink up. Cheers!'

By the time Qasim and Fuad reached 'El-Shagara' Abdul-Karim had passed out and the three of them carried him off into a taxi. When they arrived at the apartment building they carried him up the stairs and as soon as they laid him on his bed he went into a dead faint for all the world as if he had attained the death he had been seeking in the depths of the Nile.

# CHAPTER TEN

## November 1959

*M*uhammadain shivers and curls up inside his clothes which have so many holes in them that they are like a sieve. He shivers in spite of the tattered blanket. To his right his father is lying while his younger brother Hassanain lies to his left. Muhammadain is thirteen but he is responsible for his brother and his father who had been knocked down by a hit and run driver. The accident left him helpless and unable to move except by crawling or on crutches. The only work the father was capable of was to roll new cigarettes out of the butts picked up by Muhammadain. His brother then sold the re-makes at ten for one piastre. This meagre income could provide only the shelter of a wooden box on the roof of an apartment building that was itself in danger of falling down into the dark alley on which it stood in the interior of Giza.

Muhammadain wakes to the sound of the muezzin and sets off to buy bread and 'fool' and on his return makes tea and then wakes up his father and his brother. This morning his father is in a bad mood as usual, coughing and spitting continuously. And it is always Muhammadain who catches the brunt of this bad temper, his father taking every opportunity to insult him and threaten him with his crutches or slap him. Muhammadain knows that his father doesn't mean any harm and understands, vaguely, that the only way his father can give expression to his pain is by inflicting pain on him. So Muhammadain puts up with his father with more forebearance than a man would have.

When breakfast is over the looking for cigarette ends begins, with Muhammadain filling his bag with them and then going home to empty them in front of his father. After that he goes back to the street. It is tough work and full of risk as he dashes in and out of the traffic just to pick up one butt. And all too often he clashes with older boys who are in the same line of business, not to mention problems with the police.

*Bus stops are the best places so Muhammadain waits at the terminus of the bus line and in the minutes between the bus's arrival and its setting off again he dashes on board. He gets in between the seats and just like a worm he gets underneath them as well, with the result that when he gets off again he has cleaned the bus of every cigarette butt.*

*A bus comes in packed with passengers. They tumble off headlong and as usual Muhammadain gets on board, diving under the seats. When he looks up he sees a huge boot and rising from it the figure of a huge bus conductor who snarls at him. 'You little thief, you criminal, what are you doing here?!'*

*'I'm just picking up cigarette ends! Honest.'*

*'Is that all. Let's have a look at what's in your hand. I'll bet it's a wallet you've nicked!'*

*'No! It's just a bag for the ends!'*

*'No, it's not, you filthy son of a bitch.'*

*The huge boot comes down on his right hand and Muhammadain screams. The conductor presses his boot and Muhammadain bursts into tears. The boot presses down harder and Muhammadain hears his fingers breaking. He abandons his bag and rushes off like a wolf cub, howling. As soon as he gets in and before he can explain what has happened his father shouts at him. 'Come here, son!'*

*Muhammadain comes close to him.*

*'Why are you back so early! Where's the bag? Have you lost it? Lost it, you filthy son of a bitch!!'*

*The crutch comes down hard on his left hand and Muhammadain hears again the same sickening crunch that he heard on the bus.*

'I wish you'd written your story last year, Abdul-Ra'ouf,' says Fuad. 'I'd have borrowed it and shown it to Michel Aflaq. He'd have been delighted with it. He doesn't recognize bourgeois literature. He only recognizes literature that advances the cause of the toiling masses.'

'That's not what I had in mind. I've described something I saw with my own eyes once.'

'You mean you saw a child having its right hand and its left both broken within one hour? My God, where was that?'

'It was about three or four years ago that I saw what happened on the bus. I don't know if the boy's fingers were really broken or not but I wouldn't be surprised. The other details are all made up but it's close to the truth. What do you expect of a child who spends his days picking up cigarette ends? That he's going to be the son of a managing director?'

'He might be picking them up so that he could sell them for himself alone.'

'That really is a bourgeois outlook. A child wouldn't expose himself to all that risk if there were not real need.'

'So, what's the solution, Abdul-Ra'ouf? We said Socialism is the answer but you say it is all atheism and rejection of God. We said, "Soak the rich and give it to the poor" and you said that was Communism. So what is the solution?'

'Islam.'

'But how? This is a Muslim boy in an Islamic country and you've seen what happens to him at the hands – or the feet! – of a Muslim man.'

'Who told you that Egypt is an Islamic country?'

'What did you say!?'

'Who told you that Egypt is an Islamic country?'

'What do you mean?'

'Where is Islam in this state?'

'Abdul-Ra'ouf! I know about your sympathy for the Brotherhood and I know about the tragedy of your brother. But don't be stupid! If Egypt isn't an Islamic country, then where is Islam to be found? In Israel?'

'I don't want to talk about this with you. You're drugged by Nasser's propaganda!'

'And you're drugged by Hassan Al-Banna.'

'See what I mean? We've started trading insults!'

'There's no need for insults. We can talk calmly. I just want to know what you mean when you say that Egypt is not an Islamic country.'

'Your view of Islam is that it is just rituals: prayer, fasting, Ramadan and the Eid but this is only a part of Islam not the whole. Islam is where you are entirely governed by God's revelation.'

'That's what the Sheikhs say in the Kingdom of Saudi Arabia and everyone calls them reactionaries.'

'This is not just the Sheikhs. This is what God Almighty revealed to His Prophet Muhammad (peace be upon him) in the Koran. "THEY WHO ARE NOT GOVERNED BY WHAT GOD HAS REVEALED ARE INFIDELS WHO REJECT GOD." Well, isn't that as clear as daylight?'

'Shame on you, Abdul-Ra'ouf! I've read the Koran as much as you have and in that verse it is the Jews and Christians who are being talked about!'

'And what is the difference between the Muslim and the infidel except in following God's Law? When the Muslim ignores God's Law is there any difference remaining between him and an infidel?'

'I can't believe my ears. You think a Muslim is an infidel if he does not implement every detail of the Sharia. That really is fanaticism.'

'That is Islam. Call it whatever you like!'

'But who told you that Egypt is not ruled by God's revelation to man? The law of civil status is taken entirely from the Sharia? Can't we consider the provisions of criminal law the same as the exemplary punishment mentioned in the Sharia?'

'That's just rubbish.'

'No, it is very precise language which we study in the Law Faculty.'

'Forget the Faculty! Take a look around you. Is this an Islamic society? Portraits of Nasser everywhere! The broadcasting programmes from beginning to end are about him. Gamal Abdul Nasser's *The Philosophy of the Revolution* is a set book at all levels of schooling. Compare the number of times the media mention the name of Gamal Abdul Nasser with the number of times they mention the name of the beloved Prophet of God, Muhammad (peace be upon him) – then you'll know you are living in a society that knows only the name of Islam.'

'Let's say this is not, after all, an Islamic society. An Islamic society comes along which suits you perfectly. How will this society resolve the problem of Muhammadain?'

'Fuad, an Islamic society is not just a Presidential decree from your friend! The Islamic solution begins from the cradle with a comprehensive Islamic education which teaches the child to worship God not the Dictator. It teaches the child the principles of Islam not the Devil. Just take one Tradition of the Prophet: "HE IS NOT A BELIEVER WHO SLEEPS AT NIGHT SATED WHILE HIS NEIGHBOUR GOES HUNGRY." If we were to teach that in schools the way we teach the trivial nonsense of Nasser nowadays do you think there would be the likes of Muhammadain? If everyone were to take care of his neighbour would anyone go hungry?'

'No, hold on a minute! Who is stopping the preachers in the mosques from teaching the principles of Islam? Here you have the foremost mosque in the Islamic world and the greatest Islamic scholars.'

'No, we have Ulema who are just officials of the state. The most senior of them, the Sheikh of Al-Azhar, has the rank of Deputy Prime Minister and all the others have corresponding ranks. They are Ulema whose standpoint changes according to the policy of the state. If Gamal Abdul Nasser befriends the USSR then they will put out fetwas urging peace but if he turns hostile then they will declare Holy War against the atheistic Communists.'

'Aren't there any men of principle in Egypt?'

'Yes. In gaol.'

'Abdul-Ra'ouf, I've never known you paint such a terrifying picture of things before.'

'These are the facts. The regime you admire so much is fighting against Islam in a way that's never been known before in the history of Egypt. The President is the greatest enemy of Islam.'

'And how did he achieve this?'

'Isn't it enough that he had innocent martyrs murdered? Awda and Faragli and the others in the group? Isn't it enough that one of his gang asked one of the martyrs to read the Fatiha the wrong way round in the massacre they called a trial?'

'OK, let's assume that Gamal Abdul Nasser made a mistake there. But what about his achievements such as getting British troops out of Egypt. Nationalizing the Canal. Rearmament. The High Dam. The Union with Syria.'

'Qasim was right when he said they had brainwashed you. The British left as a result of the Brotherhood fighting them for thirty years. And the nationalization finished up with a battle lost by your friend. And that battle opened up the Gulf of Aqaba to Israeli shipping and brought in UN forces to guarantee Israel's protection. The High Dam was planned by a minister from the Wafd. And as for union with Syria – well, that's built on sand.'

'I can't see any difference between your views and the hallucinations of Qasim. Looks to me as if all reactionaries are as one.'

'All infidels are one community.'

Majid whispered. 'Fuad, I've got a secret. Can you keep it to yourself? During the summer vacation I joined the Arab Nationalist Movement.'

'That's a surprise.'

'With the Arab nationalists I found what I had been missing with the Ba'ath.'

'Have you forgotten how we used to laugh at them, when we were Ba'athists, and make fun of their slogans, "BLOOD, IRON, FIRE!" We used to call them the Shish-Kebab Group, do you remember?'

'The Ba'athists cannot stand competition from anyone. Anyway, that is not the slogan of the Movement. It's "UNITY, LIBERATION, REVENGE." '

'What's the difference between the Movement and the Ba'ath?'

'The first is that there is no spirit of hostility to Gamal Abdul Nasser in the Movement, as they consider him to be their actual leader. And the second is that the Movement is more accurate in its analysis of the nature of the conflict going on in the Arab Nation about the Ba'ath. This stage requires a gathering together of all social forces into one rank united against imperialism and its child, Israel. When a unitary state exists then we can discuss the nature of its economic and social system.'

Fuad looked doubtful. 'As far as I know the founders of the movement are George Habash and Wadia Haddad, both Christians. Do you remember the talk we had about minorities?'

'Things are different now. This is a purely Arab movement and it has not imported its ideas from France. It grew up in the furnace of resistance to Zionism. At the beginning the aim was revenge but eventually it became clear that revenge would only be achieved by liberation from imperialism and comprehensive unity of the Arabs. That was the logical progression.'

'But I was talking about minorities.'

'This movement isn't like the Ba'ath. There are no academic stars, such as Aflaq. Habash and Haddad are just members in the leadership of the Movement. And don't forget that one of the founders is Dr Ahmad Khatib, from Kuwait.'

'I thought he was a Syrian. Are you sure he's a Kuwaiti?'

'For God's sake, Fuad, a colleague in the Movement told me. Do you want me to produce his passport?'

'A colleague in the Movement? You mean a Comrade, don't you?'

Majid's face went red and he made no reply. Fuad laughed. 'Here we go, the same old story!'

The door opened and in came Qasim. The two of them stopped talking immediately. Qasim could see why right away and plunged in, 'Don't you ever get tired of talking politics?'

'So what do you want us to talk about?' said Fuad angrily. 'Chicks and cars?'

'Isn't that better than conspiracy?'

'Conspiracy? Who's conspiring?'

'Both of you: Fuad against the Bahrain government and you against the government of the Kingdom of Saudi Arabia!'

'We're talking about the future of the Arab Nation! About freedom and unity. The recovery of Palestine and you are calling this conspiring!'

'The future of the Arabs is nil if they're led by people with the ridiculous views you have!'

'And, pray, what are your wonderful views, oh most honoured philosopher?'

'My view is that governing should be left to the legitimate, experienced rulers. That we should study and then return to our countries and be productive. You, Majid, are studying medicine so why don't you concentrate on that and then go back and serve your country? Isn't that more useful than politics and talking nonsense?'

'My pan-Arab work doesn't come between me and medicine. And in the future it won't come between me and practising. But what's all this support for the rulers of the Kingdom and Bahrain? Did they pay you?'

'That's all you're good for, you revolutionaries – insults! Let me ask you a question, Majid. What's your allowance from the Saudi mission?'

'About 35 pounds.'

'Yes, that's the basic allowance but doesn't it come to about 50 pounds with the other allowances for books, clothes, tickets and other things? And didn't you tell me that last month you met Prince Fahd the Minister of Education when he was in Cairo, you asked for a raise and he agreed?'

'Yes.'

'So what more do you want? What you are getting is about the same as an

Under-Secretary gets in a ministry in Egypt. Don't you thank the government that gave you that?'

'That money belongs to the people. The Arabian people in the Peninsula. It's not just a handout from the government.'

'There is no one Arabian people in the Peninsula! There's over one hundred tribes and over one hundred peoples. There is a Saudi people but if it hadn't been for Ibn Saud there wouldn't even be that.'

'I'm not talking about Ibn Saud, I'm talking about the present situation.'

'So, what don't you like about it? You are a student and your allowance is twice as much as the pay of the Dean of your Faculty.'

'There's no comparison. Egypt is not an oil state, nor has Gamal Abdul Nasser got a secret oil well in his garden.'

'In the Suez war Nasser wasted the equivalent of twenty years' income for the Kingdom of Saudi Arabia. Do you know what would happen if that Arab unity that you are always going on about came about? Your allowance would be distributed among the students of Jordan, Yemen and Tunis and all you'll have left would be three pounds or four at the most.'

'It doesn't matter: for unity all sacrifices are easy.'

'All right, then why don't you start making sacrifices now? Why don't you dispense your allowance among the Arab students in Cairo who are really in need? There are thousands of them.'

'It's a waste of time talking to you.'

The next evening Abdul-Karim woke from his stupour with a splitting headache and shivering. He called out in a trembling voice. Fuad came in and as soon as he felt his forehead he knew that rapid action would have to be taken. He phoned Mr Shareef who arrived with a doctor who examined Abdul-Karim carefully. Turning to Mr Shareef he said, 'He has severe bronchitis, we'll get him into the Islamic Charity Hospital at once.'

Abdul-Karim was for ten days between sleep and waking, between a dream and a nightmare. He would close his eyes and see Farida in her white wedding dress, walking by his side, singing 'Oh, my heart, this is the first day you have been in love and the first day you have been blessed with happiness!'

The two of them were being accompanied in procession by a beautiful dancer. Was it Nagwa Fuad? Maybe. They sat down on the couch but when Abdul-Karim turned to her she was transformed into the shape of an officer like Sergeant Atiyah or the famous personality of Riad Qasbagi. The officer put hand to pocket and brought out a huge revolver and opened fire. Abdul-Karim screamed and the nurse came along with pills and an injection. He woke and saw his friends, they talked but later he could not recall a thing. He had another dream and this time saw his father smiling as he gave Farida in marriage. The face of Sergeant Atiyah appeared. This time he stabbed him with a knife and Abdul-Karim screamed. The nurse came back with more pills and injections. Then the pills and injections ceased, his temperature dropped and his appetite returned. When he left hospital he had no feelings whatever towards Farida, neither love nor hatred. It was as if his attack had driven out love for Farida and made it evaporate with the fever.

It was Thursday night and the Bahrain Students' Club was packed. But in the library there was a strange scene as three students were carrying a basket on the tips of their fingers, talking only in whispers.

Abdul-Karim turned to Fuad. 'What's this, a new game?'

'Yes, it's a new fashion. Anis Mansour wrote in *Akhir Saa'a* that he had seen a tribe in Indonesia that summoned spirits in a basket. So everyone has started summoning spirits.' He noted Abdul-Karim's disbelief. 'The way it was explained by Anis Mansour was like this: you get an ordinary cane basket. You draw a face on a big piece of paper and then mark a cross on it. You then close the mouth of the basket with the paper, and take a pencil and insert it into one of the holes at the base of the basket, tying it if necessary. Then three people sit down and touch the basket with their finger tips calling on the spirit. The spirit comes and fills the basket, which then tips forward with the weight. Then the writing begins.'

'The spirit? Do you believe it?'

'Me? Do you think I've gone mad?'

'I'd like to see it for myself.'

'OK, come on in but be sure not to laugh or to make fun because the spirits don't like that.'

When Abdul-Karim went in he greeted everyone and was encouraged to sit down. He quietly took a chair and watched. The main 'medium', Jaafar Alawi spoke respectfully. 'Has the spirit come?'

The basket wrote, 'Yes, peace be upon you!'

And all present responded, 'On you be peace and the mercy of God!'

'O noble spirit, who are you?' asked Jaafar.

'Shawqi', writes the basket. 'The Prince of Poets.'

' "The Prince of Poets"! You are most welcome! May we ask questions?'

'Please do,' writes the basket in large letters.

The page is filled up and a clean sheet of paper is brought.

'What poems are nearest to your heart?' asks Jaafar.

' "Nahj Al-Burda." '

'And what is the most beautiful line you have written?'

> ' "There is for red freedom a door
> Made red by every bloodied hand which knocks." '

'What is your opinion of Hafez Ibrahim?'

'He is my dearest friend and is with me here.'

'And Al-Mutanabbi?'

'I haven't seen him here in the world of the spirits.'

'Who, in your opinion, is the greatest Arab poet?'

'The Prince of Poets. For all time.'

The dialogue goes on for some time and then the basket writes 'Good-bye!'

Jaafar announces that the spirit of Ahmad Shawqi has departed. Abdul-Karim puts a question to the mediums.

'Can you summon up the spirit of my grandmother? On my mother's side? Her name is Fatima Hajji Easa Bulbool.'

'We'll try. It's best if you hold the basket with us,' says Jaafar.

'No, no, no.'

The mediums made a murmuring sound which he cannot hear. Their faces show their intense concentration. Two minutes go by. Then the basket begins to shake and to move and then starts writing, 'Peace be upon you!'

'And on you be peace, oh excellent spirit!' says Jaafar. 'Are you Fatima Hajji Easa Bulbool?'

'Yes, I've come for Karimee.'

When Abdul-Karim read the word 'Karimee' on the piece of paper he turned pale because no one ever called him that except for his grandmother and since she died when he was nine he had never heard the name.

Jaafar turned to him. 'Say something! Ask a question!'

Abdul-Karim hesitated and then, faintly, said, 'How are you . . . Grandma?'

'Very well, God bless you!'

Abdul-Karim went even paler and his heart raced because he had never heard anyone use that way of saying 'God bless you' in Bahraini dialect since her death. 'Have you any advice for me?' he whispered.

'Forget her! This she-devil is of no consequence. She has gone to hell.'

Jaafar then noticed that Abdul-Karim had begun to sweat and shiver and so he dismissed the spirit and brought the seance to a close.

Abdul-Karim decided to get to know the world of spirits, and to throw off the bonds of the flesh and worldly cares. When he put this to his friends he found nothing but derision.

'Spirits!' screamed Yacoub to his face, 'You loony! The guy holding the basket was causing the movement. There are no spirits.'

'OK, then how did they manage to know the expressions that my grand-mother used to use?'

'Listen, Abdul-Karim, it was not your grandmother who invented these expressions, they are used by all the old dears in Bahrain, at least among the Shia.'

Despite this Abdul-Karim made his way to Ahmad Fahmy Abul-Khair, the leader of the spiritualist movement in Egypt. He had written many books on the subject. He was welcomed by the spiritualist, who had never before met anyone from Bahrain and hoped that his guest would be the first of many spiritualists on the island and gave him signed copies of his books. He spoke of spiritualism.

'My son, there are two bodies, the material or earthly body and the ethereal or spiritual body. At death the ethereal body or the spirit separates from the earthly body. This ethereal body is like the air in that no one can touch it or see it and no one can make contact with it except through spiritualist mediums.'

'But why, sir?'

'The reason is that the medium is a person of special gifts, able to secrete "ectoplasm" and it is through this matter that the spirit is embodied to speak and to bring about the various spiritualist phenomena that we know.'

'Sir, how is it possible for all this to happen through the use of a basket?'

'Ah yes, the basket of Anis Mansour. The actual means is of no importance. The important thing is that there must be present a medium who produces, knowingly or otherwise, the ectoplasm. The more densely this matter is present the more actually the spirit is able to become embodied. In some cases where the medium is particularly gifted the spirit is able to become completely embodied, and to assume the shape of our human body exactly. It has been possible to take photos of spirits that have become embodied.'

'Here in Egypt?'

'No, up to now there has not been a medium of this standard in Egypt. But there are many documented cases in Europe and America and you will see the documents and pictures in my books. Why don't you attend one of our seances and see for yourself what takes place? We meet here at my house every Friday evening in a darkened room and listen to classical music, concentrating on the ethereal world. The spirits then come to us and speak through the medium.'

'They speak?'

'Yes. It is the medium who moves his tongue but it is the spirit which speaks.'

'You mean that if the spirit is French then the Egyptian medium will speak French?'

'That can happen. But spirits, especially the higher ones, know all languages. All the spirits which come to us speak Arabic.'

'What do you mean by the higher spirits?'

'The more the spirit is able to be free from this world with all its lusts and seductions the higher it is.'

'Why is the room darkened?'

'In the light the ectoplasm loses a lot of its vitality. This is the reason why ghosts do not appear in the daytime. Ghosts are bound to this earth, spirits which are unaware that they are dead and therefore keep coming back to the places they lived in.'

'How many attend a seance?'

'Between ten and twenty people.'

'Isn't there a danger?'

'Danger? You mean of a spirit taking on the body of one of those present? No, no!' said the teacher, kindly. 'The spirits that visit us wouldn't harm anyone.'

When Abdul-Karim turned up he was astonished to see Dr Othman Khalil Othman, the Professor of Constitutional Law in the Faculty of Law and another man, one of Egypt's leading surgeons and also a well-known film producer. The teacher explained that the leading spirit for the group tonight would be that of a man who had lived in the Egypt of the Pharaohs, called Mira. The medium would be a man who worked in the Fire Brigade. When he woke from his trance he would not recall anything the spirit had said through him.

As the seance began those present sat in a circle and the lights were dimmed except for one lamp which gave out a dim glow. The music started up and Abdul-Karim began to feel afraid. He concentrated on the medium and found that under the dim light the medium's face was shrinking so that his features almost disappeared. The medium closed his eyes and then began to speak hoarsely in Classical Arabic. 'Peace be upon you!'

'And on you, Mira,' replied the teacher. 'What will you talk to us of this night?'

'I wish to speak of the spiritual significance of the movements of prayer.'

'Have you ever asked yourselves why prayer calls for certain physical movements? Why does prayer not take place while a person is upright and not moving, or sitting down immobile? You have taken for granted the movements in prayer. The fact is that there are spiritual considerations to the movements of prayer. Various areas of the body have differing degrees of spiritual intensity, but the principal centre of spirituality is the brain which gives out and receives radiations. Here there are three spiritual regions: the forehead, the top of the head and the neck. The spiritual capacity of the brain cannot be utilized if man is content simply to stand. Sinking to the knees utilizes the spiritual energy in the top of the head while the prostration utilizes that of the neck. Returning to the upright position restores the balance to the three regions of spirituality. If you had spiritual gifts and were in a darkened room watching a man praying you would see how the radiations are concentrated around the head in prayer, and how radiations enter and leave the head.'

Dr Othman Khalil Othman interrupted. 'Mira, prostration and kneeling are peculiar to Islam: what about other religions?'

The medium replied for Mira. 'That is a very important question, Doctor. There is prayer in every religion and in all prayers there are physical movements. If you were to contemplate prayer in all religions you would find they all require the movement of the head so that all three regions are exposed to radiation. What I am talking about is regular prayer, not meditation or silent prayer.'

'So it is true, then, what they say, that the soul departs the body by way of the head?' asks the surgeon.

'Absolutely. If you saw the soul departing the body of a person about to go to sleep or one about to die it would be the same. The soul just returns to the body after sleep. You would see the ethereal body leaving the material body via the head.'

There were further questions with new answers containing terms unfamiliar to Abdul-Karim. Abdul-Khair then said, 'Mira, tonight we have a guest who wants to ask some questions.'

'I noticed that. Welcome, Abdul-Karim! You have come from Bahrain, the Land of Delmon, the most spiritual region in the world.'

Abdul-Karim's heart almost stopped through panic. 'I was in a seance and there was a visitation by a spirit which said it was that of my grandmother who died when I was a child. How can I know if that was genuine?'

'Spirits are the souls of human beings and human beings can lie or tell the truth. You should demand proof.'

'She called me by a name which was not used by anyone else.'

'That is sufficient. Dr Othman, is that not regarded as sufficient evidence?'

'It may not be categoric proof,' said Dr Othman, laughing, 'but it would be regarded as compelling evidence.'

Abdul-Karim continued. 'I should like to continue to be in contact with my grandmother. Is there not another means apart from the basket?'

Mira replied 'I can see around you a halo of ectoplasm and you are rather gifted, spiritually. You don't need the basket. Automatic writing would be better.'

'Automatic writing?'

'Mr Abdul-Khair can explain that to you.'

There were many more questions and answers until the medium began to murmur and to groan. When he awoke the seance was at an end.

Mr Abdul-Khair explained to Abdul-Karim the nature of automatic writing which needed nothing but a blank sheet of white paper and a pencil. The pencil is placed in the hand which should then relax totally until the person is unaware of it. The ectoplasm emanating from the hand enables the spirit to move the pencil so that a dialogue can take place. Abdul-Khair explained that it was better for the experiment to take place in a quiet room with no spectators and in a dim light.

On spiritualism Abdul-Karim found everything he was missing in the material world: affection and understanding, excitement and knowledge. Every night he would be absorbed in a long dialogue with his grandmother, asking her about death, life after death, the relationship of the dead to the living, and the spirit world. Her spirit would answer most of his questions but sometimes say it was 'not permitted' to get on to certain subjects. She refused to answer questions on the grave, on heaven and on hell. In spite of himself Abdul-Karim found himself asking about Farida.

'That witch! She's put a spell on you!'

'But I was in love with her before she knew that!'

'She put a spell on you so that you would marry her. Then she got married, but the spell remained until I brought it to an end. I fought with the evil spirits and overcame them and that was how you were cured.'

'Who cast the spell?'

'A witch in Imbaba.'

'Grandma, do you know Imbaba?'

'Of course I do, Karimee.'

As soon as he awoke each day Abdul-Karim would be looking forward to his evening with his grandmother. Each time dozens of pieces of paper would be filled and he would learn scores of new things: for example she told him that ever since he arrived in Cairo she had been looking after him. It was she, for example, who had stopped him throwing himself in the Nile and had prevented his father throwing him out of the family home in Bahrain. She told him that she would make him the happiest person in the world. She would get him the exam questions, provide him with all the money he needed, have every girl he wanted fall in love with him. And in return she wanted nothing except for him to set aside two hours every night so that she could talk to him via the pencil.

Abdul-Karim did not ask his grandmother's spirit for any evidence that what she was saying was true but the proof became visible. The phone would ring and she would say, 'It's for you!' There would be a knock on the door and the pencil would would say, 'It's Mr Shareef, carrying a large bag!' And sure enough it would be Mr Shareef with fruit. Or the pencil would write, 'Tomorrow a letter will reach you from my daughter, with forty pounds.' And sure enough the next day a traveller would arrive from Bahrain with a letter from his mother with that very sum. Abdul-Karim felt that he had become different from the rest of the human race, a man who could read the future.

His friends noticed how he was locking himself away each evening and the preponderance of books on spiritualism. They saw how dark he was becoming under the eyes because of the way he would stay awake every night till morning. They saw the extraordinary amount of paper he was getting through every night and began to fear that Abdul-Karim was going mad. They agreed that a trial must be held like the one they had had for Yacoub the previous summer but this time Yacoub would be part of the prosecution.

'Abdul-Karim. You've been in a strange state now for weeks! Ever since you came out of hospital. Has your brain been affected by your illness?'

'What do you mean?' said Abdul-Karim angrily. 'Have you seen me going around beating people with a stick? Well, I can promise you that you are the first one I'll go for.'

'We're not joking, Abdul-Karim,' put in Fuad. 'We're very worried about you. What's all this about spiritualism?'

'Spiritualism is a science. It is studied in the universities of Europe and America.'

'But you are locking yourself in every night and scribbling on paper all through the night. Do you really believe you are talking to your grandmother?'

'Absolutely.'

'Your grandmother's in her grave,' screamed Qasim. 'She's buried at Ras Rumman!'

'Her body is there but her soul is here.'

'That's just your unconscious working, man,' said Yacoub. 'That's what is asking the questions and giving the answers.'

'She told me lots of things I did not know. How could that be if I was just talking to myself? The letters she tells me about, and what is in them, before they arrive. The people I can identify before they actually come in. The phone calls where I know who's calling even before I pick up the phone. These are just a few examples.'

'Oh, for God's sake,' said Yacoub, breaking the silence that followed this, 'I had thought it was just a matter of self-delusion but it's more serious than that, apparently. Abdul-Karim, you'll have to go and see a psychiatrist.' Qasim and Fuad agreed.

At this Abdul-Karim looked around the faces of his friends, and leapt to his feet angrily, rushing off to his room and locking the door.

He grabbed pencil and paper. The world clouded over and he became once more a small boy, huddling close to his grandmother who hugged him. The pencil began to move.

'I know. I heard what they were saying. They are devils, too. They are your enemies. They joined in the spell on you. And now they want to kill you.'

Abdul-Karim returned from the fancies of his childhood to the pencil that raced across the page, the words almost unreadable.

'They'll come in now and kill you. With knives! Just like a sheep! They are going to break the door down now. But don't be frightened. I'm with you. Open the window and jump. I'll hold you up in my arms! Jump now!'

As loud screams come from his room the others rushed forward. Abdul-Karim heard their knocking but could not move. Seconds went by and the knocking got louder. His screams became more intense and then he gripped his right hand with his left and snapped the pencil. He tore the paper and got up to open the door. 'Help. Help!'

'What's happened?'

'The pencil. The spirit! My grandmother. She asked me to kill myself!'

# CHAPTER ELEVEN

## December 1959

*R*ashid had expected that the previous pearling season would be his last. When he was under water he often felt dizzy even after one minute. He had to pull on the rope before he had gathered in the usual collection of oysters. He was aware that the pearl-fisher could seldom go on diving after the age of forty. In the off-season he had tried to find other work but where? Pearl-fishing was the only work on the island. He had tried to persuade the master of his vessel to switch him from being a diver to being someone who stayed on board and pulled in the divers when they jerked the rope. The master had been adamant, though: a job like that needed strong arms and the muscles of a young man. And so before the season began Rashid came down to put his name down with the other divers. He took the usual advance of pay which he then spent within days. As usual he did not know if he would be able to make repayment at the end of the season or have to remain in the debt of the master.

The life of the pearl-diving industry was strictly regulated. The master was the one who was responsible for the vessel and all in it. When the divers brought in the oysters the entire catch went to the master and every week a small trader who bought the pearls and sold them on to the big traders in Manama and Muharraq came by in his boat. God alone knew where the pearls finished up. Some spoke of distant countries such as France, England and America, while others spoke of them going to Indian maharajas. Rashid would hear of the amazing prices some pearls would sell for and could not believe it. 100,000 rupees. 200,000 rupees! The world of pearl-diving was full of myths, truth and lies.

And from this wealth Rashid saw only what was enough to pay his debt and a trivial sum in addition. At the end of the season, the master, the only one on board who could read and write would settle the final accounts and allot each one his share after the advances had been deducted. Sometimes

*Rashid would get 200 rupees and he would have to live on that for the rest of the year. But if it had been a poor season the return might fall as low as 100 rupees. In rare seasons his share might rise to 400 rupees.*

*Before they put to sea his 7-year-old daughter, called Al-Dana ('The Pearl') would cling to him, saying that the other girls in their quarter would ask her where her father was and she wanted him to come with her so that she could show him off. Rashid laughed as he embraced her. It was not the custom in the industry for the diver to get his share in actual pearls but this daughter of his he considered to be finer than pearls.*

*The pearling vessel put out into the lagoons and went about its usual routine. Rice and fish. Dates with weevils in them. Brackish water. The 'nahham'. The sea shanties. And in the evening, coffee together and the seamen's tales.*

*Every sailor would relate his adventures, one swearing that he had several times seen 'Abu-Daria', the sea-spirit, in the shape of a monkey smoking his 'kedu'. Another would interrupt to swear that he also had seen the spirit and then there would be a debate on how big the spirit was. The first would say no bigger than a small monkey while another would swear he was a giant. When it got round to discussion of the nature of the spirit all agreed he was kindly. Equally all would agree that the only way to get rid of him was to beat the coffee mortar: at the very sound Abu-Daria would be terrified and dive into the sea, leaving his 'kedu' behind, the smoke still rising from it.*

*Or they would get on to the subject of the awesome whale which could swallow up whole ships and their crews, with several of the pearling crew claiming that they had actually seen it. It was, they said, two or three times bigger than the pearler but none could recall seeing it swallow a ship. Some claimed that the terrific waves it caused had swamped and sunk numerous ships. They might then get on to the subject of the other huge, terrifying whale and again there would be fierce debate: some would claim that the two whales were in fact the same while others asserted that the second was distinguished from the first by its love of human flesh.*

*Images of the whales would fade from Rashid's mind and the image of his daughter would come to him. He decided now that he would break with tradition at the end of the season. He would ask the master to pay him his share with a pearl for his daughter instead of in cash. How would he live for the rest of the year, though? God would resolve that problem for him. There were rumours about a foreign company coming to extract oil from the mountain. He might find work with them.*

*The pearling days went by wearily and with every dive Rashid knew that he was getting nearer to his end: the dizziness he felt as soon as he touched the sea-bed; the pressure in his veins, blood almost bursting through; the headaches. But he persevered and stayed under water, collecting the quantity expected, or even twice that. The master gave him a smile of encouragement and he became more hopeful of getting hold of the pearl.*

*There it was! A gigantic pearl oyster, a queen among pearls. Rashid gathered it in, amazed at how heavy it was. He put it in the sack around his neck, but then felt dizziness overcoming him and pulled on the rope. When he came to he was on deck and the gigantic oyster had been opened and he could see the fabulous pearl, the most beautiful he had ever seen in his life. He took the pearl and with wavering steps approached the master. 'Master, the pearl for Al-Dana!'*

*With that he collapsed and all the other pearlers came running.*

*'Rashid is dead! May God have mercy on his soul.'*

*'Dead? But he has only just been diving!'*

*'When he came up he was dizzy!'*

*'There is no God but God!'*

*The body was wrapped in two pieces of cloth and taken astern. The master turned to one of the sailors and asked, 'What did he mean: "Master, the pearl for the pearl"?'*

*'He had gone crazy, master, before he died. May God have mercy on his soul!'*

Abdul-Ra'ouf looked at him, smiling. 'So, welcome – you have joined the realists. Have you been persuaded of the views of Michel Aflaq?'

'Well, it is just a snapshot,' said Fuad, 'as you would say. It's a scene from the pearling era. I heard the story from my father and he began as a pearler.'

'Your father began his life as a pearl-diver!?'

'Yes. Why are you surprised? He was only a teenager at the time, but he is a self-made man. He abandoned pearl-diving and learned to read and write and later he worked for one of the small pearl-traders, becoming one himself. But when the world slump started and the Japanese artificial pearl came in the pearling empire collapsed. You can see the relics of it in our shop.'

'So, what you're saying is that he was one of the exploiters? A bourgeois?'

'He saw both sides. The life of the diver and the life of the trader.'

'So what were these two lives like?'

'The diver's life was miserable: suffering, poverty and debts. But there was no alternative: the only other choice than the sea was hunger and begging. The master's life was better but only relatively, and only then if he owned the boat. The pearl-trader was comfortably off, what we'd call today the middle class. As for the big merchants, they were small in number, no more than four or five in Bahrain.'

'And now? Has oil taken the place of the sea?'

'Yes, but I don't know which was better: the pearling days or these days.'

'At least these days there is no hunger.'

'But is the refinery worker these days happier than the pearl-diver?'

'Fuad, this story has reminded me that I've been thinking for a long time of some literary work we could do together. We put together a collection of our short stories.'

'That's a neat idea. Has anyone beaten us to it?'

'Put your trust in God! Ten from you, and ten from me.'

'What do we call it? We need a catchy name. A name that brings together Egypt and Bahrain. How about "The Pyramids of Bahrain"?'

' "The Nile of Delmon"?'

'Just a minute! Delmon! "A Papyrus from Delmon". What do you think of that?'

' "A Papyrus from Delmon". The two authors, Faud Tarif and Abdul-Ra'ouf Buhairy, present to you, from the heart of Manama and from the depths of Upper Egypt, the literary sensation of the season "A Papyrus from Delmon".'

'And who will be the publisher?'

'I'll talk to Mr Abdul-Bari. I think the Writers' Club will be interested.'

When Shereen started at the university there was much more opportunity for Qasim to meet her. Attendance at lectures became the golden excuse to fill the entire day and fortunately her father was too busy as Dean to keep an eye on her. When Nash'at's car came on the scene – known, for reasons unknown, as Ba'kooka – previously unknown opportunities presented themselves. Qasim would borrow the car and together they would drive off for lunch or take a drive along the road to the Pyramids. He would recall an article he had once read by Ihsan Abdul-Quddous called, 'Where shall I kiss my beloved?' of which the main theme was that for all its enormous size Cairo was no place for lovers. There was nowhere a man could safely kiss his girlfriend. If he held a girl's hand in a taxi the driver would stop and throw them out. At his parents' home? Impossible! At her parents' home? Not feasible. So, 'Where shall I kiss my beloved?'

Qasim discovered as Abdul-Karim had before him that the cinema was the ideal place. But it was a matter of planning. If the cinema were crowded the chances of a kiss vanished because for him to even move closer to her would immediately bring on jeers from those nearby. Qasim learned that the 10.30 were the most appropriate screenings since no one was there apart from lovers. The only other suitable place was Ba'kooka, parked away from prying eyes, whether of busybodies or the Vice Squad whose members Majid called the Egyptian Mutawwas.

When the first kiss took place, in the Cinema Kursaal, Qasim was taken aback by the affect of the short contact of their lips: Shereen began to shudder, then started to groan, and she almost fainted. It struck Qasim, that this was a bit exaggerated. Was it possible that just one kiss could lead to this collapse. But the reaction was genuine and Qasim realized that he was dealing with a young woman who was very quick to take fire. Every time they approached kissing the same symptoms appeared. Shereen would whisper, 'I can't!' 'I can't stand it!' and then there were floods of tears.

It was difficult for Qasim to analyse his feelings for Shereen: he certainly missed her when she was not there and enjoyed her company when they were together and the kisses which were so explosive for her touched him as well but he could not pretend that he loved her. Whenever they met she told him that she loved him but he was unable to reciprocate. Then hints began to be dropped: 'Wouldn't you like to meet Daddy?' 'When are you coming to see us at home?' These were questions which seemed innocent and natural but in fact they were nothing of the kind. What would he say to her father after meeting him? What would he do when he visited their home? Engagement! Dowry! Marriage! Prison! Quick, get the hell out of here.

Using all the tact he could muster Qasim explained to Shereen that there was absolutely no question of marriage: he was still a student with two years yet to go before his degree and then another two years or more before his Master's. After that he would have to work and establish himself and only then would it be possible to think about it. Shereen said that she understood perfectly. Then they would meet and there would be a kiss and she would explode like a volcano, groaning and murmuring, 'I can't take it!' Qasim was in a state of confusion: she could not ... what? Kiss him, or stop at that? And why did she say, 'Shame on you!'? Had he done wrong? Then the hints would begin again but in a differnt form: 'Mama would love to see you.' Quick, get the hell out of here, man!

Qasim picked up the ringing phone and heard a pleasant female voice.

'Is that Mr Qasim?'

'Yes.'

'I am Ilham, Shereen's mother.'

'Welcome, Mme Ilham. It is an honour.'

'I have to see you.'

'Certainly.'

They agreed on a rendezvous at Groppi's on Adli Pasha Street and Qasim was knocked out when he saw the beauty who came in, the image of Shereen, but more appetizing and mature. He was unable to conceal his surprise. Ilham noticed this, explaining she had married at the age of 16 and had Shereen when she was 17 so the age difference was not very great. Qasim could not take his eyes off her face except to admire her body. He had never felt such an overwhelming lust just through being near a woman. He prayed to God to deliver him from the Devil, began to blush and became confused. This is a married woman. His girlfriend's mother! Where had this burning desire come from? What diseased part of his unconscious had it come from?

Ilham spoke for a long time. Qasim was unable to remember the words but he remembered that she expressed her anxiety about her only daughter who had become so attached to him that she was nearly hysterical, and could no longer eat, or study or sleep. He remembered her saying that if he truly loved her daughter he would get engaged to her or give her up. Qasim explained that there was no question of getting engaged as his father would cut off his allowance and he would then have to give up his studies and go back to Bahrain. It would be years before he was ready.

The meeting lasted for more than two hours and ended with a definite promise from Qasim that he would end the relationship with Shereen and would not contact her or allow her to contact him.

The following days were difficult, full of tensions and scores of calls from Shereen. In the end Yacoub had to admit to her that Qasim was there but did not want to talk. Shereen did not give up and did not give up her attempts to meet him in the usual places. Qasim felt prickings of conscience: wasn't he the one who had started the relationship? Wasn't he the one who encouraged her? He tried to justify the situation: he had not promised her anything, not engagement nor marriage. Quite the opposite. Ever since their first date he had taken care that everything should be clear. And now here he was, he found himself guilty, a criminal when there was no crime.

His conscience hurt him more he thought about Ilham. Ever since he had first seen her he was thinking about her, day after day, hour after hour. He woke up at night with a strange lust and he closed his eyes he would see her in front of him, half-naked. He was ashamed of this animal instinct that was making him desire the mother of his girlfriend. What if Yacoub knew about this. He could almost hear what he would say: 'Didn't I tell you that every male child longs to have sex with his mother, whether he's aware or not?' God's curse on Yacoub. And Freud. And sex. And Shereen. And Ilham!

Qasim complained to Nash'at about it. 'You've lived with this story from the beginning. How do you explain what has happened?'

'Everything's fine,' said Nash'at, simply. He had an unshakeable faith that all women were . . . 'If you like Ilham and she likes you, what's the problem?'

'Nash'at! She's my girlfriend's mother!'

'Your previous girlfriend. If I were in your place I'd switch to the mother: at least with her there are no problems of marriage and headaches.'

'Nash'at! I'm talking about my feelings, not hers. Who knows? She may think of me as a son!'

'No, no, no! Don't you remember the story of our friend Fuad and Mme Khairiyya? Wasn't he like her son? You have two choices: either forget both of them, or forget the girl and concentrate on the mother.'

'Nash'at: I just can't. Having an affair with both girl and her mother! I'm not just an animal!'

'So – forget them both! The world is full of women!'

But his attempt was stillborn when Ilham contacted him. They agreed on the same place as before and Qasim went along fully expecting to hear more details of the tragedy, Shereen being unable to eat or sleep or study and living in torment: he would have to change his mind and resume the relationship and get engaged to her. He went along with all his answers but found Ilham looking more beautiful than before and he was astonished at how their conversation developed. She said very few words about Shereen: she had, she said, begun to understand the situation. Then she began to talk about him and thanked him for the way he had sacrificed his happiness for the sake of her daughter's. She said that she had been thinking about him but then the conversation took an astonishing new course: she began to complain that life was monotonous with her husband, who was twenty years older than she was, and that she regretted her lost youth. She needed a man friend who understood her and whom she understood. Qasim began to tremble, barely replying until it was time for them to part.

Ba'booka made a turn before reaching the plateau where the Pyramids stood and then went down the road leading to the secret airport, a road that no one used at night. The moon was vertically above, as the car stopped with Ilham sitting beside him. The voice of Umm Kalthoum rose from the car radio, redolent of all earthly desires, and the torment of centuries of drought, thirst and hunger.

Ilham came closer to him. He kissed her and she groaned. 'I just can't!' He looked down on Ilham. 'Shame on you!' she whispered. The moon disappeared behind a cloud and emerged again. He contemplated her face and then felt terror: the face had turned into Shereen's. How had she got here? Then the face of Ilham came back. The moonlight faded and then came back as Umm Kalthoum's voice rose to its crescendo: 'I think of you ... I think of you ... I think of you ...'

He found Shereen on his left and Ilham on his right, each winking to the other and laughing. Then the girl whispered, 'I just can't!' The mother said, 'I can't stand it!' and suddenly Umm Kalthoum was singing, 'Shame on you ... Shame on you ... Shame on you ...'

He woke up to find Yacoub's hand on his forehead.

'For God's sake. We get shot of Abdul-Karim's nightmares and get landed with Qasim's!'

'Thank God for that. It was only a dream!'

Yacoub laughed as he looked down. 'Looks like it was some dream. You'd better go and wash your pyjamas!'

After his terrifying experience with spiritualism Abdul-Karim turned to Abdul-Ra'ouf to seek an explanation.

'Abdul-Karim: why don't you come for the Friday prayers with us? Come to Roda, the Malik Saleh mosque. That's where I pray with Fuad. Afterwards, we can call on the Imam, Sheikh Radwan. He can answer your questions.'

Abdul-Karim laughed: the whole world was upside down. First he agrees with his girlfriend on marriage and as soon as he's out of the country she marries someone else. Then his grandmother asks him to kill himself. And now they want him to pray in a Sunni mosque. In Bahrain, the Shia believed that in the whole island there was not a single person other than his father who was properly qualified to lead the prayers. But still his father would not lead the prayers, he was so modest. OK, if the world was upside down he would be upside down, too: he'd pray on a Friday with the Sunnis!

After the prayers Abdul-Ra'ouf, Fuad and Abdul-Karim went to the Sheikh's apartment next to the mosque where the Sheikh listened attentively to the story of Abdul-Karim. When he had finished the Sheikh went over to a shelf crammed with books, and handed one to Abdul-Karim.

'This is *The Spirit* by Ibn Qayyim, probably the only book in our whole heritage that deals with this subject so comprehensively. Take it with you. It's clear what happened to you was the jinn playing games. Everything that you hear in both East and West about spirits is to do with the tricks of the Devil. The aim is to lead man astray and bring him to perdition.'

'How is that?'

'I've read everything written by Abul-Khair and Dr Ali Abdul-Galil Radi as well as books translated into Arabic and this is my conclusion: the jinn, what people call spirits, try to convince people that there is no such thing as the true religion. Their object is to seduce and lead man astray and bring him to Hell.'

'But, Sheikh, the spirit asked me to kill myself!'

'Exactly. Is there a grandmother who could ask a grandson to commit suicide?'

'Do you believe in the survival of the spirit after the death of the body?'

'Certainly. The life of the Prophet proves that. The Prophet Muhammad (praise be upon him) spoke with those infidels who had been killed at the Battle of Badr and said that they listened to him. See how precise is the Koran on this: "Behind them is a Partition till the day they are raised up." The Partition is a dividing barrier. The living have their world and the dead theirs. That of the dead is unseen and we know of it only what is stated in God's Book.'

'Only through visions can we make contact. In Ibn Qayyim's book you will find countless examples. But seances do not bring spirits: they bring the jinn, as you have seen for yourself. Don't repeat such an attempt but remember God's Word: "And pursue not that of which thou hast no knowledge." '

'Sheikh Radwan, I haven't been able to get any sleep since this happened to me, I have been so afraid.'

'My son, I'll teach you a prayer to God which you repeat before going to bed and all your fears will be dispelled through the influence of The One God. Write it down: "I seek refuge in the face of God the Great, than Whom there is none greater, and in His words which are perfect and cannot be exceeded by any good deed or the acts of the depraved. I seek refuge from the evil which He has created, from the evil of what is both within the earth and comes from it, from the evil of what comes from the heavens and rises thereto, from the evil of the misfortunes of day and night, with the exception of the harbinger of good fortune. O Merciful One: I take refuge in the perfect words of God from all Devils and pests and from the Evil Eye." '

Before going to sleep Abdul-Karim wondered to himself if this prayer was to be found in Shia texts and decided to ask his father when next he saw him. He recited the prayer three times and felt a profound reassurance. He slept deeply and calmly.

Yacoub had almost lost hope that Izzat would contact him as every time he enquired Izzat would say that he must wait. The last time he tried Izzat told him not to contact him any more. Months went by and then the phone call came.

Yacoub raced off to the small apartment in Abbasiyya and was delighted to find that the interview was not a preparatory one or routine because he found Izzat and three young men waiting. From his reading he knew that he was now on the verge of joining a cell.

'It took some time,' began Izzat, 'as we had to investigate you. And the situation overall was very bad, although things are now improving. Most of the comrades are now out of detention.'

The comrades. 'The comrades'. The words sounded sweeter than the patter of rain. Yacoub had now become a member of the worldwide family of those fighting exploitation and oppression.

'From now on,' Izzat went on, 'you'll have no more contact with me at all. Ever. I mean that absolutely. You'll only have contact with the comrades here: Ramiz, Rameses and Iskander. Of course these are their "party" names but for now they'll be sufficient. Later you will learn their real names. Your own party name is "Shibli".'

'What sort of a name is that? Can't I choose a name for myself?'

'No. That's your name. Finished. You'll have to get used to discipline. And now I'll leave the apartment and leave you in the hands of Ramiz, who is in charge of the cell.'

Ramiz spoke of the necessity of taking the most extreme precautions and of some things that were forbidden. It was forbidden for anyone to keep at home any book relating to Communism. Any who had books like that must burn them. No one must talk of his party activity with anyone outside the cell: and that meant mother, father, brothers and sisters. He looked at Yacoub and added, 'And girlfriends, too!'

Yacoub realized that the investigations into his background had been carefully done, and smiled. The list of forbidden things got longer and eventually it was agreed that the next meeting would be at Iskander's apartment in Boulaq. This too was taken up with precautionary procedures and the group listened to a lecture by Ramiz on how to be sure there was no surveillance and how to shake it off if there was. He told them to presume that all phone conversations were monitored and that all mail, domestic and foreign, was opened while all concierges could be taken to be working for Intelligence. He said that just one remark could lead to arrest; a number of comrades had been 'blown' because they had talked when under the influence of alcohol. He gave Yacoub another meaningful look. Yacoub wondered when the real work would begin and what assignments would be given to each of them. 'All in good time,' Ramiz replied.

Yacoub had never felt such ecstasy as he now felt as he left the apartment and followed the routine for checking on surveillance. He walked along normally then suddenly stopped to tie his shoelace. Bending over like this allowed him to see clearly those walking behind him. He carried on and then let his handkerchief drop from his hand. He stopped and went back to pick it up, looking to see if anyone walking behind him was behaving strangely. He then carried on walking until he reached the third stage in the process when he stopped at a phone in the little grocer's store and while pretending to make a phone call examined everything around him.

Everyday life became a delightful adventure: tearing up his Marxist books page by page and burning them when no one was in Apartment Freedom; the double role he was playing as an apparent devotee of Abu-Nuwas and an existentialist while secretly being a party combatant; the enjoyment he felt when he attacked Marxist views and said how they had let him down; the astonishment of the gang at this complete change; the happiness he felt when he heard of the achievements of the comrades in Iraq in fighting the bourgeois who wanted to hand Iraq over to Nasser and their efforts to educate Abdul-Karim Qasim and recruit him to the 'cause'; the joy he felt as he read between the lines of articles in the press with a Marxist slant which only the élite of the élite, namely himself, Shibli and the comrades, could appreciate.

As it was unanimously agreed the constitution could be amended and Majid Zubair became an associate resident in Apartment Freedom. Abdul-Karim proposed that a party be thrown on this occasion but no one was keen. Nash'at was busy with Hilde who had become his 'Swiss peasant girl'; Fuad, after his experience with Shahenaz, refused even to talk about girls; Qasim was in a quandary, lost between the girl and her mother, even though he was actually refusing to meet either of them; while Yacoub was leaping from book to book.

Qasim treated Majid to a 'celebration', however. 'Majid, we have some Saudis in the Faculty. They are really something, just amazing. One of them says he belongs to "Young Nejd" which is seeking the independence of Nejd. Another says he belongs to "Free Hejaz" which is seeking the independence of Hejaz. What sort of a country is this?'

'These are just regional, separatist tendencies that will disappear when total Arab unity comes.'

'Disappear?'

'Yes. Haven't you studied the growth of nations? The process begins with the family which grows and then becomes a clan, which becomes a tribe, which then becomes a people and finally a nation. All those people are still living in the tribal stage and when we enter the phase of the nation these differences will disappear.'

'And when do you enter the phase of the nation?'

'When the regime which resists Arab unity comes to an end.'

'You mean if the Al Saud were to end the Kingdom of Saudi Arabia would join the rest of the Arab nation? Rubbish. That's just cloud cuckoo land. I'll tell you what would happen if the Al Saud were finished. Hejaz would become independent under the leadership of "Free Hejaz" and Nejd would become independent under the leadership of "Young Nejd". And as for ARAMCO it will be absorbed by the Shah when he takes over Bahrain.'

'You're talking like a druggie.'

'You ought to know.'

Sheikh Abu-Zahra welcomed Fuad and began with the usual question, 'So how is Bahrain – still only two seas and not three?'

'Regrettably, Your Reverence!'

Ever since he had gained a grade of 'Excellent' in Sharia Law in the second term of the previous year Fuad had had special attention from the Sheikh. 'What are you doing in Sharia this year?'

'To tell you the truth, since you left we have become like orphans.'

'How's that?'

'Dr Mukhtar's book is too complicated, and his lectures even more so. There is not one student who understands the set book.'

'But Dr Mukhtar is a distinguished scholar.' His smile, however, indicated that he was of the same opinion as Fuad.

'Reverend Sheikh, there are a number of subjects that are bothering me. May I ask you about them some time?'

'Such as what, my son?'

'Arab nationalism and Islam. The view that the regime in Egypt . . .'

'Listen, Fuad,' the Sheikh interrupted. 'I have a lecture just now. Why don't you come to the house tomorrow?'

So the next day the Sheikh, after they had finished their tea, said, 'All right, then, go ahead!'

'Firstly, is there a contradiction between Islam and Arab nationalism?'

'Of course there is, my son.'

'But wasn't Muhammad an Arab?' asked Fuad terribly disturbed by the reply and needed more time before he could go on. 'Wasn't the Koran revealed in Arabic?'

'My son, it is good manners every time you mention the name of the Prophet of God to say, "The blessings and peace of God be upon him"!'

'I am sorry.'

'There is no doubt that the Prophet was indeed an Arab. Some scholars say that anyone who denies the Arabism of the Prophet is an infidel because he is denying something that is an essential and known fact. Moreover the Koran was revealed in clear Arabic. But you have to be precise, Fuad, in the terminology you use. You did not ask me about Arabism, but Arab nationalism.'

'Sir, what is the difference?'

'There is a huge difference. It is part of God's rule in creation that there should be numerous types and colours, such as Arabs, Persians, Indians and Chinese. The problem with Arab nationalism is that it wishes to transform this multiplicity into multiplicity of loyalties. The pan-Arab nationalists want to abrogate loyalty to Islam in favour of loyalty to nationalism. This is not permissible. There cannot be alongside loyalty to Islam loyalty to some other belief, not nationalism, not Communism, nor internationalism.'

'If Arab unity is based on Islam and is to be the nucleus of Islamic unity, then it is a blessed thing. But if it is based on local Arab identity and tribalism then it is to be rejected. Arab tribalism is no different from any other historic tribalism.'

Shocked, Fuad was silent. He had expected to hear from the Sheikh anything but opinions such as these. Eventually he went on, 'But sir, what do you think of those who claim that the Egyptian regime is not governed by Islam?'

'Do you want to land me in trouble?' laughed the Sheikh. 'Who are you? The Secret Service? Have they even reached Bahrain?' He went on, seriously, 'Actually those who say that are right.'

This was another violent slap in the face for Fuad and asked, 'But reverend sir, Egypt is a bastion of Islam and in his *Philosophy of the Revolution* Gamal Abdul Nasser speaks at great length about Islam and the Islamic Circle.'

'There is no need to talk about individuals,' says the Sheikh, smiling. 'OK. No need to mention names. Here we are talking about the principle. No country is Islamic which does not impose Islamic punishments, or use the Islamic Sharia for its government and which does not take the Koran and the Sunna as the basis for its entire existence.'

'So the Kingdom of Saudi Arabia is the only Islamic country in the whole world?'

'Didn't we agree that there was no need for names?'

Fuad was struck dumb and depressed. The Sheikh realized that his pupil had been shocked and tried to soften the blow. 'None the less, Fuad, there is no need to worry. There is no need to call everyone infidels. It took the Prophet Muhammad thirteen years of effort in Mecca to teach people the principles of the unity of God and the Islamic Sharia was only put into effect in Medina. There is no need for haste, as in the end victory is guaranteed. God Almighty guaranteed it in His Holy Book: "It is He Who hath sent His Apostle with Guidance and the Religion of Truth to proclaim it over all religion, even though the Pagans may detest it." '

'But, sir . . .'

'I know that all this has been a surprise for you. But don't take it too hard. The ordinary Muslim is not taken in sin just because he gets confused. They sin who are able to implement the rule of God and do not do so. They alone are the infidels, the oppressors and the unclean.'

'May I ask one last question? What do you think of Hassan Al-Banna?'

'May God have mercy on his soul. He was my teacher and he died as a martyr. My rule is not to place anyone above God and I include him in this rule. May God have mercy on his soul!'

'But what about the Muslim Brotherhood?'

'The exam is next month,' said the Sheikh, once again smiling. 'You'd better go and study and may God guide you.'

As he left the Sheikh's sitting room Fuad felt worried. Here was Sheikh Muhammad Abu-Zahra, in the view of many the greatest scholar in Egypt, possibly the greatest scholar in Islam: how could he believe that there was a contradiction between Arab nationalism and Islam?

Abdul-Karim was running with the magazine *Al-Kawakib* in his hand.

'Fuad! Look!'

Fuad took the magazine and found the picture in the middle. It is the freebie with this issue, the 'new face': Shahenaz Shakir, with her golden hair tumbled on to her shoulders, her smile was radiant and her eyes spoke of endless green pastures. Fuad turned to Yacoub, 'Yacoub, the first part of *Al-Atla*!'

Yacoub recited the famous poem relating the end of a love based on delusion. As he listened tears pricked Fuad's eyes and he rushed to his bedroom.

Qasim screamed at Abdul-Karim, 'Now do you see what you have done!'

'What I've done?! Don't scream at me, scream at "Al-Kawakib"!'

# CHAPTER TWELVE

## February 1960

For Qasim the end of the year brought two important developments. The first was the arrival of his car from Bahrain, the car his father had promised him ever since he had got his driving licence, a white VW. It was so small that he immediately named it BAPCO after the huge road tankers of Bahrain. No one from then on thought of using any other name. Yacoub decided to learn to drive.

The second momentous development was the arrival in Cairo from Switzerland of Margaret, the friend of Hilde with whom she was to spend the end-of-year holiday. As soon as he set eyes on her he realized that Nash'at was right when he said it was mad to spend time with the 'country girls straight off the farm'. Their first meeting was at the Hunting Club in Doqqi as he sat with Nash'at and Hilde came in with Margaret. She was wearing slim blue jeans like an American and a patterned blouse. The jeans revealed all there was to know about her legs and thighs and nothing was left unannounced by her blouse about her bosom. She had the faintest dusting of freckles while her eyes had a depth of blue which reminded him of the waters of the Gulf. It turned out that she was three years older than he was, that she worked in a Geneva bank and was visiting Cairo for the first time.

Abdul-Karim in relaxed moments had already given grades for being handsome to the members of the group: he himself was 'Poor', while Majid and Fuad were 'Acceptable'; Abdul-Ra'ouf was 'Good' while Nash'at and Yacoub were 'Very Good'. It was only Qasim that he gave the grade 'Excellent'.

Qasim was pretty indifferent to his appearance and took himself as he was with all his imperfections. He was unaware that in dealing with the fair sex he had anything distinguishing in his thick, soft hair, his sporting and slim frame or his wide black eyes. He did not notice the impact of his appearance on women until after his experience with Ilham or rather her experience with him. After that it was clear to him that almost all the young women showed interest. Now, as soon as he was introduced to Margaret, he was aware that she was as immediately attracted to him as he was to her.

It was a happy coincidence that Margaret arrived in the same week as the VW, so every day they went off in the little car to visit all the touristic features of Cairo. Margaret savoured every experience as if she were in front of some delicious banquet. She drank greedily of the greyish sugar cane drink that Qasim refused for fear of germs, and pounced on the Ta'miyya sandwiches as if she had been born in Khan El-Khalili. She leapt on to the camel's back at the Pyramids as if she were about to get on to the Magic Carpet. And through all of this she treated Qasim as if she had known him since childhood.

To celebrate these two happy events Qasim invited the gang to a New Year's Eve party at the Arizona Nightclub on the road to the Pyramids. Most of the friends declined because exams were near: only Nash'at and Abdul-Karim who accepted, Abdul-Karim letting Qasim know that he would be bringing his friend with him. They met at one of the best front tables at the big club: Nash'at and his Swiss Peasant, Qasim and Margaret, and Abdul-Karim with Reeri who was dazzling in a lovely golden dress. Nash'at pointed over to a table at some distance from them surrounded by plants at all points.

'The nightingale's nest! That's the table for Muhammad Abdul-Wahhab. It's always reserved for him whether he comes or not.'

Qasim had decided that beer was not right for this occasion so a bottle of Champagne was brought.

The party began and they put on their New Year funny hats and masks, throwing balloons at one another, hurling mock hand-grenades and blowing whistles. Suddenly Nash'at whispered, 'Fuad, Karim! Look. Abdul-Wahhab has arrived.'

And there at the isolated table sat the great musician surrounded by a crowd of friends. Reeri asked Abdul-Karim to ask for his autograph for her, but he insisted she should go herself. She came back beaming: on the menu he had written in a beautiful, clear hand 'With best wishes for health and happiness in the New Year, Muhammad Abdul-Wahhab.'

Reeri carefully put the sheet of paper in her handbag as if she was dealing with a jewel.

The programme of entertainments went by, each chosen carefully to suit the tastes of the Egyptian clients, the Arab visitors and the foreign tourists. There was Oriental dancing, followed by a Spanish group, then an 'oud' player demonstrating his skill with scales, Rock and Roll rounded things off. A stand-up comedian was followed by a magician and the evening flew by. Qasim could hardly take his eyes off Margaret. His leg touched hers but he could not tell whether he had made the first move or Margaret but what seemed like armies of ants marched from his leg to his brain. He held her hand and she squeezed his, so that he was seized by that overwhelming desire he had first known when he saw Ilham. His hand was now on her shoulder and her leg was, like a snake, coiled round his. The MC announced that it was nearly midnight and the New Year was about to dawn. The countdown began and the lights were dimmed before coming on again brightly. Every guest embraced his female neighbour and Margaret embraced Qasim, her lips holding his in a kiss that began in 1959 and did not end until 1960: a kiss that lasted a year and was over in a flash.

Nash'at took off his Swiss Peasant in Ba'kbooka and Qasim with Margaret beside him set off in the VW, with Abdul-Karim and Reeri on the back seat. Margaret's hand slid to his leg and he had to concentrate with all his might on the road. Groans rose from the back seat and Qasim smiled to himself in the darkness: no question, Reeri's company was a lot more fun than 'grand-ma's', and safer, too. When they reached the apartment Reeri went with Abdul-Karim to his room and Margaret went with Qasim to his.

That night – or rather that morning – Qasim found everything that he had been dreaming of for years. All his expectations, all his aspirations. He did not get a moment's sleep and neither did Margaret. His thirst was slaked as never before. So was his hunger sated. The world was not present any more, only two young bodies, raging, giving and taking, giving pain and pleasure in their generosity and pleadings for more. Qasim left the Old Year a boy and entered the New Year a man.

'Wine today and on the morrow labour.' The phrase went through Qasim's mind but he had forgotten who said it: Abu Nuwas? Tomorrow came and the intoxication was over. Margaret disappeared as if she had been a ghost of the old year who had been scared off by the sight of the new. She left behind only the memory of the perfumed night. Qasim knew it was useless to try to make contact with that charming ghost, knew that something as marvellous as this could happen only once in a lifetime.

A few days after the party Qasim noticed the scattered yellow spots on his underpants and at first thought that he might need spectacles. But then came the burning sensation and now there could be no illusions. He hurried off to the specialist who had treated Abdul-Karim. He gave him an examination and then said, smiling, 'Ten shots of penicillin.' Then he added, 'What's with you guys? Don't you go for women who are clean?'

The hangover had gone and now here was something far worse: gonorrhoea. Like a madman he roared, 'Nash'at. It's impossible. A nice little Swiss piece and she's got gonorrhoea!'

'Are you sure you didn't sleep with anyone else?'

'Course I'm sure.'

'Are you sure you couldn't have picked up the infection from somewhere else: the bathroom?'

'The doctor says the chances of that happening are one in a million. When Qasim got his we all said he deserved it as he was picking girls up in the street – but this sweet little thing. She works in a bank, she's a university graduate, how did she pick up gonorrhoea?'

Angry thoughts chased around Qasim's head. Gonorrhoea! From Margaret! And after his first screw. And what a piece she had been. The loveliest girl he had ever seen! What miserably bad luck he had with women. Whores he could not come near. A young woman who goes on hunger strike, insists on getting married, faints as soon as she's touched and a mother who's chasing her own daughter's boyfriend. And now this one: a charmer from the Alps coming with her New Year present.

These days every talk between Fuad and Abdul-Ra'ouf seemed to end in a row as each tried in vain to explain what to him was crystal clear. Fuad could simply not accept that Abdul-Ra'ouf for all his intelligence and education believed that the Muslim Brotherhood could lead the Islamic nation into the future. They only cared about the implementation of the Sharia. What was their economic, social and political programme? Did they have the modern Nasserite vision of development? Did they have the capacity for modern Nass-erite planning? Could they get the masses moving as Gamal Abdul Nasser did?

Islam, according to Fuad's understanding was to be found in the programme of Gamal Abdul Nasser not in that of Hudaibi and his group. Was not Islam in itself the greatest revolution in history? Did it not liberate women from the custom of female infanticide and the other traditions of the Jahiliyya? Did not Aisha command armies? Did not Umar bin Al-Khattab confiscate the wealth of the governors? Was not what was going on now in Revolutionary Egypt the translation of Islam into practice? Islam was just not texts to be interpreted by the religious elders as they saw fit. It was progressive and revolutionary.

Could not Abdul-Ra'ouf see how Gamal Abdul Nasser embodied the principles of Islam? Could he not see how he was fighting against imperialism as a powerful believer with integrity? Could he not see how he was uniting Arabs from the Atlantic to the Gulf, fragmented though they were? Could he not see the new factories? The schools and universities? The High Dam? The modern army? Could Hudaibi do this? Why he had not been been able to persuade his daughter to wear Islamic dress?

Abdul-Ra'ouf tried desperately to explain to Fuad that he could not see reality, was seeing only what he wanted to. He tried to make clear that in Egypt there was no social justice, only dictatorship and rule of a police state. He tried to show him that building schools was only doing harm if the syllabuses were filled with glorification of the dictator. Putting up factories was useless if their production was plundered by a handful of officers. And this Army, if it was not defending Islam, was only another agency of repression for the state. He tried to get rid of the rose-tinted spectacles with which Fuad was looking at Gamal Abdul Nasser.

They agreed to announce a truce for a minimum of three months, during which neither of them would raise the subjects of Nasser, or the Muslim Brotherhood or the relationship between Islam and Arab nationalism.

Every day Majid became more enthusiastic about the Arab Nationalist Movement and insistent that Fuad should join it. 'It is the natural place for you to be. You'll not regret it.'

'Remember my experience with the Ba'ath? I am not up to party discipline.'

'I told you – we consider ourselves as a movement, not a party.'

'That's just playing with words.'

'No. Look, you saw the Ba'ath. A left wing and a right. A Syrian Ba'ath and an Iraqi. A military one and a civilian. We are one mass movement. We don't consider ourselves as an élite leading the masses, we *are* the masses. And our sole leader is Gamal Abdul Nasser.'

'I don't think I'm ready for a new political commitment. I am just a Nasserite.'

'And in the Movement we are all Nasserites. Next week Dr Ahmad Khatib will be in Cairo. Why don't you come with me to meet him?'

'I don't need another Teacher. Those in the Faculty are enough for me.' But he went.

The meeting took place in the apartment of Barrak Al-Nafi, a Kuwaiti studying medicine with Majid. Dr Khatib turned out to be under 30 with dark features, prescription spectacles and boundless energy. Introduced to Fuad he exclaimed 'What's this, a bag of bones? I'll prescribe you some vitamins!'

'I'd forgotten you were a doctor,' replied Fuad. 'You and Dr George Habash, and Dr Wadia Haddad, and tomorrow Dr Majid Zubair and Dr Barrak Al-Nafi. What is this: a political movement or a doctor's trade union?'

'Who better than doctors to diagnose the ills of the nation?'

'Yes, and the prescription is: Unity, Liberation and Revenge. Is that it?'

'Do you have a better one? I like nothing better than a debate. Except maybe "mumawwish"!'

'To start with: why the Movement? Why set up a barrier between the masses and Gamal Abdul Nasser?' asked Fuad.

'Firstly we started in the late 1940s. Secondly, we don't regard ourselves as a barrier between the leader and the masses. We are a bridge between the leader and the nation. We believe that at this stage the leadership should be in the hands of Gamal Abdul Nasser, and of him alone.'

'Second question: what is the Movement's attitude to Socialism? Are you capitalists? Or veiled socialists?'

'Ever since we were students at the AUB we have been asking ourselves that question. We had only 3 or 4 members and we did not call ourselves a Movement. The question of socialism has been our preoccupation since then. We have often discussed it with our Ba'athist brethren. We are convinced that social justice will never be achieved under capitalist exploitation. A formula must be found to reconcile the interests of the individual and those of the group. But we have reached the conclusion that it is better to postpone the whole subject and not to make socialism a slogan or an objective.'

'How long will postponement last?'

'Until the Imperialists have left the homeland, until there is unity and Palestine is liberated. We are beginning with the political revolution and we shall end with social and economic ones. To talk at this stage of socialism does not serve the cause and will simply divide the Arab world into two camps, one of the rich and the other of the poor. The poor may be pushed into the socialist bloc and the rich into the capitalist bloc. We have to be extremely cautious and at this stage the absolute priority must be given to combating imperialism.'

'Even so I can detect hints of sympathy with socialism.'

'Our movement is open to all theories and opinions. We don't have ready made moulds and we have not devised our ideas in ivory towers. They have been made through experience. We have the capacity to develop and to change. That is what makes us believe that our movement is different from the others.'

'Among the things that worry me, Doctor, from my experience with the Ba'ath is that most of the members are from Syria, Lebanon and Iraq and almost nobody has any idea about the rest of the Arab world, about our region for example.'

'In our movement we are committed to realism and a scientific outlook. Don't forget we are doctors. We are fully aware of the divisions in the Arab people. We know how to deal with these differences.'

'Don't you think that our area in particular has very special features?'

'Brother Fuad, we are talking about a homeland stretching from the Ocean to the Gulf. More than 100 million people. What is our area? 100,000 in Kuwait; the same in Bahrain: we are a drop in the Arab ocean, a couple of small tribes and without the depth provided by the Arab homeland that's what we'll remain.'

'Dr Ahmad,' cut in Majid, 'Fuad is very concerned about the relationship between Arabism and Islam. We'd love to have your opinion.'

'This is another fundamental topic. Let me affirm that there is no one in the Movement, even among our Christian comrades, who denies that it is Islam which has given the Arab nation its heroic qualities, its history and its spiritual values. We have never felt any contradiction between Islam and Arabism.'

'And what about the Sharia? The role of Islam in the unified Arab state?'

'We believe in freedom of religion and the right of every Arab to embrace and practice it. But remember that freedom is indivisible: if I give the Arab man freedom of religion then I have to give him the right to reject any authority imposed on him in the name of religion. I can't just let the Muslim impose his opinion on the Christian, or the Sunni on the Shia.'

'So the Sharia will be regarded as simply ritual and rites not to be implemented in practice?'

'What is Islam? As I understand it, Islam does not differ from what we are advocating and believe in. We both say Unity, Liberation and Vengeance. Only the words chosen are different. I was born in a conservative environment and I have never felt that there was any conflict between my principles and my religion.'

As they left Majid asked Fuad what he thought of Dr Ahmad Khatib.

'Well, at least he's a young man who can laugh and joke and admits that he does not have all the answers. If I had to choose between him and Michel Aflaq I'd choose the Doctor.'

Yacoub thrived on revolutionary activity and was thrilled when Ramiz asked him to host one of the meetings at Apartment Freedom. He chose an evening when there were no visitors and none of the residents was at home. This meeting was devoted to a lesson on Molotov cocktails, the bombs which had knocked out so many Nazi tanks. He had thought that making them required a great deal of skill and a variety of raw materials. It turned out that it was simply a matter of a bottle filled with petrol with a filler soaked in the petrol. When the bottle was thrown and smashed into a solid object it broke up and was transformed into a bomb which hurled flames all around it.

This was the wonderful thing about revolutionary activity. This was the difference between odes and bombs, between words and volleys of shots, between an unarmed people and a people fully armed. Just an ordinary bottle and a small quantity of petrol and an armoured car or a building could be destroyed. If only the masses could be made revolutionary in one day. If every oppressed person were given a Molotov cocktail and told to throw it at the nearest symbol of exploitation at the same time on the same day what would happen? The tyrants would fall and in one day the masses would be victorious!

But how to get Molotov cocktails to all? How to train them in their use? How to urge them on to movement? It was here that the role of the party came in and here could be seen the importance of organization, but here too could be seen the need for extreme caution. Every activist was surrounded by dangers. Yacoub had never imagined until he joined the party how much effort was required to produce just one pamphlet. The stencil machine had to be in a place known only to a few for safety's sake. A printing machine, ink and paper could not be bought at one time or in one place by one person. And after all that came the writing and printing and the phase of distribution, the most dangerous stage. It was essential to choose the appropriate time and place to throw out the pamphlets or to stick them up. The early hours of the morning in a place where the maximum number of people gathered with the minimum of policemen was a difficult combination to achieve. As well as the pamphlets there was the problem of writing slogans on walls, just as complicated an operation: there was the secret transformation of the paint-sprayer into a writing instrument, the selection of the walls, the choice of words and then the choice of writer and the time. Any mistake could lead to years in gaol.

At the end of the meeting Yacoub enquired of Ramiz about real bombs and when they would learn how to make them. He said there was no need for real bombs yet. Yacoub then said that he had some questions on the relationship between the party and religions. Ramiz answered that the meetings were not for questions of philosophy and anyway he was not an expert but that he would arrange for Yacoub to meet the party's supervisor in Egypt, Mr S.

Reeri had now become a regular guest, coming to Apartment Freedom at least twice a week. It turned out that she had told Abdul-Karim some fibs on their first meeting. Her father who really had died in a car accident was a government employee not in the military while her mother actually did have to look after a small boy and three girls. She had actually begun 'work' at 16 – four years earlier, not five as she had originally said – and really had finished Intermediate schooling and produced for Abdul-Karim her diploma.

When Abdul-Karim had got in touch with her at the end of the previous year he had not analysed his motives. He was in need of some diversion after his ordeals, and Reeri had come along to do that. She brought jokes, smiles and laughter and a great deal of understanding. For hours she would hear him relating the story of what had happened to him, listening with sympathy and affection. And when he heard the story of her bitter experiences of every day he understood the truth of a proverb which spoke of the misfortunes of others and one's own. The sight of Abdul-Karim and Reeri exchanging their tragedies was an endless source of enjoyment to the others.

When did their relationship, based purely on commerce, become friendship? When did Reeri begin to change her style of dress and her behaviour? When did she lose the characteristic signs of her profession and when did old Zakaria the concierge begin to treat her as a student in the Faculty deserving of respect? When did she begin to go into the kitchen and help Aisha? Abdul-

Karim could not answer any of these questions as everything happened without any planning or encouragement.

Reeri, 'The Swiss Peasant', were the two ladies of the household: one from the far edge of the Delta and the other from the Swiss Alps. Hilde brought flowers and cloths for tables as well as cheap oil paintings. Reeri brought, with new and high standards of cleanliness, order. Mr Shareef, with evident pleasure and curiosity, noted all these changes.

'Fuad, where did this oil painting come from?'

'They sent it from Bahrain.'

'And who bought this window-blind?'

'I did, sir,' replied Qasim.

'How did Aisha learn to cook Wiener Schnitzel?'

'From the cookery book, Mr Shareef!'

Mr Shareef shook his head.

What changes female presence can make to the lives of four bachelors living like Bohemians. None of them had ever noticed the chaos in all parts of Apartment Freedom until it disappeared. None had ever paid any attention to the pile of dirty washing in the bathroom until it vanished just as no one had ever noticed that toiletries, shelves, places for soap and brushes were absent until suddenly they were all there. And in the same way no one was aware of the holes in their clothes until they were mended.

Abdul-Karim was proud of the changes which Reeri had brought to Apartment Freedom in general and to his life in particular. She took all his ties, threw them in the waste-bin and bought him another set. She brought him shirts in bright colours and insisted he should buy new spectacles with smart frames. She guided him towards a new barber. The little touches she added here and there – the new cupboard, bookshelves, a small rug, a flower-vase – transformed his room from a large prison cell to a cosy retreat.

In spite of their ripening friendship based on sex and the spirit, there was one no-go area for discussion, her 'work'. She refused to take anything from him, and he, from time to time, would insist that she accept some little present, a bottle of perfume, a sash, or a ring from Fuad's father's shop. But what about her 'work'? Was she still doing her old job? Had she found new work in some other field? Abdul-Karim smiled as he remembered what she had said when he asked her what her mother thought of her going out of the house:' She doesn't ask and I don't say . . .' That was the height of wisdom.

It was nearly midnight and Fuad lay in bed engrossed in Yusuf Idriss' latest book as the phone rang. He stumbled out of bed. Opening his door he found the rest of the Apartment in darkness. He picked up the phone, scarcely bothering to hide his irritation said, 'Yes?'

'Who are you?'

'Fuad.'

The voice was feminine, disturbing and musical but he replied irritably. 'Can I be of any assistance?'

'We are at your service.'

'Who are you?'

'Madiha. The Nice One.'

'The Cheeky One.'

'My, we are witty, aren't we?'

'Too kind. Can I help you?'

'Is Susu there?'

'Listen, Madiha the Cheeky One, she isn't here.'

'You aren't Egyptian, are you?'

'Of course I am: Farid Asri.'

'It doesn't sound like it.'

'It doesn't sound like I am an Egyptian? Or not like Farid Asri?'

'Are you making fun of me? Either you are from the Hejaz or else you have a bad temper!'

'Stretch out, my dear Mr Ahmad!'

'Oh, where is Susu?'

'Now listen, you! It's midnight and tomorrow I have to be up early, I'm off to college!'

'Which one?'

'Law.'

'Are you a student there?'

'No, I'm on the door!'

'Hmm . . . a doorkeeper and you can read. You'll do someone proud! Who?'

'Your parents!'

'You're going to make a complete mess of things, you Hejazi.'

'And you are going to wear a veil for me, you foul-mouthed broad!'

Fuad did not know why he didn't close this wrong number call: all he knew was that he just wanted to go on with it.

'That's enough. Where is Susu?'

'Didn't you hear me! She's dead, and I hope you are soon, too!'

'How awful. Same to you!'

'Yeah, go and ask the Imam to arrange it!'

'Why are you so aggressive?'

'You can talk, you poison-tongued woman!'

Her laugh rang out, clear and thrilling.

'No, listen, you are really funny. I'll ring you tomorrow. What's your number?'

'Wasn't it you who called me?'

'I was calling Susu and it was you I got! Hidden misfortunes.'

'OK, take down the number! What time will you call?'

'I don't know. When I feel like it.'

And with that she put the phone down.

Fuad had some experience of pestering phone calls and if he found a ready response could go on for hours. He insisted that he extracted material for his stories from such calls but this call was something else. Sexual desire was transferred by phone to his body. Before tonight he had never known real lust overwhelm him just from a phone pest.

Sheikh Abu-Zahra smiled as he welcomed an anxious Fuad.

'Reverend sir, I have a question about the Hadith of The Prophet Muhammad on flies.'

The Sheikh exploded, 'What's all this about the Hadith on flies! Have we liberated Palestine? Liberated Kashmir? Have we united the Islamic world? Have we put an end to all our problems so that we have only the Hadith on flies to bother us?'

Fuad was startled by this outburst and stammered. 'I'm sorry reverend sir. I just wanted to know if The Prophet Muhammad (peace be upon him) actually uttered this Hadith.'

'Has anyone ever forced you to eat from a vessel that a fly has fallen into? Has any government ever put out a decree for the execution of anyone refusing to eat from such a vessel? Did the Prophet Muhammad (peace be upon him) ever say that anyone who did not would suffer in Hell? My good friend, put all this out of your mind.'

Fuad blushed to his roots. The Sheikh calmed down and even smiled a little. 'This Hadith, my son, has been the main preoccupation of the Orientalists, they have written whole books on it, and they still point the finger of suspicion because of it. That's why I was angry. They have investigated this Hadith as if all the holy books of the Sunna contained nothing else.'

'But is it a sound Hadith?'

'It comes in the books of sound Traditions. But it is one of those based on only one authority and in the Hanafi school such Hadiths have value only for thought or supposition. There is nothing obliging Muslims to accept all such Hadiths. Al-Bukhari, may God have mercy on him, did not put many of the Hadiths in his collection even though they fulfilled his conditions, and the same goes for the Imam Muslim, may God have mercy on him. It was this which Al-Hakim put right. Some scholars have spoken of the chain of Tradition. There is a study by the late Muhammad Rashid Rida. If you can't find it let me know and I'll look for it in my library. And remember: there are things more important than flies!'

Nash'at had warned Fuad and Abdul-Karim that if they did not study French they would not pass the French section of the exam on Civil Law and would fail thus in the whole subject. As a result of this insistence they joined the Berlitz School and each of them paid in advance for 20 lessons. The secretary told them that the teacher was French and it was no use talking Arabic to him.

The elderly teacher, M. Denteil, had a scowling face and a fiery temper. As soon as the lessons began Fuad and Abdul-Karim realized that their hopes for success in French were slender. At every lesson there was wrath in French which the two students did not understand although they were able to imagine his drift. The last straw came over the question of the pronunciation of the letter 'O' which they both pronounced in the English way. M. Denteil practised the correct sound for them time after time. Suddenly he smashed his fist on to the table and shouted, 'Are you human beings or donkeys!'

Fuad was so astounded he could not speak but Abdul-Karim replied quietly, 'The donkey is your father!' There were no further Berlitz lessons.

Nash'at was very put out. 'You're going to fail! Listen to you guys! Find someone else. I'm ready to teach you!'

At this they replied with one voice, 'We'll fail. We'll fail!' And Fuad added, 'Well, even failing is to take a position. It's making a gesture!'

# CHAPTER THIRTEEN

## April 1960

Q asim always liked to listen to the views of Nash'at's father, Muharram
Pasha when he visited. Muharram Pasha delighted in talking with
this young man, a capitalist from Bahrain who seemed the only wise
person in a generation which Gamal Abdul Nasser had deprived of the gift
of thinking. They would talk in the garden of the large villa on the Nile.
Although land reform had deprived Muharram Pasha of most of his wealth
the routine of the villa seemed not to have changed since the days of the
Monarchy: the place abounded with servants, coming and going and dressed
in the height of elegance.

'Oh, Pasha, I wish you would explain to me how the *coup d'état* succeeded
and how they were able to remove King Farouq.'

'My son they did not get rid of King Farouq. It was the King who removed
himself. Forget the claims that have now become official history. Before the
Revolution there were about 1,500 officers in the Egyptian Army and
the group of the so-called Free Officers was no more than 40 officers who
had 20 or 30 sympathizers, that is less than 5 per cent of the officer total.'

'So, how did they manage to take power?'

'It was a risky venture. In the beginning they had only limited demands
but the collapse of the King gave them encouragement. Do you know how
many tanks took part in the coup? Less than 30. Less than 20 armoured cars.
They were able to take over GHQ thanks to the information that Abdul-
Hakim Amir had got. They then took over the radio station and as soon as
the first communiqué went out the King caved in.

'But how did the King react?'

'At the time he was in Alexandria. The Army, apart from a handful of
officers, was loyal to him as were the Navy and the Air Force. If the King
had proclaimed that he was advancing on Cairo to put down the rebellion

the coup attempt would have failed within hours. Instead he phoned the US and British Ambassadors and they both advised him to abdicate.'

'But Pasha, wasn't there great popular support for the coup?'

'No. But the King stayed in Alexandria until the tanks surrounded the Palace. Ten tanks! The Palace Guard could have destroyed them easily. Instead the King surrendered and abdicated. Even the coup plotters had never dreamed of that.' The Pasha was silent for a moment and then went on. 'Don't forget, Qasim, that the King was just a big child.'

This coming from one of the most prominent figures in the Royalist regime, was unexpected. The Pasha noticed Qasim's surprise.

'Do you know how the King spent most of his time? Driving fast cars or playing with model trains or his stamp collection.'

'So what is being said about him these days is untrue?'

'Not a tenth. They say he was blotto most of the time but in fact he never drank alcohol. They say he stole and plundered the wealth of the State but that is fabrication. There was a great commotion in the Chamber when repairs to his yacht cost half a million pounds. But now *Mahrusa* is the Republican yacht *Hurriya* and if anyone asked about the cost of its upkeep he would disappear for good.'

'And what about . . . well, the other things?'

'Women? He liked to seem to be a Don Juan . . . a new woman every night. But he was just like a child that wants all the kids in his area to see his new toy. It was just a charade. As for those books about him – all their authors used to fawn to him. If you only knew the huge sums they used to get from the Palace!'

'What about the stories of the useless weapons?'

'My son. The King was surrounded by thieves. Pimps! I don't rule out them being involved in financial scandals but as for him – he just wasn't interested in money. If you offered him the choice between a million pounds and a new car for 5,000 pounds he'd choose the car. Since they removed him he has been living on allowances from the Kingdom of Saudi Arabia.'

'But, wasn't there a popular wish for change? Wasn't there resentment?'

'Grumbling? Of course there was. And now the whole country is grumbling. And it will be the same in 1,000 years. The emotions of the masses are like quicksilver. One word can turn them away and one word can bring them back. Ten years ago every time the King's red Rolls-Royce appeared the people would cheer. But now all you see is rent-a-crowd.'

'So why did the regime fall so easily?'

'Because it was weak, not because it was tyrannical. I know what is taught in universities now and I have warned Nash'at against believing it. They teach you that tyranny leads to revolution. Rubbish! They teach you that hunger leads to revolution. Nonsense! The French Revolution happened when oppression had ended and concessions had been made. The same with the Russian Revolution: it did not break out because of the tyranny of the Czar but because the Czar was feckless. The latest example is Iraq: I've been told that King Hussein sent King Feisal a list of the officer conspirators and the King did nothing. And they murdered him. The King knew all about it. The names of the Free Officers were given to him more than once but he took no action. The Prime Minister merely sent for Gamal Abdul Nasser and gave him a reprimand! If the King had jailed the 10 officers he would have remained *in situ.*'

'How do you explain his failure to act?'

'God created some men strong and others weak, some courageous and some cowards. But the coup plotters learned that if there is the slightest initiative now, up go the scaffolds and the detention camps open.' The Pasha paused and his gaze wandered far away, to the horizon, perhaps to Italy where the deposed King lived, the boy/man, and he sighed. 'Remember this, my son: it is weakness that brings revolutions, not tyranny, or hunger.'

Qasim left. The more he thought about these final words the more he believed Pasha was right.

*Khalid kicks the stones imagining that each one was a ball being launched towards his opponent's goal. He crossed the narrow lane making for the large open space, then walked to the main street where the Oriental School stood. On the corner stood Ghaloom's shop in a strategic position to catch all the students as they went to and from school. Khalid takes his daily allowance, 4 annas, and wonders how to spend it. He decides to buy 2 annas' worth of King chewing gum and to keep 2 for some bread and jam in the cafeteria. He puts out his hand to take the chewing gum from Ghaloom but his bag bumps against the jar full of sweets. It crashes to the floor, scattering pieces of glass all over. Ghaloom screams. 'Look what have you done? Pay up! Come on, 5 rupees!'*

*'Five rupees. I haven't got it!' Khalid stammers.*

*'All right, then, Come with me!'*

*Ghaloom indicates a door at the back of the shop leading to complete darkness. Go in there with him? Why? Khalid looks at the spiteful face and the fierce glare. He shivers. Does Ghaloom want to kill him over a jar of sweets? 'Bring me 5 rupees and you get your bag back,' he says, snatching his schoolbag.*

*The day begins with the arithmetic lesson and the teacher, counting the homework book says, 'Khalid, where's your book?'*

*'I'm sorry, sir, I left it at home.'*

*The teacher sends him to the headmaster who tells him to put his hand out and brings down the cane on it, twice. Khalid fights back the tears and goes back to the class.*

*The next day it is the same in the Arabic lesson. The headmaster. The cane. And a message for his father.*

*Khalid stands rooted to the spot and unable to raise his eyes as his father reads the message carefully. Khalid's heart is pounding. His father had never given him a beating or even scolded him. Would this be the first time? His father looks at him with more regret than anger. 'Where did the schoolbag go to, Khalid?' Khalid does not speak, as he remembers the spots on Ghaloom's face and the dark at the end of the store. 'Did you lose it? Where did you lose it?'*

*The broken jar, the glass scattered around. And 'Come with me!' He blushes and does not speak. His father sighs. 'I'll give you to tomorrow. Go and look for it and don't come back without it!'*

*Tomorrow. That's when Sheikh Muhammad Saleh in the Religion class would be having them memorize the verse from the Koran: 'If those who worship Me ask about me I am near, to respond to the prayer of anyone who invokes Me.'*

*A thought flashes into Khalid's mind. 'Sir, does God respond to every call on Him?'*

*'Yes, if it is from a believing heart.'*

*'Even from a small boy?'*

*'Even from a child.'*

*'Even if it was asking for 5 rupees?'*

*The whole class bursts into laughter. The Sheikh smiles. 'Yes, even 5 rupees.'*

*Behind the cafeteria counter, out of sight, Khalid closes his eyes and bends all his feelings to the heavens, whispering, 'O Lord! O Lord! 5 rupees! Please, O Lord! O Lord! O Lord! 5 rupees! Please, O Lord!'*

*As the bell goes announcing the end of break Khalid is still in prayer.*

*When he leaves school he makes a detour to avoid Ghaloom's shop. He kicks an empty tin can which flies off, making a beautiful sound. He goes after it and kicks it again. It flies up and lands next to the wall. He goes after it and sees the banknote. A brand-new 5 rupee banknote thrown away. He picks it up and races off to the shop. 'Take your money and give me my bag!'*

*He clutches it as he races home. He does not stop to kick stones but runs along muttering, 'O Lord! Thank you! Thank you, O Lord!'*

'You're really into committed literature now, Fuad. You'll never abandon it.'

'Well, yes, Abdul-Ra'ouf, but the story is only something I saw for myself.'

'How old were you?'

'Eight. Seven perhaps. I don't remember.'

'And was there really a man called Ghaloom?'

'His real name, I think, was Abbas. He's still there.'

'So Khalid was you? I thought so. Did Abbas actually ask you to go inside with him?'

'Yes.'

'What for?'

'At the time I thought it was to beat me or to kill me. But now, maybe only Yacoub has the answer.'

'Listen, Fuad. We have enough stories for the collection and Mr Abdul-Bari has agreed to the idea in principle. He has agreed to print the book in the summer: 3,000 copies. We'll get 10 per cent of the net profits.'

'If there are any . . .'

The night after the first phone call the phone rang. It was Madiha. It was the same the next night and the next. Their chattering turned into flirting, then turned into amusement until it became a part of the nightly routine. At just on 11 the phone would ring in Apartment Freedom and Madiha would whisper from the penthouse in the Zamalek Tower building, or else he would call her from the apartment. They would then talk until midnight and beyond.

How many nights? 50? 60? They lost count but their talk which had begun with cheerful insults became weightier stuff. The phone had come to have a number of different functions: it was a confessional, a stage, a music, a book, a bed. The black instrument had become means of addiction for them both. Fuad felt embarrassment at himself and at such adolescent stupidity and at the delicious thrill of lust the phone created. Madiha swore that she had not made a nuisance call since she was 15 but now neither of them could either break the habit or propose meeting.

They knew everything about each other that it was possible for a girlfriend and boyfriend to know, who had never seen each other. She suggested they should exchange pictures but the idea remained in suspense for a while. Neither wanted to take the initiative. Then she gave him the name of a photographer. He went there, giving praise to God that the prescriptions of Dr Ahmad Khatib had brought about certain improvements in his appearance. But then came the bill: 30 pounds! This bill had drained all his funds completely but he was happy with the result as the photographer had managed to hide his defects and emphasize his good points.

He sent her his photos and then hers reached him, in the form of a small album showing her life from when she was a little girl in her school smock, right up to the previous week. Here she was, wearing a bridal dress (did she have to send this one?) and here was another one of her with her girlfriends. And here was one in front of the Pyramids. She made no comment on any of the photos but neither did he, and their nightly phone calls went on.

Madiha Mazhar Rashwan! Maybe she had been expecting a shout of amazement from him when he heard the sound of her father's name but he had never heard it before. He admitted this fact to her but she was pleased rather than angered. It turned out that her father was a famous businessman who owned a major hotel in Zamalek. He also owned an even grander hotel in Alexandria, the Sevio. Her mother had died when she was 5 and her father had vowed to bring her up and to foreswear other women. The girl's requests were commands.

This went on till she was in Intermediate school but then her father married again and a new woman came between them. The father had hoped that his new wife and his daughter, who was only a few years younger than she, would develop a relationship like that of sisters. But war broke out between the two women from the first moment. There was a let-up when Madiha joined the English Department of the Faculty of Arts. The atmosphere of the university gave her scope to escape from the home which had become unbearable. She became very taken with her English tutor, Dr Sidqi and he with her. Their wedding took place with incredible speed: the father was very keen to accede to her request and the stepmother wanted to get rid of her while Madiha herself was very keen to have her independence. However within weeks Madiha realized that she had simply exchanged one prison for another.

Dr Sidqi was barely 30 but began to behave like someone from Upper Egypt of advanced years. He forbade her to continue with her studies (was he afraid she might come to admire some other lecturer?) and then forbade her to wear her usual clothes, requiring her to dress more modestly. He kept on insisting that he wasn't going to be a kept man: he wanted her to leave the penthouse which her father had rented and furnished and presented as a wedding gift and to live with him in his tiny apartment but she refused. It ended in divorce within the year. Madiha stayed in the penthouse with nothing to relieve her loneliness except the nurse who had brought her up. She tried to go back to her studies but discovered that she had lost the will. Then she made an agreement to work for her father in his Star Hotel in charge of PR but on her terms, mainly that she would be free to come and go as she pleased. For this work her father paid her 300 pounds a month (which, according to Qasim's information was more than the salary of a government Minister). She broke off all contact with her stepmother (who was now going from one doctor to another in the hope of having a child) and saw her father only in the hotel. The arrangement which suited all parties.

At first Madiha was very happy with her freedom and with her job but within a few months, at the age of 23, she began to display all the symptoms of middle age: feelings of being hemmed in, boredom, loneliness, and sleeplessness. On top of that her open car no longer gave her the thrill that it used to. Nor was the Gezira Club any longer that dreamy, romantic port of call of old. Every day became like any other, the chatter of her girlfriends was all the same, and all dresses looked alike and the only exciting thing in her life nowadays was the nightly rendezvous with the strange young man, 'The bad-tempered Hejazi'.

He pored over his pictures, and especially his favourite, the one of Madiha in her bathing-costume. No objective observer could have described Madiha as being beautiful nor as being ugly: she had a small frame and Fuad laughed as he imagined her standing alongside him. Still her body was full and he wondered how she had got into that bathing costume. She had almost no hips and her face joined her torso in such a way that her neck could hardly be seen. Her bosom was large while her features were an extraordinary mixture of Roman and negroid. Her hair was crinkly and short while her nose being slightly raised gave her a rather superior look. Her lips, in the African manner, were heavy while her eyes were narrow, almost Asian. And yet this bizarre mixture emerged in her final photo as being very attractive, a woman who caught the eye and held the attention.

Then suddenly one April night, when the temperature was between cold and warm, at nearly midnight, as they were in the midst of their banter she said, 'Wait for me downstairs. I'll be with you in a quarter of an hour and take you to the penthouse.'

The phone was replaced and Fuad had to put his fingers in his ears to stifle the pounding of his heart.

Yacoub opened the door to Apartment Freedom to welcome his guest but as soon as he saw his face he froze to the spot, 'You, Mr Sab . . .'

'S! Mr S!' the visitor said interrupting him with a laugh.

The visitor began the discussion in Yacoub's room. 'When I leave here, please forget that you have met me. No one will believe you if you talk, but I am quite sure that you won't.'

'I swear on my honour.'

'Right, let's begin. What are the questions that are troubling you?'

'All right, Mr Sab . . . Mr S, I mean, I'll tell you everything that is going round in my head about religion. I am a Communist and will remain one till I die but still I can't deny the way I was born and grew up. I was born a Muslim and took in Islam with my mother's milk and I can't simply get rid of this part of myself. I embraced Communism in the search for freedom and arrived at Marxism after many stages of intellectual journeying. At every stage I was looking for a doctrine that protects the freedom of the individual. I then discovered that such freedom could be found only under the umbrella of Communism. But I don't want my Party work to be at the expense of my freedom. If I want to pray I'll pray and if I want to fast I'll fast. If I decide to be a Marxist Muslim I'll be a Marxist Muslim. Do you see what I am getting at?'

'I thank you for being so frank. Dialogue has no meaning unless it is freed from ritual courtesies. Before we get into details let me clarify three positions which people often misunderstand thanks to capitalist propaganda. Firstly, it is not true that Communism means profligacy and the breakdown of morals. The USSR is more conservative than any capitalist country and more than some Muslim countries, while China is more conservative than the USSR. In China – and I have visited it more than once – the police will arrest you if you hold your wife's hand in the street. Secondly we in the Party are not just copies of each other, according to one common view which is wrong. Every one of us has his own interests, his own intellectual tendencies and his own private life. We have general principles in common but there is a lot of disparity between us. Thirdly, as regards the Party's attitude to religion, we concentrate on religion as an establishment or institution.'

'Every religion begins with ethical principles calling for kindness, justice, compassion, charity and so on. And we have no objection to these. Many of them are not in contradiction with the essence of socialist thought. But any religion, immediately following the death of its Prophet, becomes transformed into an institution with its pyramid structure, its priorities and its vested interests. That's where the problem starts. The religious institution becomes a reactionary institution working against the interests of the masses and for the benefit of the exploiters.'

'I may, for the sake of argument, agree with the first part, the transformation of religion into an institution but I cannot understand the second part. Why is the religious institution of necessity a reactionary one acting against the interests of the masses?'

'We could discuss the reasons for that for months. But the important thing is that this is the actual historical model followed by all religions. The religious institution becomes an institution which simply trades in the commodity of the next world. "This world below is a vale of tears: only have patience. God will reward you in Paradise. He will grant to you gilded palaces. Have no care for this transient world below. It is for those who deny God. Do not object to that which is pre-ordained by God. Know your place. God wanted there to be rich and poor." Isn't that the gist of the message that every religion puts out? Isn't the result that the masses are induced into a state of narcosis? It is this which has caused the Party to say, "Religion is the opium of the masses." '

'But sir, Islam differs from the other religions.'

'Religions may differ but religious institutions don't. Look at Egypt. What was true of the attitude of the religious establishment to the governing apparatus in the time of Rameses The First applies to the religious establishment's attitude to government in the time of Gamal Abdul Nasser!'

'How, then, do you explain the attitude of the Muslim Brotherhood?'

'It was not satisfied with the role of junior partner but aspired to a monopoly of power. Do you really think that Hassan Al-Banna was concerned with the workers and peasants? If the Brotherhood had taken power they would have established the most hateful form of reactionary capitalism.'

'Islam differs from all other religions. Islam is concerned with this life and the after-life equally.'

'In theory. In the Koran. In the Hadith. But what about real life? Come with me to a mosque, here in Cairo, or New Delhi, or in Jakarta – and what do you hear? Will you hear a sermon about oppressed workers? Will you hear a call for the formation of Trade Unions? You will hear all about the torments of the grave and the vipers of Hell and the palaces of Paradise but you will never hear a single word about the torments of factory life or the vipers of Imperialism. You will not hear the view of Islam – you will hear the views of the clerical establishment.'

'But there is no clerical establishment in Islam, sir!'

'The Prophet Muhammad was hardly dead before the clerical establishment made its appearance and made its alliance with political power. From the time Abu Hureira became an official working for Muawiya to when the Sheikh of Al-Azhar became an official working for Gamal Abdul Nasser – it's all the same kind of relationship.'

'I beg your pardon!! No, really, sir – you are exaggerating and making generalizations. Haven't there been revolutions in Islam? Haven't religious scholars been put to death? Haven't those learned in the Sharia been gaoled? And haven't some men of religion been in the vanguard of the struggle?'

'All that is merely the exception to the rule. Go to Mr Adbul-Rahman Al-Sharqawi and he will give you a lecture on Abu-Dhurr Al-Ghafari, Sulaiman Al-Farisi and the socialist revolutions in Islam but all that is merely exceptional cases. Some men of religion have stepped out of line and have been executed – but most have lined up with authority. And I am not just talking about Islam: I'm talking about the religious establishment everywhere and at all times. You are studying sociology and you'll soon be graduating. Has there ever been a society where the religious establishment has not lined up with the governing one?'

'We don't study that aspect.'

'Well, read about it now – go to any encyclopedia and look up religious establishments. What you will find is that the religious and the ruling establishments are always two faces of the same coin.'

'But the clerical establishment may actually divide against itself and rise in revolt. Take Martin Luther.'

'Martin Luther actually pronounced in favour of the slaughter of peasants! Such clerical rebellions as his either fail or if they succeed they become a new clerical establishment which joins an alliance with the ruling establishment. Did you know that the Queen of England is actually Head of the Church?'

'Anyway, you haven't answered my main question: what about my own attitude to religion? Can I bring together Islam and Marxism?'

'You can pray and fast day and night just so long as your own attitude to religion does not clash with Marxist thought and the interests of the masses!'

'As a matter of fact,' said Mr S, rising to his feet, 'if we want to infiltrate into your reactionary part of the world it is in our interests to have party members who pray and fast night and day.'

Yacoub started at the next Friday lunch. 'I'd like to raise a question. It's the relation between religion and the masses.'

'Oh, you mean the relationship between Islam and Arab nationalism?' said Fuad.

'No, I mean religions in general. I had a discussion last week with some of the other students and some of them took the view that religions inevitably become transformed into institutions and that these again become transformed into reactionary institutions which join up with the governing circles against the masses.'

'That's the view of Marx and Lenin,' said Abdul-Ra'ouf calmly.

'All right,' said Yacoub, blushing. 'That's the Marxist position. That's what I want to talk about.'

'I don't know a lot about religions in general,' said Abdul-Ra'ouf. 'All my information concerns Islam. If you want to discuss the situation in Islam, go ahead.'

'Hasn't Islam been transformed into a clerical institution that has made an alliance with the ruling power?'

'You can't put the question in that way,' said Abdul-Ra'ouf. 'You can't just generalize. Are there any specific examples?'

'Haven't scholars in Islamic law all through history been in alliance with the ruling class?'

'Anyone with a vague idea of Islamic history could reply to the charge but that's what "the colleagues in the Faculty" lack. Take a look at the four main schools in Sunni Islam and their Imam's view of the ruling power. The Imam Malik was beaten until his shoulder was dislocated. Abu Hanifa was subjected to all manner of persecution and Al-Shafi escaped only by a miracle, while Ibn Hanbal nearly died of his beatings in prison. These are the greatest of our religious scholars. Is this collusion with authority?'

'But these are only exceptions.' Yacoub was parrotting an earlier debate.

Over and over again identical issues were aired, conflicting and confusing answers offered as they parried over the same old ground ...

'I don't deny that these positions exist. But what I object to is the confusion between the attitudes taken by individuals, who are at bottom only officials, and Islam itself. These people represent only themselves.'

'So who represents Islam, then?' Yacoub demanded.

'That's the difference between Islam and Christianity. There is no official spokesman for Islam. In Egypt there's a Mufti for the country who puts out scores of fetwas every day but these fetwas only bind him and those who are persuaded of his authority. They don't bind me. Nothing binds me except the Koran and the Sunna.'

'Not everyone is like you. The majority follow the views of the men of religion. And if they make common cause with authority the mass of the people follow suit.'

'I'll go back to a matter I've been talking about with Fuad for a long time. People should be given a genuinely Islamic education. If we teach the Muslim that he must follow the Koran and the Sunna and there is no obedience due to anyone in opposition to the will of God it is no longer possible for anyone to speak on behalf of God.'

'Abdul-Ra'ouf! All this is merely theory and wishful thinking. Look at the reality.'

'I'll make it easy for you,' says Abdul-Ra'ouf, butting in, 'The Sheikh of Al-Azhar, the Mufti and the rest are merely state employees employed by the President. I've said this so many times to Fuad already. But do their views in any way commit Islam? No! The standpoint of Islam is embodied by those Sheikhs who led the struggle against the French in the past, and now it is the Muslim Brotherhood who have that role.'

'Yes, but there are those who say that Hassan Al-Banna was allied with everyone even with King Farouq just to make sure he got into power.'

'If that had happened he would have been Sheikh Al-Azhar and would have been still alive today.'

'But still you can't deny that the examples you have given don't change the facts. You are talking about theories and I'm talking about actuality.'

'Yacoub!' interrupted Fuad. 'If we want to talk about the difference between theory and practice we'll not find any more glaring examples than the leaders of the USSR who are living the lives of Kings and Czars.'

'That's a cheap fabrication!' retorted Yacoub angrily. 'Anyway that's not the subject we are on.'

'Oh, yes it is!' said Fuad. 'It's human nature that as time goes by any revolutionary loses his fire. If we have to be harsh in our judgements then our harshness should be directed at human nature not at Islam.'

'OK,' said Yacoub. 'Just give me the name of one Sheikh who puts out fetwas against the feudal landlords, just one Sheikh who gives his support to the workers.'

'No, this is a matter of defining our terms,' said Abdul-Ra'ouf. 'You put your faith in things you consider to be in the interests of the masses and anything at variance with them you consider to be feudalism and exploitation. For example you believe in nationalization . . .'

'Of course. Is there any other way of bringing about socialism?'

'Ah, now, we are getting to the point. Who said that socialism has to be in the interests of the masses? Who told you that social justice will be achieved by nationalization? That's only your opinion. I think it is just the myths of Marx and Lenin! If a Sheikh came along and issued a fetwa against nationaliz- ation that would not mean that he is against the masses. All it means is that he takes the view that nationalization contradicts Islam. And the true Muslim cannot believe that there is anything in Islam that is in conflict with the interests of the masses. Who was it who created the masses? God. Who revealed the Koran? God. How could there be any conflict?'

'You are digressing. We were discussing the alliance between men of religion and power.'

'We've gone into that and you've not proved there is such an alliance. But we have proved to you that the greatest scholars in the history of Islam have been against authority.'

After lunch Yacoub thought to himself, 'The next time I'll have some questions to put to Mr S that he is not expecting.'

After a year of profound thinking the idea of forming a business had intensi- fied in Qasim's mind. It was not a part of his plan for the future that he should be content with the wealth that his father had accrued. He intended to multiply it many times over and he did not plan to wait till he had graduated before beginning. When he discussed the idea with the others in Apartment Freedom there was no response. In fact the only one who accepted his idea was Nash'at who listened intently.

'It's a gold-mine, Nash'at. Every month hundreds of bewildered visitors come to Cairo, from the Kingdom of Saudi Arabia, from Kuwait, Bahrain, Qatar and Dubai. The idea is to set up an office for providing services for them. The expenses will be minimal and the profits huge.'

'But what will the office do, exactly? What kind of services will it provide?'

'The office will provide everything the visitor needs: meeting at the airport, hotel bookings, medical appointments, escort girls, guided tours, car hire, renting apartments, and any other services needed, so long as they are legit- imate, naturally. We'll get paid the actual invoice value plus 10% of the value of any invoice paid via us. Trust me, I've done my homework. The office won't be official so that we don't get into the hassle of registration and taxes and all those headaches. It'll just be an ordinary apartment with no notice outside. Secondly we'll only have the minimum of employees, three at the most. Thirdly, we'll not be providing the services ourselves but will be calling on existing offices – car hire firms, tourism bureaus, airlines, and so on. That way we'll cut down on overheads.'

'But how will visitors know about the office if it does not officially exist?'

'Leave that to me. We'll put the word out and let people know the phone number. In no time at all every visitor will know about our office.'

'And who will manage it?'

'To start with I'll be there myself three or four hours a day till we find a reliable manager.'

'And the other employees?'

'I've found two of them. One used to work in the Saudi Embassy and knows most of the Saudi visitors and the other used to work in the Hilton and knows about all the Cairo offices that service tourists. Both have agreed to work on probation for a month at 30 pounds a month.'

'What about expenses?'

'That's all there is to it. There is nothing but rent, the cost of some simple furniture, and salaries. The entire capital needed is 1,000 pounds and I already have 700 – that is to cover all expenses for one year even if we don't get a cent in income. You can come in as a partner for the rest. I'll guarantee you'll get annual profits equal to your share.'

'I've got about 400 pounds.'

'So let's get started right away. Tomorrow! We'll take turns managing.'

Qasim did not sleep that night. He'd let his friends focus on political parties and ideologies and the One Arab nation but he would go his own way: he knew the true priority in this world, the one thing that concerned everyone, male and female, capitalists and communists, rulers and ruled, believers and atheists, the one thing that did not need any theories or mottoes, the fundamental fact in this life, was MONEY.

Reeri blushed and lowered her eyes as she murmured, 'A little present for you, See Karim!'

As he unwrapped the coloured paper he found a certificate in a frame from the Institute of Hairdressing in the Ministry of Social Affairs to the effect that Mlle Enayat Radi had obtained the diploma for hairdressing from the Institute. He then found a message in another frame from the Personnel Manager at the Hilton informing her that she has been appointed to a position in the hotel beauty salon at a month salary of 25 pounds.

Abdul-Karim looked at her with pride and she blushed even more. Then he sighed and kissed her. 'Congratulations, darling. A thousand times.'

It was only later that Adbul-Karim realized that for the first time he had called Reeri 'Darling'.

Suad and Fuad remained in contact. He would meet her once or twice a month, in the lecture hall or the cafeteria or in the place where books were given out. Sometimes he would invite her for a cup of tea and they would exchange news and rumours. This time, however, she seemed to be depressed. She tried to smile as she said, 'I hear you've joined the "Shish-Kebab" movement. Congratulations!'

'It's a lie!'

'Thank God for that! You're too smart to join those ruffians in "Blood. Iron. Revenge." '

'What about you? What about the party?'

Suad was silent for a moment and then sighed. 'You were right, Fuad. You were so right, Fuad. Nasser and the comrades are really at loggerheads now, so the comrades have resigned and Syria is now back in the hands of the feudal landlords.'

'In the hands of the feudal landlords? How? When?' he stammered, astonished.

'Syria is run by the National Union, owned by the "5-Company".'

'Is this because the Ba'athists lost in the elections for the National Union?'

'Elections? What elections? Abdul-Hamid Serraj appoints and fires whom he wants. It's very ominous. There's going to be a catastrophe. The supporters of the union have gone and the only people left in the field are the big landowners, traitors and opportunists – and the secret security people.'

'I sympathize, Suad. But I can't see any catastrophe. Gamal Abdul Nasser's popularity hasn't been affected and the union hasn't got any weaker. In fact some say that Gamal Abdul Nasser's popularity has increased since the Ba'ath ministers resigned.'

'The only ones to say that are traitors and hirelings. We had high hopes of Gamal Abdul Nasser but he has broken all his promises.'

'Suad! Gamal Abdul Nasser didn't promise you a thing! He told you he would not acknowledge any political party, including the Ba'ath. He told you he would not allow any political organization except for the National Union. It was you who staged a coup against him.'

'That's just propaganda. He started playing around with the Syrian Army, transferring all the Ba'ath officers to Cairo or dismissing them. Then he started concentrating the activities of the whole security apparatus on the Ba'athists so that Syria became a huge detention camp for the supporters of union.'

'I just can't believe what I'm hearing. Is it you talking? Are you really attacking the union at the first sign of a dispute between the Ba'ath ministers and Gamal Abdul Nasser!'

'What union, Fuad? The union has lost the support of the masses and has become a tool of Serraj. There is no meaning in a union run by the secret service!'

Fuad rose. What had happened to the Ba'ath? What had happened to Syria? What had happened to Suad? What catastrophe was she talking about?

# CHAPTER FOURTEEN

## August 1960

_____

When Fuad opened the door of the convertible he looked for a long time at Madiha who stared back and at exactly the same moment they burst out in laughter. The car raced away and within minutes they were in front of Zamalek Tower and then within moments they were in the penthouse occupying the tenth floor.

'What's this!' exclaimed Fuad. 'A football stadium?'

Fuad had never seen in Egypt or anywhere else an apartment as luxurious as this.

'What do you do with all these rooms?'

'I'll take you on a tour. This is the main salon. That is the dining room. Here is the small salon. There is the kitchen and its annexes. That is the nurse's room. Here is a guest room. And this is my room.'

'Ten rooms? All for you alone?'

Fuad felt a moment's sympathy with her ex-husband. No one could live here without feeling that he was just the husband of the lady of the house.

Fuad now knew that he was just about to end his long and bitter sexual deprivation. They were alone on her huge bed. He moved closer and so did she. It was all much simpler than he had imagined . . . 'The people knew its way forward . . .' Was he hearing this sentence from the nurse's radio? 'It is the people which has unified its country . . .' Or had this come from his sub-conscious? She was groaning and was crying out. He understood only some of what she was saying. Her nails sank into his shoulders. He exclaimed at the pain but she clung more closely to him. She carried on crying out until she fell into a brief doze, from which she soon awoke, and then the crying out began again.

Fuad entered a new existence. He had come into the world of 'Arpège', which he could smell everywhere – on the cushions and sheets, even the walls and the curtains. He had entered a world in which pleasure was continually being renewed: the phoenix which rose from the flames. And every time he was burned there was a more marvellous taste than the previous time, while his return from the flames was each time more beautiful. He discovered the continent of the body. He had imagined that desire was concentrated in just one part but now he realized that his whole body from head to toes was a mass of cells throbbing with desire. And her body: how was it possible for this tiny frame to have every inch transformed into a waterfall of pleasure, into endless wedding feasts?

The days and nights passed in delirium. When did he go back to smoking which he had given up from his first week in Cairo? He drank beer for the first time since the first party at Apartment Freedom. Where did the time go? Where did they dine on Friday night? What's the name of that little dance hall tucked away on Pyramids Road? What's the name of the floating restaurant on the Nile? When did he begin to wear flowered shirts? And when did she teach him the tango? When did he drink his first glass of champagne? And when did he start to sleep in her bed every night? How did everything else vanish – studies, politics, friends, family? Nothing in the world remained but Madiha. Madiha's car, Madiha's penthouse, Madiha's 'Arpège', Madiha's nurse. Had he been a man of reason up to now and with Madiha had a period of madness begun, or was it the other way round? Nothing mattered now but that body, perfumed with 'Arpège', that African mouth, firm and strong, this magnificent bosom. Where was this law of diminishing returns that Dr Rifaat Mahgoob talked about in the Faculty? The second apple doesn't give you the same pleasure as the first, the third not as much as the second, etc... No, Doctor! This apple is different. The second is more delicious than the first, and the third more delicious than the second. Why shouldn't he invent the law of increasing returns? And how had his name been transformed into Duda! Then to Didu, then to Fudfud. And how did Madiha become Hidaya? Then to Dahha! Then Madhuwa!! Had her nails left all these marks? Had her teeth left all these signatures? How had he got through all the years up to now coexisting with this beast of sexual desire?

Had he been a mixture of Mr Hyde and Dr Jekyll? Had he been a man/wolf waiting for the full moon over the penthouse so as to be transformed into a wolf/wolf, liberated and launching attacks with the freedom of a wolf? Where was his control? How could he press her to him, oblivious to everyone, when they were dancing? How could he kiss her in that little dancehall ignoring other people's looks? And what were these expressions that came to him during that delicious raging fever? What was this bizarre dialogue going on, 'I hate you!'... 'I hate you more!'... 'You savage!'... 'You beast!'... going on during the dialogue of the bodies... And the nurse... was she really in a deep sleep in spite of this festival going on...?

As soon as Fuad arrived back at Apartment Freedom he knew that one of the apartment's Nuremberg Trials was just about to be held. He decided to let the storm that was about to break over him blow itself out if only because his nights of Arpège had exhausted even the capacity to speak. It was Qasim who took the initiative.

'Will you just take a look at the calendar. It's the last day of May and there are only three weeks to exams. You haven't even opened a book yet. Do you want to fail?'

'Fuad! What's happened?' said Yacoub as Fuad kept his eyes on the floor. 'We only see you once a week, sometimes once every two weeks. What's happened?'

'Are you in love?' asked Abdul-Karim. Fuad merely looked at the ceiling. 'OK, fine, we understand! Congratulations! We've all been in love and all suffered for it. But your studies. Your future. Have some time off. Ask her for some study leave till after the exams.'

'Oh! go to hell!' shouted Qasim as Fuad looked at his hands. 'Go ahead and fail! Waste your life just for the sake of having a wild fling.'

As soon as Fuad heard these last words he felt that something had snapped, that something made him take up an ashtray and fling it in the direction of Qasim. It missed him by a miracle but then Fuad grabbed Qasim by the neck and began to throttle him. Then everything became confused, everyone got into a tangle of arms and hands, and voices were raised until suddenly Fuad rushed to his room and slept.

However trial proceedings were not over. This time the judge was Mr Shareef who came straight to the point.

'Listen, Fuad, there's a limit to everything. I am responsible to your father for you and for your studies, so if you don't pay heed to your work I'll have to go to Mazhar Rashwan Bey and ask him to get a hold on his daughter.'

Fuad closed the door of his room and finally got down to his studies telling Abdul-Karim to tell Madiha if she got in touch that he would not be emerging until after the exams.

When the results came out it was as expected by Nash'at, that Fuad and Abdul-Karim failed in Civil Law. But Fuad, contrary to expectations passed in the other subjects even though his grades were 'Fair' in everything but Sharia Law where he was given a 'Good'. As usual Abdul-Ra'ouf received 'Excellent' while Qasim, Yacoub and Nash'at got 'Good' grades. Majid passed all his exams, and so went into final year Medicine.

For Fuad, though, the results made no difference, just like a breath of wind on the depths of the ocean. It was as if this person who had, for the first time in his life, failed in one subject was someone he did not know. His only concern was to stay near Madiha and so when his friends left for Bahrain he remained in Cairo. For the first time he told his father a lie, claiming that he had to stay behind to have medical tests for his stomach and his eyes.

This second honeymoon passed even more sweetly than the first. He now knew her body very well and knew how to arouse its desire and she knew how to excite him to the point of causing pain all over. She knew when she should launch her assault and when she should allow him to catch his breath again. The third honeymoon was even more delightful than its predecessors as now the frenzy and delight of coupling had changed into a slow and pleasurable savouring of each other. He was now just as happy to be with her in a public place as he was to be in bed with her. Their old dialogue based on curiosity and suggestiveness had become an exchange of thoughts on the meaning of life, death, love and happiness. He now went with her to her office in the hotel and she would go with him to the empty Apartment Freedom, or to the Faculty which in the summer vacation had changed into a village of ghosts. But each and every day would end with the two of them in the same bed, between the white sheets, where the cloud of Arpège would lift him up with her to the highest peaks.

It was only in the fourth month that the law of diminishing returns began to come into effect. Fuad had no idea how or when the viper made its way into the penthouse: it was not as if fighting was something new since they had had rows from the beginning of their relationship on the telephone. But now an innocent disagreement would turn into a bitter competition, each intent on inflicting the maximum psychological harm. There as also jealousy which had been there from the beginning of their relationship from the first telephone call. But it now took the form of blazing rows when he would tear up her wedding photos and she would rip pictures of him with Suad. He would interrogate her on everything she had done in the period between the divorce and when she met him and she would not accept him going out by himself. He tried to stop her going to the hotel.

The most serious crisis began between the perfumed Arpège sheets. Any time that she wanted him he was ready and normally she was available every time that desire seized him but now headaches would intrude just before Zero Hour or he would be overwhelmed by fatigue the moment he saw a gleam in her narrow Asiatic eyes. The spontaneity and madness disappeared, replaced by planning ahead. Loud cries and groans were things of the past.

One morning as he picked up his clothes and left the penthouse there were no embraces. She watched him calmly. There was not even a farewell.

Abdul-Ra'ouf greeted him warmly. 'I always knew you would come back. Thank God you're safe!'

'What do you mean by that?'

'You were just away on a trip and I was sure that it would come to an end. But I hadn't expected it would last all these weeks!'

'And how do you know that it's over?'

'Just by looking at you. That primitive gleam has gone out of your eyes, and your mouth doesn't have that hungry look any more. And it isn't magical any more that you have lost your virginity.'

'You're talking, Abdul-Ra'ouf, as if you had been through something like this yourself.'

'Maybe, but don't the expect details in my next story. When are you leaving for Bahrain?'

'How did you know? I've made a reservation for next week.'

'And I know something else, Fuad. I know that you'll not write to her and she'll not write to you. And when you get back you'll not ask after her and she'll not ask after you.'

'You've become a fortune-teller, then?!'

'Yes. Isn't that the job of the artist? She was your first woman and, in spite of her being married, you were her first man, so all those desires that had been suppressed simply exploded with the force of a volcano. They then died out.'

'The amazing thing, Abdul-Ra'ouf, is that everything should be over just like that. I'd been expecting that I'd cry a little, that she would, too.'

'What for? There was no love, not even friendship, it was just that the two of you were so parched and needy.'

'It was just an incredible experience.'

'Well, yes... but in the whole world is there any more wonderful experience than a hungry man meeting a feast? But even the hungriest person would not claim that he was in love with the dining-table!'

'OK, let's drop the subject. What about our book?'

'You'll find it ready when you get back. 3,000 copies!'

Fuad had never before seen his father looking so care-worn or noticed the progress of old age across that face that was always so kindly and smiling. His father reminded him, 'I've reached 70, Fuad! Not much time left!' With a sigh he went on, 'What sort of a state is this. When Nasir decided to leave the shop and open his own travel agency I said to myself that nothing would be different so long as he was still living nearby but now he wants to give up the house and move to Qudaybiyya. And now there's only you and Khalil left,' he went on, sighing. 'Will you abandon me as well, next?'

Knowing that Khalil was on the point of working independently Fuad preferred to say nothing. Then he rose and kissed his father on the head. 'Everything that happens will be for the best, God willing. What you wish is what will happen.'

For Qasim this summer in Bahrain was totally different from the previous one, an unbroken round of pleasure. When he talked to his father about his Cairo project he was delighted to find this evidence of a commercial spirit so early in his son and decided that the time had come for him to begin his practical training. He sent him to the Accounts Department in his firm and told the manager to brief Qasim on all the details of the work. He began to take him with him on his daily rounds and introduced him to bank managers and to those in charge of foreign companies working in Bahrain. But the main assignment he entrusted to his son was to supervise the 'Bustan' project. This venture proved that Muhammad Sadafi was ahead of all his competitors. He cleared all the palm trees on a huge plot of land he owned in the Khamis area and built 50 villas which he then furnished and put up for rent at 600 rupees a month. No one had imagined that this project could succeed or that a single tenant would pay such a steep rent but as soon as the villas were built nearly all were let. Qasim's father asked him to go every day to work at the project site and to see to making good any deficiencies and making sure that the tenants were comfortable.

As he moved around the villas and got to know the tenants Qasim discovered a rich trove of pretty young English girls, some staying permanently with their families and others on visits in the summer holidays. He made the acquaintance of Jean, the daughter of the dentist at BAPCO, and Daphne the daughter of the surgeon working at the Naim Hospital. Then there were Heather the daughter of the Customs Director and Susan the daughter of Mr Cook, the manager of the Electricity Station, not to mention Mary, the daughter of the Production Manager at BAPCO. He had use of a luxury car, a launch belonging to his father which he would borrow each Friday to take them on fishing and swimming trips, and 'parties'. Qasim lived in one of the unoccupied villas and asked his father for permission to have Nash'at visit him, with the result that the Bustan villa became an outstation of Apartment Freedom, and indeed became a Villa of Freedom where the friends gathered each evening.

The first party began quite by chance with a spontaneous suggestion by Jean who took on the job of inviting young men and women. Each guest was to bring their own drink and dinner consisted of traditional Bahrain Tikka sandwiches. It was a very successful party that went on until dawn. Very soon these parties became a Thursday night fixture and as the word spread amongst the Bustan villas guests began to arrive with and without invitation. Married couples would come and adolescent boys and girls as well as visitors to Bahrain, male and female, so that sometimes there would be 80 or even 90 people there.

Soon the inhibitions of the sexes were loosened in the hot and noisy atmosphere, as bodies were crushed together to the sound of throbbing music and the beer flowed. Qasim could not believe how easily things developed:

at the second party he suggested to Jean that they go upstairs and within moments they were on the bed. At the next party he made the same suggestion to Heather and the experience was repeated. Nash'at discovered that these opportunities were available and while swearing to himself that he would not be unfaithful to his Swiss Peasant made frequent trips upstairs.

Yacoub neglected the young girls and concentrated on the mothers. He had no less success than his friends. He would wait till the husband had reached an advanced stage of inebriation or was occupied with some other woman and would then propose a turn around the garden to the wife. He would then pounce in some dark corner on the grass. Yacoub did not feel that he was engaged in sex but was on revenge: he was not bedding Mrs Henderson or Mrs Stone or the rest of the greying ladies so much as raping the colonial empire.

Abdul-Karim and Fuad refused to join in these goings-on but contented themselves with looking on from a distance but even they were not safe at the end of an evening from the advances of wives in their cups. By the end of the vacation Qasim and Nash'at had accounted for all the girls living at the Bustan while Yacoub had gone through most of the wives. It was with heavy steps that Qasim got back to Cairo. What a summer it had been.

Fuad thought for a long time about the stormy emotional experience he had been through, but with detachment and without pain. What concerned him was to know how he had let go of his life in this way when up till then he had never done anything rash. He had never ever missed a single day's study and was seen as a model of balance and discipline ever since he was a child. How had he managed to spend so much time day after day, month after month, hardly getting out of bed?

He came to the conclusion that the dividing line between madness and reason was very fine, liable to be broken at any moment. So after deep meditation he took a vow that from now on, till the end of his days, no matter what his preoccupations were or what came up to seduce him or what challenges surrounded him, he would keep an eye open for this fine line to make sure that it was not broken and that the worlds of reason and madness were actually kept apart.

# CHAPTER FIFTEEN

## September – October 1960

When the friends returned to Cairo it was for the beginning of their graduation year. Fuad and Qasim decided to complete their studies in the USA after finals. The only thing remaining was to get Fuad's father's agreement but Fuad was confident that with a little patience he would be able to persuade him. Abdul-Karim had decided to open a law office in Bahrain whereas Abdul-Ra'ouf planned to work as an assistant lecturer in the Faculty before going on to his doctorate abroad. Nash'at wanted to join the Council of State while Yacoub was eager to get back to Bahrain to begin another phase in the class struggle there.

The friends decided that this year would be quite different from previous ones and that they would begin serious study from the first day and to go to all lectures even Discussion. Fuad and Abdul-Karim began to study French but this time with a teacher chosen by Mr Shareef and Fuad began the new year of study happy in the knowledge that the graduating students would be taught by the very best of the teaching staff all considered to be the 'Giants' in Law in Egypt whose lectures it would be a great pleasure to attend and whose books were the last word on their respective subjects.

For Fuad there were a number of pleasant surprises. The collection of stories had had a warm welcome in literary circles and Dr Shakir Ayyad had written an article on them in the Short Story Club. They had been mentioned in a weekly radio programme while Mr Saleh Gowdat had praised them in *Al-Musawwar*. The back page of *Al-Ahram* had also had a reference to them in an article. The two students were overwhelmed to find that they had now become literary figures, and became intoxicated by this new world, enjoying every moment of their sudden fame.

In the first week of October the really big surprise came when Fuad was told by Abdul-Ra'ouf that the Dean of the Faculty of Arts, Dr Sabir Al-Sayyid, had admired the collection of stories so much that he volunteered to present the students to his own teacher, Dr Taha Hussain. Fuad was thunder-struck. Taha Hussain? Dr Hussain gave a monthly lecture to post-graduate students in the Faculty and that he was in the habit of calling on the Dean beforehand. It was there that they were to be presented.

The first thing that stuck Fuad about Taha Hussain was the smart way he dressed. He wore a dark-grey suit, carefully pressed, a red tie, speckled with black and the fez which by this time was worn by almost no one in Egypt. The years had not taken away vitality from his features, he still had a touch of glow in his cheeks. He was much slighter than Fuad had imagined. He had pictured someone huge.

The Dean presented the two students to Taha Hussain, who shook them warmly by the hand. The Dean said, 'Your Excellency, Fuad is from Bahrain!'

'Ah!' said Taha Hussain, 'Do you know the story of these lines?

"Kings have given me a crown of pearls, the pearls of
    Bahrain, and of its coral
A palm tree – a sign that the Orient still has meaning
This city with its bedu origins and its modern buildings. . . ."

When the Dean said that he did not know the lines Taha Hussain said, 'Tell him, Mr Fuad.'

'Mr Fuad'. From Taha Hussain.

Fuad told the story. 'When Shawqi was made "The Prince of Poets" Bahrain presented him with a gold model of a palm tree, whose dates were made of silver. Some of the pearls were from my father's shop and he still remembers the tree.'

'Your Excellency, I never before heard you quoting from Shawqi,' said the Dean.

'May God have mercy on his soul! He was last of the master-poets.'

'But Dr Taha, you yourself attacked him,' said Abdul-Ra'ouf.

At this Taha Hussain gave a long and ringing laugh as he quoted some lines of poetry about those who are forever attacking all others. Then he sighed as he added, 'That is all in the past. Today I am in the same position as the ancient poet Labid who at the end of his days wearied even of people asking him how he was.'

Abdul-Ra'ouf ventured to ask a question. 'Dr Taha you have written most forms of literature. Which form is the nearest to your heart?'

'You may not believe me when I say this, but it is poetry. But my relation-ship to poetry is like that of Khalil bin Ahmad when he said that good poetry was beyond him and he could not bring himself to write bad verse. It's for that reason that I have said farewell to poetry.'

'But why poetry in particular, Dr Taha?'

'Because poetry is the very summit of concentration. In just one line you can summarize a lifetime. You could write a whole book on just one line of Al-Maari.'

At that moment Taha Hussain's secretary came up. 'Your Excellency, it is time for the lecture . . .'

Before leaving, Taha Hussain said to Fuad, smiling as he shook his hand. 'Mr Fuad, what news of Ibn Malik?'

Fuad laughed. 'He's fine, Doctor Taha, and sends you his best wishes!'

They left the office hardly able to believe that they had just spent almost a quarter of an hour with the doyen of Arabic literature. 'What was "Your Excellency, The Pasha" all about?'

'Well,' said Abdul-Ra'ouf, 'he was a Minister, had you forgotten?'

'But didn't they abolish titles like that?'

'No, Your Excellency. Anyway, what's this about Ibn Malik?'

'A secret between Taha Hussain and myself. Did you hear him call me "Mr Fuad"?!'

'Mr Fuad who is Ibn Malik?'

'It doesn't concern you. OK. Just read the Golden Ode of Tarfa bin Al-Abd!'

The next surprise came in the same month when there was an interview with Abbas Mahmoud Al-Aqqad. Their book really had changed their lives. Doors opened and they met luminaires of literature whom they had only known as photos in newspapers and magazines. Mr Abdul-Bari came with them to the salon of Al-Aqqad, held every Friday at noon. The small drawing-room was packed with visitors and in the midst of them was Abbas Mahmoud Al-Aqqad, wearing yellow pyjamas which had seen better days. Around his shoulders he wore his famous woollen scarf and sat, with his left hand inside his pyjamas. As soon as Fuad saw the faces of the disconcertingly male and female admirers he was reminded of the salon of Michel Aflaq. Of those present here he only recognized Anis Mansour and Saleh Gowdat. The two young writers were introduced by Mr Abdul-Bari to Al-Aqqad who rose to shake hands. As soon as his eye fell on the title of the book he questioned Fuad, '*A Papyrus from Delmon*? Is the book about Gilgamesh, then, Your Excellency?'

'No, sir,' said Fuad, blushing furiously and stammering. 'We chose the title to symbolize both Bahrain and Egypt.'

'Who is Gilgamesh, sir?' someone asked.

'Your Excellency has not heard of him? A famous entertainer.'

Al-Aqqad laughed again as he told the story of Gilgamesh. There could not be in the whole of Egypt ten persons who had not heard of Gilgamesh, and yet here was Abbas Mahmoud Al-Aqqad telling the story as his own.

Fuad was astonished. There was another question, 'Why doesn't Arabic literature have its legends, sir?'

'Where did Your Excellency get such a nonsensical idea?'

Fuad was amazed to hear such an insulting response but the questioner
was not; it seemed that it was a regular occurrence to hear patronizing
comments in this distinguished salon. Al-Aqqad then launched into talking
about myths and legends in Arabic literature, starting with the legend of
Khurafa and ending with that of Ali Zaibaq, the whole flowing as if it were
a lecture that Al-Aqqad had spent days in preparing carefully.

Fuad gathered all his courage and decided that he would face any wounding
reply from Al-Aqqad. He asked, 'Sir! The Arab world these days is overwhelmed by different intellectual currents and we young men are lost and
confused. I'd like to ask you your opinion of the relationship between Arab
nationalism and Islam.'

Al-Aqqad fixed him with an unfathomable look and replied 'Your Excellency, we are Arabs and we are also Muslims.'

'But isn't there a contradiction between faith in Arab nationalism and belief
in Islam?'

'Listen! The only contradiction, Your Excellency, is between a condition of
slavery and one of freedom, between despotism and justice, between dictatorship and democracy. But manifestos, saving your presence, are no more than
slogans.'

Before Fuad could recover from the shock of such brutal simplicity Al-
Aqqad went on 'There is no substitute for liberty. Anything put forward as
an alternative is dictatorship. Putting forward Islam as an alternative to liberty
is a counterfeit Islam. Saying Socialism is an alternative to liberty is a false
form of justice. If they suggest that either nationalism is an alternative to
liberty then you can be sure that is a hotch-potch of ideology. And you are
asking me about nationalism, good sir! Just look at what Hitler did in the
name of nationalism! And look at Mussolini!'

The questions and answers went on, with Al-Aqqad talking on every subject
as if he were a master of each. At 2 precisely he got up. So did every one
else.

'I'd heard before that Al-Aqqad was controversial but I'd never have
imagined this. He wasn't just talking about Hitler and Mussolini. Everyone
knew exactly what he meant. Any one else who talked like that would spend
the night in gaol. If not the year.'

'We've missed the Friday prayers,' said Fuad, looking at his watch. 'Doesn't
Al-Aqqad go to the prayers?'

'Good sir, kindly drop these ridiculous questions,' was Abdul-Ra'ouf's
reply, with a sly look.

'And what was his hand doing inside his pyjamas?'

'Didn't I say "Good sir, kindly drop these ridiculous questions"?'

Yacoub sat at the wheel of his little VW in a narrow side street off Bab El-Hadid, taking glances at his watch every minute. Nine o'clock came and nothing happened. Five more minutes went by and still nothing but then the door opened and a woman's face appeared, with eyes shaded by thick prescription spectacles. 'Shibli? Mervet!'

Yacoub looked at her cautiously. 'Have you got the newspaper?'

'Here. Friday's news.'

Yacoub relaxed. The pass words had been exchanged. 'Jump in.' Mervet got in beside him and the little car shot forward.

This was his first assignment for the Party, to put out leaflets condemning the big landowners who had come back to the countryside in spite of land reform. The leaflets spoke of the peasants' sufferings and called for the dissolution of the cooperatives and for giving them the right to form trade unions as well as the nationalization of the remaining landholdings. About 1,000 copies of the leaflet were stuffed into Mervet's handbag but for concealment she had knitting hanging out of it. They had been given four main points for distribution: Giza, Boulaq, near Tahrir Square, and Shubra El-Khaima. Fortunately as the instructions did not stipulate sticking up the leaflets and hurling them out of the car was a relatively speedy operation and less dangerous than putting them up on walls. Yacoub selected a street, looked out carefully in all directions and whispered 'Now.'

Mervet threw out a bundle of leaflets and the VW sped off to the next target. The same scene was repeated and shortly before midnight they had completed the assignment. Yacoub took Mervet back to the place they had first met.

When he got home Yacoub had difficulty in getting to sleep. He imagined what would happen when morning came, crowds gathered and the leaflets were discovered. He could imagine the rage of the police as they saw them scattered on the pavement and visualized a conference being called immediately at the Ministry of the Interior, perhaps attended by the Minister himself. In his mind he followed the route of the leaflet as it arrived, by the end of the day, at the desk of Gamal Abdul Nasser. He could imagine the joy of the oppressed as they read the phrases urging them to be steadfast. He smiled to himself as he imagined the terror that would now grip the new landowners. Every leaflet was a blow aimed by the masses at their enemies. Every one was a dagger. The phase of actual class combat had now begun for Yacoub and he took an oath, before he fell asleep at dawn, that this struggle would last as long as he lived.

Abdul-Karim knocked Fuad's door. 'Fuad, there's something personal I want to talk over with you. I don't want the others to know. Will you keep the secret?'

'I promise. What is it?'

'I'm seriously thinking of marrying Reeri and I want to talk it over with you. What do you think?'

Fuad was silent, embarrassed, but Abdul-Karim persisted. 'Come on, tell me: what do you think?' Fuad went red but remained silent.

'Oh, come on, Fuad. I must hear what you think of the idea.'

'What do you want me to say, Abdul-Karim? If you've decided why ask my opinion? I think you know very well what I think.'

'I want to hear it from you.'

Fuad sighed. 'OK, but you must listen calmly and not get mad. Firstly, you're graduating in a few months and then you can open a law office and be self-reliant. That's not the problem. Your father will be angry and maybe disown you. But even that is not the main problem.'

'So, then, you approve,' said Abdul-Karim, relieved.

'I've not finished yet. I've no objection to Reeri: she's a nice girl and well-behaved and she loves you. But I think you'll be doing her wrong by marrying her and harming yourself too. There's no need to beat around the bush, Abdul-Karim. I know she works in a hairdresser's now and isn't on the game any more, but what about the past?'

'I've forgiven her for the past.'

'It's not a matter of forgiving: can you forget?'

'I have done.'

'Let's suppose that you have. Others never will.'

'What's it to do with other people? *It's my private life.*'

'Since when did other people respect anyone's private life? Did you lot respect my private life with Madiha? Remember that people are merciless. Do you know what people would say if you married Reeri? They'll say he married a . . .'

'Stop!'

'So, you understand what I meant. You don't want to hear it but that's what they'll say.'

'I won't take any notice of what people say. My happiness is above all else.'

'This marriage won't bring you happiness.'

'Why do you say that? You can't imagine how happy I am with Reeri.'

'Things will be different in the future. There'll always be something to remind you of her past. And people to remind you. Let me be hard on you. Have you any idea of the number of clients she had when she was "working"?'

'I don't know and don't want to know.'

'You can take it she had dealings with hundreds.'

'Don't be ridiculous, Fuad!'

'You'll always be a prey to all kinds of painful questions: did she know so-and-so? Did she have a good time with so-and-so? How can I be sure she's not being unfaithful to me? How do I know she won't go back on the game? Your life will become hell, and so will hers. She will be the one who suffers.'

'I have complete trust in her.'

'I don't think she'll agree to marry you even if you ask her.'

Adbul-Karim looks at him in astonishment. 'How do you know? Have you discussed it with her?'

'No. It's just what I think, that's all.'

'I have talked about it with her, in fact, several times. And each time she has turned me down – hard.' His friend frowned.

'She did that because she's smart, Abdul-Karim, smarter than you.'

Qasim had never imagined that his first commercial venture ever would turn out so successfully. No sooner had the office opened than requests poured in. The man who came from the Hilton was promoted manager and the number of employees rose to five. Monthly revenue soon reached 500 pounds of which profit was about one-third. Qasim felt a thrill of a new kind as he counted the money. In addition to this exhilaration he felt a strange possessiveness towards this money that prevented him spending it. How could a man squander money he had struggled to make? He opened a special account for the office profits and did not spend a cent of it.

Nash'at had much the same feelings even though he was used to getting all he needed from his father. The money coming to him now from the office had a special flavour and he too found it very difficult to spend any of it. The two friends became ever and ever closer as they met at the office at 4 p.m. each day and worked till 8. After the office there were other activities. They learned lessons in public relations that they could never have learned in any college. They learned the differences between dealing with someone sick and someone in good health, someone rich and aristocratic and someone who was *nouveau-riche*, between men and women. They frequently found themselves at the canon's mouth dealing with some angry client, male or female. Nash'at discovered commercial and diplomatic talents that he had not suspected.

He suggested opening a small office at the airport with just a desk and one employee. This actually doubled turnover. He then suggested employing a female secretary to take over receiving the clients and answering phone calls and this also turned out to be really effective. One day as the friends were talking about the future of the office Fuad said, 'Listen, Nash'at, after I go back to Bahrain the office will be yours entirely. I'll sell you my share in it for what I put in, 700 pounds. After all, 'What am I going to do with Egyptian pounds when I am in the States?'

'There's no hurry. Just think about it.'

'No more discussion – the office is all yours. Are you going to carry on running it in the same way?'

'No. I think we are going to need a proper birth certificate. We'll have to register the office formally and give it a name. Taxes are hardly worth talking about. Only about 100 pounds a year.'

'OK, but how are you going to manage, with your job in the Council of State and your work in our office?'

'That's right!' said Nash'at, with a look of mock panic on his face. 'The law forbids having jobs in both the private and public sectors. What am I going to do?'

'You've got some of the finest legal brains in the country in the Council of State. Why don't you consult them?'

'I've got an idea. How about "THE COUNCIL OF STATE OFFICE FOR SERVICES"!'

And with the office the friends discovered a world filled with sweet little things: girls working in tourist offices and others working in banks and hotels. Both of them discovered that the real problem for them was not how to find girls but how to stay away from them. How had the hunter suddenly become the hunted? Money!

Qasim hesitated before bringing up the subject with Nash'at but then he took his courage in both hands.

'Look, I don't want to meddle but since we got back from vacation I've not seen you with the Swiss Peasant. What's up?'

'Yes, she really was a peasant,' said Nash'at. 'Do you know what she said to me when I got back from Bahrain?' ' "You either marry me or you leave me".'

'What's unusual about that? That's what Farida said. And Shereen.'

'Yes, but I thought it was only Egyptian peasant girls who said that sort of thing. They're so keen on marriage. Funny, but this girl's Swiss and she knows it's impossible for me to marry her.'

'It looks as if marriage is something that is really deep down in the heart of every woman whether she is from Switzerland or from Upper Egypt. What did you say to her?'

'I told her to go to hell. Said I couldn't marry her. If she was happy for us to be friends, fine, she's welcome but if she was insisting on marriage she'd better look out for some nice Swiss gentleman.'

'So – you as well, Nash'at.'

'Well, what do you want me to do? Marry her?'

'Someone from the East would never marry a woman he had slept with before marriage, unless he was mad.'

'Well, I'm from the East and I am not mad. I've not made a fool of anyone and not cheated anyone. Having a good time OK, but marriage – no way.'

'And so now you've got a new girlfriend, one of the girls from Mina House. She's very nice looking, but watch it! She too shows every sign of wanting to get married.'

'I'll never get married to a girl I fool around with!'

'Have you made that clear to her?'

It was hopeless . . . they could not find it . . . All the efforts of the employees in the office, all the endeavours of Qasim and Nash'at, and all Mr Shareef's support and that of the Pasha. The Persian carpet Qasim had brought from Bahrain was lost. And now Qasim cursed the day that he had decided that Apartment Freedom needed an Isfahan rug. He had paid 300 rupees for the rug and bringing it with him on the flight from Bahrain had been wasted, time money and effort too. He had been ready to pay the customs dues which would be 100 per cent of the original price. He had brought the original invoice, the sum due and all the documents.

At the airport the Customs officer had looked at him coldly and before pronouncing, 'That's a carpet!'

Qasim tried to answer him just as coldly. 'Yes, I know.'

'The Customs dues aren't paid here.'

'Where are they paid?'

'At Customs at Saptiyya. Instructions. Go to Customs at Saptiyya in a week's time.'

One week later, armed with the receipt from the airport, Qasim went to the Customs at Saptiyya. But he did not find the carpet. A week later he returned but he did not find his carpet. One of the officials said, 'Go and see the Main Customs at Giza. Maybe it went there by mistake.'

'The Main Customs?'

'This is just Airport Customs. The area Customs is at Giza.' There no one knew anything about the carpet. Nor at Saptiyya. Nor at the airport.

Qasim screamed in Fuad's face as if he were responsible for the loss. 'Chaos. A shambles. That's the administration of your great Leader. They've pinched my carpet.'

'The money of the exploiters is for those who have nothing. This is the society of sufficiency and justice,' said Fuad, clearly enjoying Qasim's discomfiture. It made him even more enraged. He screamed, 'Thieves and robbers!'

# CHAPTER SIXTEEN

## December 1960

---

The voice on the telephone was soft and quiet. 'Fuad? How are you, my son?'

'Professor Ibrahim?' said Fuad, recognizing the voice at once. 'Welcome back.'

'I have a message for you from your father. Will you drop by to collect it, or shall I call on you?'

'No, Professor, I'll call on you. Where are you staying?'

'At the National. Come right along now!'

Everyone in Bahrain called him 'Professor Ibrahim'. There was only one. The famous poet, and writer. Ever since his childhood Fuad had known him as they lived in the same quarter and he called in at his father's shop almost every day. He had given lectures at the secondary school when Fuad was a student and after reading his stories had encouraged him to write. And now Fuad scribbled a lengthy dedication on a copy of *A Papyrus from Delmon*, jumped into the first taxi that came along, ignoring the instructions of Mr Shareef about economizing.

In the lobby of the hotel he was met by Professor Ibrahim, with his spare frame, his broad smile and widely-spaced, clear eyes. He embraced Fuad with warmth. 'Welcome, my son! How are you keeping.'

'Very well, indeed, sir, and how are you?'

'Praise be to God! And here's your letter from your father.'

'Thank you, Professor! Cairo is illuminated by your presence. Is your trip for business or pleasure?'

'It's business, my son. I'm representing Bahrain in the Arab Writers' Conference. I was the only one invited.'

'What is the programme for the Conference?'

'The usual, my son. Speeches and recommendations, tomorrow and the day after. Then we meet the President.'

---

'Gamal Abdul Nasser! When?'

'At noon on Thursday, when the Conference is over, at the Presidential Palace.'

'The Kubba Palace, then. Professor Ibrahim!' said Fuad, an idea coming to him like a sword. 'Can I make a request of you?' A flicker of caution appeared on the visitor's face.

'A request? I'm at your disposal, my boy.'

'The greatest wish in my entire life is to meet Gamal Abdul Nasser. This is an opportunity that won't be repeated. Please! Have my name registered with the delegation and take me with you to meet him.' The Professor did not speak. Fuad went on. 'Please! Please, Professor Ibrahim! I've written scores of stories and published a book. Here it is, in front of you. The book was well received by the critics. I can be considered to be a man of letters, isn't that so?'

'That's right, my son. I consider you to be a man of letters, without a doubt.'

'So, Professor, please help me. Put my name down with you in the Conference. Tell them that I am someone who has joined the Bahrain delegation at the last minute.'

The visitor's face twitched with conflict. He was torn between the desire to fulfil the wish of this young writer, the son of his friend, and the need for strict discipline. He was not given to sudden, spontaneous acts. 'My son, it is too late. The Conference starts tomorrow.'

'Professor, the one responsible for the Conference is Yusuf Siba'i. He's a friend of yours. Just one word from you and my name will be on the list. Please, Professor Ibrahim, this is my only opportunity to see Gamal Abdul Nasser. I leave Cairo this summer. Please, Professor Ibrahim.'

'I'll try, my son,' said Professor Ibrahim resignedly getting to his feet, 'Wait for me here.'

He went to Reception and picked up a phone. There was a long discussion and he waved his hands from time to time. He put the phone down and came back to Fuad, smiling. 'Yusuf Siba'i has agreed. You're in the Bahrain delegation. We meet here tomorrow at 8 a.m.'

'How can I thank you, Professor Ibrahim?' said Fuad embracing him.

The Conference proceedings passed by Fuad like a dream, starting in the Conference Hall of the Arab League with an inaugural Address by Yusuf Siba'i, followed by speeches by all heads of delegations. There was a dinner at the Officers' Club at Zamalek where Fuad saw many of the famous: Nizar Qabbani, Abdul-Wahhab Al-Bayyati, Sulaiman Al-Easa, Nazik Al-Mala'ika, Yusuf Idriss, Hamad Al-Jasir. He even had a few words with some of them. The next morning the meetings of committees began and Fuad found himself in the Formulation Committee where all the Conference's recommendations finished up. 'The Conference condemns . . .'; 'The Conference deplores . . . ; 'The Conference greets . . .'; 'The Conference urges. . . .' The recommendations were read aloud and were adopted in the Closing Session where the Professor gave the speech on behalf of all the delegations in which he offered thanks to the UAR Government.

At last the writers proceeded to the Kubba Palace in a cortege of 40 cars led by the Special Police vehicles, sirens wailing. There were crowds on the streets, waving, as Fuad sat alongside the Professor. He was going to meet Gamal Abdul Nasser, soon. He heard the Professor's voice faintly, as if it were coming from another continent. 'My son, the father of Al-Mutanabbi is not a puzzle. All the researcher needs is to be fairly smart.'

'The father of Al-Mutanabbi? We're on our way to meet the leader of Arab nationalism and the Professor's talking about the father of Al-Mutanabbi!' The Professor went on. 'Mr Shakir alluded to this but Taha Hussain, regrettably lost his way . . . And just now, my son, I am busy on a book about Al-Mutanabbi. I'll clear up this subject.'

Gamal Abdul Nasser! Gamal Abdul Nasser! Gamal Abdul Nasser!

'We're here, Professor!'

They were met at the entrance of the Palace by protocol staff who led them into a large hall, where all the writers stood waiting in line for the President. Fuad could feel the anticipation in the atmosphere, so intense that it was like a weight on their chests. Suddenly there was an electric charge in the hall as a number of officers came in: they were followed by the President with Yusuf Siba'i alongside him. The whole room burst into applause as the President smiled and moved through the delegations. He shook hands with every delegate and had a few words with the leader of each delegation. Fuad drank in all the details: the brownish face which looked even more handsome than in photographs, the bright sparkle in the eyes, the dark areas beneath them, and the touches of grey at the temples, the dark blue suit, the blue tie spotted with red. (Qasim claimed that all of Gamal Abdul Nasser's ties were of one particular luxury make and he had counted no less than 400 different ties in his photos.) Fuad also noticed a small cut from shaving on his chin.

Gamal Abdul Nasser stopped by the Professor and Yusuf Siba'i presented him. 'Your Excellency, may I present Professor Ibrahim Al-Arayyid, Bahrain's greatest writer.'

'You are welcome. Welcome to your own country,' said Gamal Abdul Nasser, putting out his hand and smiling.

However the Professor who had now been freed from the prison of Al-Mutanabbi, was not content merely to shake hands but launched himself upon the President, embraced him and kissed his forehead. Gamal Abdul Nasser was taken by surprise for a moment but then said, 'I hear you have written a wonderful epic about Palestine.'

'*The Land of Martyrs,*' replied the Professor, barely audible. 'I shall send Your Excellency a copy.' He went on, 'Your Excellency, may I present to you Mr Fuad Tarif, a young writer from Bahrain. He is studying here in Cairo.'

Gamal Abdul Nasser was right in front of him. Face to face! Eyeball to eyeball! They were about the same height! Gamal Abdul Nasser was pressing his hand firmly. 'You are most welcome. Where are you studying?'

'The Faculty of Laws at the University of Cairo.'

'Work hard! And make sure you graduate.'

In a fit of spontaneity Fuad repeated what Professor Ibrahm had done: he launched himself upon the President and kissed his forehead. There was a smile from the President who was prepared this time as he said, 'You are welcome. Welcome to your own country!'

Just one fleeting moment in a lifetime and Gamal Abdul Nasser had moved on to the next delegation. Fuad suddenly felt dizzy, and was afraid he would faint in front of everyone and caught hold of the arm of Professor Ibrahim.

As Abdul-Karim awoke he could hear the telephone ringing. He put on the light and peered at his watch: 3 a.m. Who could be calling at this hour? The ringing went on so Abdul-Karim got up, and grumbling, picked up the phone.

'See Karim? See Karim?'

'Yes? Who is it?' His voice was heavy with sleep.

'It's Enayat's mother, See Karim.'

At first he did not know who was Enayat's mother, but then he remembered Reeri's real name.

'Please hurry, See Karim! Please hurry. She's had an operation and is in a very bad way!'

Abdul-Karim felt something very close to paralysis strike him and was unable to speak. The mother was telling him the story in a disjointed way. 'We are at Qasr El-Aini, Ward 5. By the Prophet. Please hurry, See Karim! Oh, Lord! Please keep her for us!'

Abdul-Karim put down the phone and rang Majid who only replied when the phone had been ringing for several minutes.

'Majid, it's Abdul-Karim!'

'What is it? It isn't dawn yet!'

'Yes, I know, sorry to disturb you but Reeri is in Qasr Ei-Aini, Ward 5. She's in a bad way. Come right over. See you at the entrance.'

Majid and Abdul-Karim stood by Reeri's bed. She opened her eyes and smiled as she whispered 'How are you, See Karim?'

Before he could reply she had closed her eyes again. Majid asked him to wait while he went to enquire what had happened. The minutes passed painfully as Reeri talked in her sleep. He put his ear close to her mouth to catch what she was saying. Nurses took her pulse and blood pressure every 15 minutes. They refused to answer any of Abdul-Karim's questions. Her mother carried on praying. 'Oh, Lord!! Please keep her for us. A prayer at dawn! Oh, Lord, look kindly upon us.'

Abdul-Karim asked her about what had happened and she burst out. 'My son, she came home in the late afternoon from work, and said she was tired. A bit later she got up and started vomiting. She started screaming, "My stomach! Mother!" I said I'd get the doctor but she said there was no need. She sat down, crying and still vomiting. Then she fainted. So I brought Dr Butrus. His clinic is opposite our building. As soon as he saw her he said, "Qasr El-Aini, right away." We brought her here as the sun was going down. As soon as the doctors saw her they said, "Appendix. Immediate operation." They took her to the theatre and the operation took four or five hours. When they brought her out – you can see how she was. I asked the doctor if she was going to be all right and all he could say was, "May God be kind, madame!" Oh, Lord! Please keep her for us.'

Majid came back and asked Abdul-Karim to come for a walk with him in the hospital grounds. As they left the hospital daylight was beginning to steal through and Cairo was about to begin a new day. 'I didn't want to talk in front of her mother, Abdul-Karim. Reeri's condition is hopeless. She has peritonitis.' As Adbul-Karim looked blankly at him Majid went on, 'I'll tell you what that means. She had a severe inflammation of the appendix but hours before they could get her to the hospital it burst and when they performed the operation they found the poison had already spread to the intestine. That's peritonitis.'

'But Majid – they performed an operation. Her mother told me the operation took more than four hours. Why couldn't it save her?'

'I talked to the surgeon. He did everything possible. He tried to clean up the intestine but the poison had seeped into the blood. She's in a coma now and the doctors don't expect her to come out of it.'

'But she opened her eyes! She spoke to me! You saw for yourself.'

'That's what sometimes happens just before death when the patient suddenly wakes. It's a false hope: don't cling to it. Prepare yourself for the worst.'

'Majid, what are you saying!? She's just a young woman, 20 years of age! How can she die of an appendix operation? What about this medicine of yours? What about surgery.'

'The will of God is above all else. If she had come to the hospital when the symptoms first appeared the operation would have been a simple routine. But she came in too late. God ordained it.'

When they went back Abdul-Karim found the mother waiting for him at the entrance. She pulled him fiercely to her and embraced him and broke into shouting and exclamations. 'Enayat is dead, See Karim, and you are alive!

The girl is dead, Abdul-Karim! She died in the prime of her youth! I wish it had been me, See Karim! She didn't get married and had no children! Enayat is dead, See Karim!' She held him in an embrace. He tried to lament with her but could not. He tried to weep but no tears flowed.

Abdul-Karim found Qasim and Fuad and Yacoub waiting for him. Bad news gets round so quickly. Each one of them embraced him with no words spoken. He kissed each of them in turn on the cheeks, in silence. He went to his room, followed by Majid, but before going in he turned to his friends and said, 'The arrangements . . .'

'We'll take care of everything,' said Qasim. Majid went in with him, gave him a sleeping pill and then left the room.

Abdul-Karim could feel the drowsiness overtaking him and his eyelids flickered but sleep would not come. On the small bedside table was a picture of Reeri at the Zoo, the picture she had sent the previous summer to Bahrain. It showed her smiling at life, at people and at the animals. She died without even knowing the meaning of inflammation of the peritoneum, without even knowing the cause. She died before she could marry and have children. And it's all due to you! You bold brave, hero! Abdul-Karim, the Sheikh, afraid of what people would say. What will people say now? People remember the good points about the dead. No one will say that she had been on the game. 'Poor thing!' they'll say. She died so young!' As for her clients – Reeri? Reeri Who? Don't know her. Don't remember her. She came to us once. When? When? Forgotten. No, I'm mistaken, I don't remember anyone called Reeri. Except for the mother. And you, See Karim? You will forget me, won't you? You'll meet somebody else, won't you?

The door opened. Abdul-Karim asked, 'What's the time, Majid?'

'Go to sleep now. You must rest.'

He felt the needle, Majid went away and Abdul-Karim slept at last. Then woke, and slept again. It's just another of Abdul-Karim's nightmares. Do you know his nightmares? They are just deeply rooted childhood phobias that seep into the subconscious and cause these nightmares. Reeri has died?! Died! At 20!!? No, come on, you guys!! She was over 20, girls like her tell lies. More like 22 or 23. Does our friend take hashish, or opium? Beer? Beer causes nightmares unless you drink too much. Beer that caused this one. The one who had given up the game. She'd gone on a hairdressing course. Got a diploma. She'd become a real housewife, first-class, but without getting married. Reeri, who'd cooked for him, and knitted a blue pullover for him, bought his handkerchiefs and socks for him – it was Reeri that he had not had the courage to marry. People talk, Karim!! Shame, Karim!! What will people say? 'Yes, he married a . . . She used to be on the game. . . .' Thanks! . . . The word is well known. Begins with 'har. . . .' or 'strum . . .' Yes, that's the word, the very one. And a man when he plays around . . . well, of course, guys ... that's totally different. He becomes a Lothario, a Don Juan, a Romeo. He doesn't become a whore, or concubine, or prostitute. He becomes a 'chasseur de jupes', one of the boys, a real lad, Abdul-Karim, Fuad, Yacoub, Qasim. Oh ... and here's that real lad, Majid, in front of him. 'What's the time, Majid?'

'You must rest.'

The needle again. Reeri has gone to her rest now. The lads have looked after everything. All the expenses. Everything's on him. Birth, death. What a mess. Here in Egypt they don't bury the dead, they put them into little chambers and close the door. An ancient custom of the Pharoahs. No, it's only the rich who have those mausoleums in El-Qarafa. And the poor? They live in the dirt. Like the dead in Bahrain. There are two cemeteries there, one for the Shia at Ras-Rumman and one for the Sunnis at Qudaibiyya. One nation, except in death. We are afraid that the dead Sunnis will take the same identity as the Shia or the other way round. A Sunni never cheats, and a Shia never deals honestly. Adulterated water and pure water. Just get a load of that. They meet in life and are separated in death! We'll meet in Paradise, God willing! Do the Sunnis enter Paradise? We'll ask the reverend gentleman, the father, 'Oh Sheikh! What do you think of the Sunnis?' He doesn't answer questions like that, even when the villagers invite him to special lunch feasts, and cook him their plumpest chickens. They even keep the water he uses for his ablutions. They drink it for the blessings to be derived from it. We'll ask His Reverend Our Father for his opinion of Reeri, 'What do you think, oh Sheikh? Inflammation of the peritoneum, oh Sheikh! It's something we don't know, neither us nor you. She was a Sunni girl, oh Sheikh, and an enemy of the community. And she was on the game, oh Sheikh! Will this woman go to Paradise? A diplomat, really, is Father. Where did he study Diplomatic Law? No, the Sheikh does not have women teachers. The Sheikh marries women, proper marriage and 'mut'a' marriage. 'Mut'a' marriage! Why hadn't he just married Reeri in 'mut'a'? I married you in spirit ... Two hours ... Just two hours, Karim ... It's true, two hours isn't enough! Just wait till I graduate, and I'll go back and marry my cousin. You'll be free as air. That's a neat arrangement.

A great idea, get married, mut'a-style, but with retroactive effect. The law may OK that, except in the Penal Code. Father wouldn't object to 'mut'a: we derive benefit from you, oh Sheikh! How many mut'a wives have you had, reverend Sir? No, really! How many? Nearly 40!! Bravo! Mut'a marriage: I'll suggest the idea to Reeri and she'll agree. And with retroactive effect. Reaction is the agent of imperialism. What's that got to do with anything!!? I married you in spirit. Yes, didn't I just! Shame on you, See Karim! Drop all this stuff about 'I married you in spirit'.... The matter can be expressed in three different ways: 'I took you to wife'; 'I married you'; 'I took you for pleasure' – as has been stated by the leader of the community. Was it Sheikh Suddouq, or Sheikh Tusi, or was it my reverend father? 'I took you to wife in spirit' . . . Majid came in again, this time with a man Abdul-Karim had never seen before and he could just hear echoes of what they were saying:

'Doctor Husni, this is the fourth day. His condition is normal, pulse, blood pressure, heart and temperature, everything. But as you can see he's in another world.'

'It's shock, Dr Majid.'

'I gave him some injections and some sleeping pills. I was afraid he might kill himself.'

'Don't worry. It's just a severe shock. A couple more days and he'll come out of it.'

Dr Majid. When did he graduate and become *Dr* Majid? We've all grown up and graduated! We are really somebody now. Doctors and lawyers. The Sheikh's Law Office. No, by the Prophet! Let's just call it 'The See Karim Law Office'. Why, you have graduated, after all, See Karim. And now you're a really hot-shot lawyer! Strike up the band, H. E. The Lawyer! The Lawyer! Look at the two of them! You and me! Hey, what's the bridegroom's name, See Karim? Her name, oh Sheikh, is Enayat. And her nickname is Reeri. No, really, she is quite a flirt! Do you, oh flirt, accept to marry this lawyer? Yes, oh Sheikh, I accept. What a great lawyer, really top-notch! But we have been bad, we were on the game, oh Sheikh! But then we repented, oh Sheikh! But we've really given up the game, oh Sheikh . . . Except for See Karim, though . . . But I married him in spirit, oh Sheikh. Just two hours . . . Three . . . four . . . Don't be suspicious, ask him, he's right there in front of you. Didn't I marry you in spirit, See Karim? And didn't you marry me in spirit, until you graduated and could then marry your cousin? The Bahrainis go home to Bahrain. Lawyers go to their offices. Doctors go to their clinics. And Reeri? Reeri goes back to . . . Madam. What a shambles! But Reeri has truly repented, oh Sheikh! I heard her myself in the hospital saying, 'Oh Lord, I repent!!' With these ears I heard her – the girl who is going to be eaten by worms. Couldn't you put it a bit better than that? Don't use language like that in front of Reeri. She's still young, poor thing. She didn't get married and had no children.

Abdul-Karim opened his eyes and heard the voice of the stranger. 'I don't think he needs to go to the hospital, Dr Majid.'

At the top of his voice Abdul-Karim shouted, 'Hospital. I'm not going to any hospital.' He then fell back into a deep sleep. Why are they talking about hospital? Has he got peritonitis? Medicine is all about that sort of stuff – the hymen, the lining wall of the abdomen and now the peritoneum. Any one who doesn't die by the sword will die by the peritoneum. 'No, Dr Majid, just another couple of days. He'll be better then.'

Why don't you wake up, See Karim? You've only had a couple of tablets too many. Come on, get up. I'll be cross with you, you dozy thing, See Karim! Don't shame me! Get a move on. Shake yourself. Be a man and get up. Get up, See Karim! Come on, just for Reeri, just for Baby. By the Prophet, will you get up! Just for me, Reeri! Just for me, darling!

As Abdul-Karim opened his eyes he saw his friends gathered around his bed and asked, 'Have you had lunch?'

For some reason he could not understand, they all roared out laughing.

The lecture hall in the Kuwait Students' Club in Doqqi was packed to overflowing. Tonight, for once, a literary evening had attracted over 200 students from many countries and faculties. The celebrity everyone had come to hear was the poet Sulaiman Easa but the organizers were shrewd enough to put him on last. If they had put him at the beginning no one would have stayed after he finished. The first to speak was Abdul-Aziz Hussain, then came Abdul-Razzaq Basir followed by the poet Ahmad Abdul-Mu'ti Hejazi who recited a number of his poems, greeted with polite applause. Then came Fuad who read out the story of Al-Dana which was met with warmer applause. But when Sulaiman Easa rose to speak the hall was alive suddenly and there was loud clapping. When he began his poem 'I have carried on my lips fire and pain . . .' the hall was in uproar. His next poem 'They are my wings in the great advance . . .' caused even louder reactions. His next poem, 'I am returning to smell once more the fragrance of my country' made some in the audience call out 'Unity. Liberation. Revenge.' But no sooner had these calmed down than others began calling, 'Unity, Freedom and Social-ism'. The poet smiled and recited his poem, 'The Nation of the Renaissance Shall Never Die'. At this the audience went wild. He was a Ba'athist, Suad had told him. She was applauding enthusiastically.

While Fuad was reading his story he had noticed in the second row a young woman he had never seen before. She was tall, and unusually fair-skinned with long hair bound by a single ribbon, in the fashion of Indian ladies. She had deep-set eyes, honey-coloured. As he read his eyes wandered from the page to the audience, but he tried to avoid hers. He smiled at Suad who smiled back, and then he carried on reading the story of the diver who died clutching the perfect pearl.

Sulaiman Easa was surrounded by admirers and was giving autographs. The attractive young woman, fair of skin, with the hair in a ribbon, came to Fuad and said, 'I'm Laila Khazini, from Kuwait.'

'Laila Khazini, the poet?'

'How did you know?' she asked, clearly delighted.

'I read one of your poems in the students' magazine and another one in

*Al-Musawwar.* I did not pay a lot of attention to them, I'm afraid. I did not imagine that we'd meet.'

'I have some technical comments to make on your story.'

'Thank God for that, I've had enough of ideological ones.'

'You mention that Rashid woke and found the oyster open. How long did it take before he woke?'

'I don't know. It's a short story and details . . .'

'Details are very important,' she said, interrupting him. 'An oyster can't open when it is still alive. It has to be left a whole night for it to die. It only opens the following morning.'

'How did you know that?'

'My grandfather was in pearling.'

And this fair skin, touched with reddish tints, came from a line of pearl-divers. 'My father was a diver, too.'

'OK, then, ask him, if you don't believe me. And then, what's this in the story about dates eaten by weevils, and brackish water?'

'That's what was said.'

'Fresh-water springs in the sea floor were at all points of the pearl-diving areas. Have you never heard about "the drinkable water"? The sailors never had to drink brackish water. The pearlers had enough to put up without all this about brackish water and rotten dates. My grandfather says that the dates were of the best.'

'Your grandfather must have been an aristocratic pearl-diver, then.'

Laila laughed and they parted after they had exchanged phone numbers and she had given him the address of the dorm where she was staying. He put the slip of paper in his pocket believing that he would not be using it.

Yacoub's assignment this time was more dangerous than the last, picking up information from a Comrade at the Helwan Iron and Steel Complex then drafting a proclamation and giving it to another Comrade who would look after the printing. The more the danger the happier Yacoub felt: when would it be the time for bombs? Or at least for the Molotovs?

At the crowded Helwan station he watched the faces. A man wearing a hat and carrying an umbrella drew near. He approached the man and asked him, 'Do you have a water-melon?'

'On a knife.'

He took the small envelope and rushed to the Metro which took him back to Cairo. In his room he began to write and re-write, finishing the leaflet at dawn.

Oh honourable toiling masses

The hireling Press talks of the enormous achievement of the government in establishing the Helwan Iron and Steel Complex. But lying propaganda is one thing and the painful reality is something else. The Complex is now a frightful concentration camp in which the workers in the factories suffer all manner of tyranny, repression and terrorism. Last week three workers were gaoled just for complaining about the excessive smoke that was causing chest complaints. The manager of the Complex is Colonel Akram Shubrawi, a Fascist and an intelligence man specializing in torture. His assignment is to put down any attempt by the workers to improve their conditions. Toiling masses! Do you know what the rate of pay is in the Complex? 15 pounds a month . . .

Just before noon Yacoub took at taxi and went to the Azhaar Square area of Bab El Looq. He stood at the grocer's shop near the fountain waiting for the Comrade who would take the draft from him. An elderly man with tattered clothes stood before him and asked, 'Have the goods arrived from Alexandria?'

'On the morning train,' replied Yacoub. Yacoub handed over the paper and at that moment they were surrounded by four men, of whom one said, 'You'll both come along with us.'

Yacoub and the Comrade found themselves in a closed black police wagon as it sped off.

# CHAPTER SEVENTEEN

## February 1961

Fuad's resolve to avoid Laila did not last long. As soon as he saw the small blue envelope with the neat handwriting he guessed that the message was from her. But he put off reading it, putting it in his pocket as he set off as usual for the university. He put in his usual routine but still he could not help feeling that the letter in his pocket had been transformed into a living thing. He resisted temptation and only opened it just before going to sleep. He was startled because although he knew that she wrote poetry he had not imagined that she would compose verses about himself, let alone so soon after meeting him. Fuad was used to using other people for his writing but this was the first time he had ever found himself being used as material for anothers work.

To F.
Are you destined for my heart? Or for other women
Oh, you who are trying to avoid even looking at me?
You avoid me, as if I were a thorn, while the girls in your area
They are the flowers. . . .
While I am crushed and in tears . . .
And is there anything else but tears possible for the one who is crushed?
                                                                          L.

When had she written this? It must have been just after the literary evening. Was she referring to his failed attempts to avoid looking at her? Had she known about him before that evening? Had she read the collection of stories? Fuad was moved deeply to find himself the subject lines of verse. Would he go down in history. He thought about his own work. Who had ever heard of anyone who had gone down in history as the subject of a story? With poetry it was different. If you were mentioned in just one line of a poem that was well known, you were guaranteed immortality.

But it was not her poetry that drew Fuad to Laila because when he found his eyes straying to her he had not known that she was a poet. He had been attracted by that milky complexion, that braid of black hair, those deep honey eyes and that tall, elegant body. A palm tree from Kuwait. He had been drawn to her by the fragrances of pearls ... by the sea and by long evenings talking and by the sea-chants. And now here were these verses and each line was transformed into a sharp stab into his heart. Fuad rushed to the phone and then hesitated: wasn't it better that he should give like for like and that as a literary man he should make his reply a literary one? Maybe she preferred that her emotions should be expressed only in verse? Maybe she would pretend not to know or understand if he spoke to her directly. How do male and female poets behave? He had read somewhere once that every poet had to have a touch of madness. Maybe this madness was inherited from the devils of poetry ...

To L.

Every time he stood looking out to sea his imagination wandered freely as he visualized 1,001 things: the pearl nestling in the oyster; the shoals of fish seeking their prey; the forests of coral; beautiful maidens of the sea. He had an intimate knowledge of the sea from his childhood, where his house was only minutes away from the Sif. Before he was four years old he knew about the cycles of watering and waiting patiently and he caught his first fish, a zamrour, at five years of age ...

He entered the school of the sea and went through the various classes of knowledge, year after year. He stood before the blue waters that called to him, summoning him. He began to dive and then he learned to swim. The current would take him far out and he would feel a thrill as he was pulled towards small islands he had never seen before. Then he would feel deliciously tired. The tide pulled him in now, drawing him to the depths, but then he opened his eyes and saw all the worlds he had been dreaming of. The forests of coral and the mermaids. He walked on the bed of the sea. This must be a dream. Then he saw a palm-tree, heavy with dates. A palm tree in the sea. The palm tree smiled and spoke.

'I am Laila ...'

F.

He posted his message by mail and soon came a reply in a small blue envelope. This time he tore the envelope open immediately.

To F.

You ghost of the fortresses,
You diver in the depths,
You who have washed the sea with blood,
You who suffer torture and pain,
They said that the gleaming pearl
Grows in the oyster from a rain drop, a tear,
But I know that it is from the tears of man.

L.

He sent his reply.

To L.

When I came to Cairo I longed for nothing more than that I should have a woman friend, who would love me and whom I would love, with whom I would walk in the moonlight, with whom I would talk in the evenings as we drifted on the Nile.

But I passed through experiences some happy and some painful, that left me feeling that I have a heart, at the age of 21, which is worn out by old age and events.

I never thought it possible that before I packed my bags to travel to a distant country, a country of strangers, fate would have me encounter a woman poet of ravishing beauty who could talk of the tears of the pearl divers which turn to pearls in the heart of the oysters.

Isn't it one of the peculiarities of fate that a young man from Bahrain should meet a young woman from Kuwait in Dokki?

Wouldn't it be more fitting that they should meet on board ship ploughing the blue seas, a ship carrying the new Sindbad and the Princess of the Seas to a legendary land?

Is it not more fitting that a meeting should take place?

F.

Laila's reply soon came.

F.

Don't expect that all my messages will be in verse. I don't have a store of them. And don't expect that I'll help you to keep your distance from me. You are not the type of man who needs someone to take your decisions. Especially as you – as we – have only a few months left.

L.

He sent his reply almost in the form of a telegram:

L.
Where? When?

F.

He opened the blue envelope.

F.

Half way along the Pyramids Road there is a place known only to a few, hidden from sight, called 'The Little Nest'. I'll wait for you there, to say farewell to this year.

L.

He wrote back to her:

L.
How did you know of 'The Little Nest'?

F.

Back came another blue envelope from which he drew a sheet of blue paper stamped with the fragrance of Chanel No. 5:

F.

In her dreams he is the light of day
And the gleam of the new moon, the music of the nightingale
And legends . . . and the yearing of the seas,
A wonder: you give him this and he is jealous!?

L.

Fuad was sure that the architect who designed this place must have been in love himself, a man who despaired that Cairo did not have hideaways where lovers could hide. Fuad cursed the years that he was ignorant of 'The Little Nest'. In the middle there was a beautiful garden, and on each side there were hideaways, with wooden barriers, and in each 'nest' a table and two chairs. Each was private. Surrounded by bushes, no one could see inside and, similarly no 'nesters' could see or hear what was taking place in other cosy, secluded corners. The waiters did not hover but when summoned they would disappear swiftly.

When the waiter came Laila said 'Two beers, please!'

Seeing Fuad's puzzled face she opened her handbag and pulled out a packet of 'Kent' cigarettes and offered him one. She lit his and then her own, blowing out the smoke. She laughed. 'What's up? Are you one of the Muslim Brotherhood?'

So – was everyone who didn't smoke or drink one of the Brotherhood?

'I'm not used to cigarettes and beer. Except on special occasions.'

'And this, of course, is a special occasion?'

'It certainly is!'

It became clear to Fuad that the woman who sat before him considered herself to be the leader of the women's liberation movement in Kuwait. She had taken part in the famous incident of burning the abbayas, even though she had been very young. Now she was telling him that she was the only woman who had been arrested twice for leading demonstrations.

Fuad smiled. 'I'm really lucky with female revolutionaries, of all types and from all countries.'

'What do you mean?'

'The meaning is deep within the poet.'

'I'm a poet, a woman poet.'

'So – it's deep within you.'

'I've got nothing within me. Order lunch.'

Fuad contemplated this lovely woman as she sipped her beer and blew cigarette smoke in his face. He looked at this strange mixture of feminine delicacy and the violence of rebellion. How could these beautiful features conceal such rage? How could she reconcile these opposites: gentleness and coarseness? Chanel No. 5 and arrest? It occurred to him that he had not taken any decision about their relationship but it was she who had made all the running. She had begun to talk, started their correspondence, and chose the time and place . . .

He could not overcome his curiosity. 'How do you know this place?'

'My ex-husband discovered it. We used to come here before we married.'

Ex-husband? A small bomb burst out of the smoke. 'Your ex-husband?'

'Yes. Did you think I was a virgin?'

Fuad went red and she went on. 'Do you want to hear the story?'

He nodded. 'I fell in love with a young Palestinian, a fellow-student, and I married him. The rebel of the family revolted and they threatened to kill me but I paid no attention to them. I lived with him for six months but then I got bored and divorced him.'

'Do you mean, he divorced you?'

'No! I divorced him.'

'Just like that? You're taken with a young man, so you marry him, you get bored and you divorce him?'

'Isn't that what men do all the time? They marry, get bored and divorce their wives. Why shouldn't I do the same thing?'

'And how did you manage to live after breaking up?'

'You mean, how did I manage for money? Didn't I tell you, I'm wealthy?'

'I didn't ask and you didn't say.'

'I came out of the marriage with plenty of money.'

'From the young Palestinian?

'No, from my first husband. The Kuwaiti.'

Another small explosion. Another puff of cigarette smoke.

'Laila, you've got to be pulling my leg!'

'No, this is all true. I was 17 and one of Kuwait's richest men asked to marry me, a man over 60. He spent a year with me and then abandoned me. He left me a palace, I mean a villa, and some jewellery, a few cars and some money.'

'I don't believe a word of it.'

'Do you want to see the documents?'

'And how old are you now?'

'Twenty-three.'

'And you've been married and divorced twice?'

'Listen to the rest of it. You know who my first husband was, don't you? All Kuwaitis know him.'

'Laila, I'm not a Kuwaiti. I'm from Bahrain.'

She laughed playfully. 'Do you know what your fault is, you Bahrainis? Your conceit. You think you are the centre of the universe. Awali, Delmon, the Bride of the Gulf.'

He countered. 'Do you know what your fault is, you Kuwaitis? Your fault is that you are so perfect.'

'You've caught some of it!'

'Let's go back to your husbands. The second marriage was a love marriage – OK. What about the first?'

'It was a challenge.'

'Whose challenge?'

'The challenge of all those busybodies who said, "Don't marry him. He's older than your father." "He'll divorce you tomorrow." '

'And what about his wealth? Didn't that come into it for you?'

'No.'

'But you made no objection when you got your share of it?'

'Why should I?'

'Don't you believe in women's liberation?'

'A fundamental part of women's freedom is that they should be materially independent of men.'

'Even if this independence comes from a nice big slice of the wealth of an old man?'

'Why are you so concerned about my marriage?'

'Because I'm trying to understand you.'

'I don't think I'm too difficult to understand.'

'You are. Up to now I have three impressions. The first is the refined and romantic woman poet. The second is the rebel and the leader of the women's movement, the Huda Sha'rawi of Kuwait. The third is the young woman who married a man as old as her father and because of him becomes wealthy.'

'All these impressions are correct. But there's more.'

'I'm all ears.'

They had arrived at 'The Little Nest' at 11 in the morning. They had lunch there at 2 p.m. and had dinner at 9. She looked at her watch. 'It's 11. I'll have to get back now.'

'What for?'

'Regulations at the dorm.'

'The woman who challenges the family, society and the whole world observes the regulations of the dorm?'

'When it suits me.'

'You mean if you wanted to stay out longer you could?'

'Of course.' Her red Buick stood outside 'The Little Nest'. She took the wheel and he sat beside her. As the car sped away Fuad burst into laughter. 'Are you all right? At least tell me the joke!'

'I have a friend who lives on four pounds a month and he thinks I'm one of the richest men on earth because I get twenty-five pounds a month from my father. And I really did feel rich myself. I felt my conscience pricking me. How can a wealthy man relax surrounded by an ocean of the poor? Then I met a young woman who lives alone in ten-room penthouse. And now I've met a young woman who owns a villa and drives a Buick. Well, my conscience is quiet now.'

'What happened to the girl who owned the penthouse?'

'I didn't say she owned it: she lived there.'

'Who does own it, then?'

'I don't know. I suppose it is the owner of the building, Zamalek Tower.'

'Zamalek Tower? Do you know the building there?'

'Yes, Zamalek Lights. What about it?'

'My ex-husband owns it. I mean, my first husband.'

'Is it possible to meet any of his daughters?'

'No, but you may get to know his divorced wife.'

When he got back he wrote to Laila,

L.

Can you believe it? I can't drive a car. I must be the only man in the world who sits there like a log and lets the woman take the wheel. I have the feeling that I am just a travelling companion, a spectator. The decisions are in someone else's hands, those of the driver of the car. I must say that this situation is rather worrying. Is it now time for confession? In my life there are no stories of marriages and divorces, villas and cars. In the beginning there was a young woman I loved but then I began to feel that I was marginal compared to her political interests. Then I was in love with another woman but I found that she was only in love with her ambitions. Then it was the turn of the penthouse girl. She also drove her own car, not as grand as your Buick, but it was a convertible at least. She used to take me on drives and bring me home. We would meet only at her place or at her father's hotel. And now it is the season of the red Buick, 'The Little Nest' and the liberated woman poet who married a rich old man and accepts the presents given on divorce to exercise her right to freedom, and then marries a young Palestinian to express her freedom. The spoilt young woman who believes that people should respond to her whims: her urge to challenge, her whim to marry, and her whim to divorce.

And what about my weak self? What is my position on the map of your heart? Are we facing a literary whim that will be over after the second poem? Or the tenth?

I can't see any point in our carrying on this relationship. It was born with all the signs of death upon it. I can't see any use in a love that comes by order. You once said to me that your poems can't be produced to order: neither are my feelings.

Happy New Year.

1 January 1961.

F.

Fuad sent his letter and was then struck with a kind of schizophrenia. I hope she replies. I want her not to reply. I hope she gets mad and disappears for ever. I hope she is kind and gets in touch again. Almost every hour of the day her ghost was present. But at nights her memory blotted out all his law books and the dread of the exams. What an amazing woman. Where did that picture of the female poet go? Calm and silent love. The sadness. Noble self-deprivation 'We have a friend whom we must not betray.' 'This is your young woman, oh meadows.' But this woman was really something else. She smokes two packs of Kent and drinks six bottles of beer a day. She drives a red Buick. She married a man old enough to be her grandfather. And then she married a young Palestinian to provoke her clan. She knows a restaurant specially designed for lovers. She spends twelve hours with him there. And then she refuses to spend an extra hour to see in the New Year. She won't let his hand near hers, won't let his face approach hers. Please let her get mad and not reply.

Her reply came one month later:

F.

> I thought of you the whole evening
> And the sky became more beautiful
> The stars beflowering the universe.
> Then came the clouds
> To pour rain on my thoughts.
> Bombs, but bombs with fragrance.

L.

'Bombs with fragrance'? He wrote back to her straight away:

L.
The same place, same time. Thursday.

F.

He went there in turmoil: would she come? I so hope she comes. I hope she doesn't come. Then he saw the red Buick, glinting in the sun, like a ruby in Solomon's ring.

As Yacoub came in all his friends leaped to their feet, gathering as if seeing a ghost. In fact they were seeing someone who had no connection with the old Yacoub. His handsome face had shrunk, his eyes were vague, with dark rings underneath them. He was unshaven and pimply. He had lost weight and his hands were trembling. His friends fell on him, bombarding him with questions.

'Did they torture you?' 'What have they done to you?'
'Did they beat you up?'
'Mr Shareef told us you were in the Security jail.'
'The Pasha told us you were in the Military Prison.'
'Did they charge you with anything?'

Yacoub sat down. 'The first thing I want is a cup of tea. And a cigarette. Then a cheese sandwich. After that I'll tell you the story.'

The maidservant came. The tea and sandwich were brought joyfully and Yacoub began his tale.

'They took me in the police wagon to an ordinary villa in Abbasiyya, with no sign outside and no guard. They put me in a room with a comfortable bed and locked the door from the outside. Then they left me alone. Breakfast was a 8. Lunch at 1. Supper at 8. The food was really good and seemed to be from a restaurant. If I wanted the bathroom I would stand at the door, the guard would take me there and bring me back. There were no chains, no beating, no insults, no interrogation. Just solitary confinement. Radio? Forbidden. Papers? Forbidden. Phone? Forbidden. Visits? Forbidden. Four days later a carpenter came and put a thick wooden cover over the window so I couldn't see daylight. Then the guard took my watch. Next they put in a weak light bulb in place of the old one. Then I couldn't go to the bathroom any more. They brought a bucket for me. I became a mouse in a dark hole. I didn't know night from day. Gradually I lost my mind, or that's how it seemed to me. I didn't know if I was eating lunch or dinner. The guard never spoke to me so I started talking to myself. I'd laugh and cry. I'd confuse hours with minutes and couldn't tell the week from the day. Then I found I couldn't eat or sleep. Then I found I was spending all my time walking up and down in the room. Walking and weeping. Then I was seeing faces in the dark. I've no idea whether they were in my memory or if they were really there. Madness took hold of me. I began to see soldiers filling the room and gallows suspended from the ceiling. I could hear screaming from all directions. Then today – I think it was today – an officer came along and took me to another building. It was just a small building. He took me to another officer and told me his name was Colonel Mustapha. He gave me a very warm welcome and ordered coffee for me. I asked him about "Ramiz", "Iskandar" and "Rameses".'

'Who are they?' asked Qasim.

'That's a secret,' said Yacoub, with a bitter laugh. 'A secret. A military secret. You must know by now that I was a member of the Communist Party. They were members of my cell. Anyway the Colonel refused to give me any information. Then he told me he knew everything about me and didn't need any investigations or confessions. He said he appreciated that young people were liable to error. He said he appreciated that I had volunteered to fight alongside the Egyptian people during the Suez War. He ended by saying it had been decided to let me off on condition I left Egypt within three days.'

'Leave Egypt? In three days? What about your studies?' cried Fuad.

'I tried to talk about my studies, told him I was within months of graduating but he said the decision was final.'

'Now do you believe me. Now do you believe what I've been saying?' shouted Qasim. 'All it is, is terrorism, prisons and throwing people out of the country. They ask people to resist imperialism and if they do this is the result.'

'Talk's no use now,' said Yacoub calmly. 'The guillotine has fallen.'

Qasim shouted again 'But what are you going to say to your father? To your family?'

'Don't you think the news will precede me?' said Yacoub, sadly. 'Till the day I die I'll only have one name there, "the Communist". "The Communist did this and the Communist did that" . . .'

'It must have been a dreadful experience for you . . .' It was Abdul Ra'ouf.

'Indescribable. The worst thing is that I reached the point of breakdown without anyone noticing or caring. I was ready to confess to anything. Killing Nasser, burning down a hospital, blowing up a bridge, anything. That's the really terrifying thing. What sort of a state would I have been in if they had gone in for torture? Beatings, electric treatment, cigarette burns and all those things we've heard of. I thought if was made of solid stuff. But I broke down completely.'

'No,' said Abdul-Ra'ouf. 'What you went through was worse than physical torture. This psychological pressure only arouses the most primitive and instinctive fears. That's the cruellest torture. Anyone subjected to it will break.'

Two days after Yacoub left for Bahrain the phone rang in Apartment Freedom. Fuad answered.

'Fuad? It's Yacoub. I'm at the airport.'

'Which airport?'

'Cairo.'

'What's happened?'

'They've turned me back from Bahrain.'

'We'll be right with you.'

Mr Shareef, Fuad and Qasim set off for the airport where they found Yacoub in the airport police station. Yacoub explained what had happened at Bahrain. As soon as the official saw his passport he called over another officer who took him to the airport gaol where he spent two nights and was then told to go back to Cairo. At Cairo the official told him he could not enter Egypt.

'Beirut!! There's no other place,' cried Qasim.

It soon became clear that this was the only practical choice so they made a booking for him.

Qasim handed him a bulging envelope. 'This is from the office.' Then in a whisper, 'Capitalism finances Communism.' In spite of himself Yacoub smiled. As the plane took off Qasim fought back tears as he watched the aircraft disappear.

Majid shouted. 'You can't delay things for ever. Now is the time. You've got to decide, Fuad. I've just got back from a conference in Damascus, the conference of country delegates.'

'So – you are now a country delegate. Promotion's pretty quick with your lot.'

'This is supposed to be a secret but there are no secrets between us. I'm now the delegate for Saudi Arabia, or the Peninsula as we prefer to call it. From the whole of the Kingdom of Saudi Arabia there are only four members in the Arab Nationalist Movement, and I'm the most senior. Even in little Bahrain there are more.'

'They are trouble makers in Bahrain. So what happened in the conference?'

'We feel that the Union is in danger. The entire move towards unity is in danger. We fear that popular enthusiasm is feeble now. Can you believe it: the Ba'athists have become the enemies of the enemies of union and the enemies of the enemies of Gamal Abdul Nasser? There's an urgent need for new blood. The Movement needs you, Fuad.'

'Me?'

'Yes. I've had a long talk about this with Dr Ahmad Khatib. He agrees with me that you will be an asset. We need mature young men.'

'Mature young men! Me?'

'Fuad, drop the sarcasm. If you came in it would be based on conviction, and after all you have been through some tough intellectual experiences. You could be a really effective member with your brains and your pen.'

'My pen? Are you going to ask me to write stories about revenge?'

'We won't ask you to do anything you don't want to do. What do you say?'

'Listen, Majid. How about a compromise? Accept me as a sympathizer and I'll co-operate. But as for joining the Movement, let's leave that for the moment.'

'OK. A short transitional period and then you join the Movement officially. This is your first assignment: there is a Ba'athist refugee from Iraq, called Saddam Takriti, one of the bunch who tried to assassinate Abdul-Karim Qasim. Although he's still young some of the brethren in the Movement think that he'll soon be a star in the party. We have to know about opinions and inclinations. You are well placed to find out because Saddam is a close friend of Suad.'

'I offered to be a helper, not a spy.'

'In the nationalist Movement gathering information on the enemy is a noble assignment, not spying.'

'The Ba'ath Party is the enemy?'

'Yes, regrettably.'

Suad was alone in a corner of the Faculty cafeteria when Fuad came up to her. 'I won't disturb you long but there's a favour I'd like to ask.'

'Go ahead!'

'I'd like to meet Saddam Takriti.'

'Haven't you met him yet? He often comes here.'

'Maybe I've seen him but I haven't been introduced.'

'Why do you want to meet him? Planning to come back to the Party?'

'I've heard a lot about him and his attempt to assassinate Abdul-Karim Qasim and his escape. I'd like to see him.'

'We could meet here Thursday morning. He's generally here then.'

'Comrade Saddam. Meet Comrade Fuad Tarif from Bahrain.'

The tall, swarthy, handsome young man with piercing eyes rose and shook hands warmly with Fuad. 'All strength to Bahrain. Its population is half Ba'athist.'

'And the other half is on the way,' said Fuad, laughing.

'With the help of God.'

The three of them sat down. Saddam chain smoked. Fuad noticed a bluish tattoo on his hands. He asked about the assassination attempt which pleased Saddam, and he launched into details. Fuad then asked him about his gaol escape. This pleased him even more and he told the full story. He even rolled up his trousers to show Fuad the bullet mark from when he was hit in his escape.

Carefully Fuad asked, 'And what of the future, Comrade Saddam?'

'In three years' time the Party will be in power in Iraq and will remain there. The Arab Nation is bound up with the future of Iraq and that is bound up with the future of the Party. The centre of gravity will shift from Cairo to Baghdad. Regrettably, Nasser has shown that he is just a politician subject to the calculations of personal gain and the reports of his intelligence people. He has abandoned the revolution and leadership of the Nation and is content to be the President of the UAR.'

Fuad was astonished to hear this criticism coming from a man who was here as a guest of Nasser. Saddam seemed to read his thoughts. 'Look, this is a state of intelligence bodies, a police state. I'm sure that a whole platoon has been assigned to keeping me under surveillance. If you were to look around now you'd see three or four detectives. Gamal Abdul Nasser is no longer a leader of the masses. The only hope now is the Party.'

'Well,' Fuad asked cautiously, 'What about the Arab Nationalist Movement? Isn't co-operation possible with them?'

'They're just puppets of the secret police. We tried to reach an understanding with them but it was a waste of time. The only hope is the Party.'

'That's true. But as an interim measure till the Party comes to power can't we make use of Gamal Abdul Nasser's leadership?'

'I used to think that was possible,' said Saddam, 'and so did the comrades in Iraq. But then we had one shock after another. The day we fired on Abdul-Karim Qasim, Nasser was supposed to act and we had an agreement that he would send in aircraft. If he had sent just one plane Abdul-Karim Qasim would have fallen. But Nasser didn't budge. And then there was the uprising by Al-Shawwaf and Nasser encouraged it but then he simply stood by as a spectator while it was wiped out. If 10 planes had flown in from Syria the attempt would have succeeded.'

'How do you explain his attitude?'

'He's got used to being a President and has forgotten the struggle. Union with Syria came to him on a plate and he thought that unity would be achieved in the same way everywhere. Arab unity will be achieved only by rivers and seas of blood.'

'But the UAR has to act with the logic of a state.'

'May God have mercy on your parents. This is where the Party comes in. When it is in power the problem is over. The state can act like a state but real power will be in the hands of the Party. Gamal Abdul Nasser's problem is that all he has are bureaucratic systems and security apparatuses.'

'But what about the party in Syria?'

'All there is is the Founder and Leader and a few comrades. The rest are just dreaming of being Ministers again and at peace with Gamal Abdul Nasser!'

'Don't you think there is a possibility of peace with him?'

'With Gamal Abdul Nasser! Impossible!'

'What do you think, Fuad?' asked Suad later.

'What do *you* think – they say you're his special girlfriend.'

'Are you jealous? He's very nice-looking isn't he? You're obviously jealous. There's no need. Saddam has no time for girlfriends. His life is the Party. His girlfriend is the Party. I have high hopes for him. What is your impression of him, personally?'

'He certainly seems to know what he wants and how to get it.'

'Exactly!'

'But why didn't you tell him I've left the Party?'

'If I'd told him that he wouldn't even have shaken hands with you.'

'The spy's report, Sir,' said Fuad, saluting. 'In brief, Majid, Saddam Takriti's view is that the Party will be in power in Iraq within three years. Then the power base will shift from Cairo to Baghdad.'

'And Nasser?'

'He's finished as a revolutionary and has just continued as a President of a state based on bureaucracy and security apparatuses.'

'Security apparatuses? And Syria?'

'All there is is the Founder and Leader and a small number of comrades.'

'And what was your impression of him? Is there any hope of achieving what Saddam Takriti is talking about?'

'Yes. A one-in-a-million chance.'

Apartment Freedom had lost most of its cheer since Reeri died. With the disappearance of Hilde and the expulsion of Yacoub the place no longer rang with laughter. Flowers were noted by their absence. The bathrooms filled up with dirty clothes and the apartment with the low odour of neglect and dust. Abdul-Karim was now wearing his dark shirts again. Aisha forgot the new recipes she had learned and the place had become a depressing hotel that people came to only to sleep. Studies were pursued only in the Faculty. Qasim spent all his spare time in the office and Abdul-Karim only left the library when it closed at night. Fuad was immersed in his law books and in his new and increasingly complicated relationship.

The ties to Suad had been of mutual feelings, beginning with desire and ending with indifference. Then came the relationship with Shahenaz when there was unrequited love. Then along came Madiha. They had shared an overwhelming lust and when it faded broke up. But this new relationship with Laila was more twisted than a lizard's tail. He couldn't understand this woman and had no idea what she wanted from him or what he wanted from her.

She seemed to love him because no one could write such poetry unless they were in love. He seemed to love her because only a lover could have patience with such determined madness. But there was something missing and wrong: the affection and tenderness that could only come from a woman. That flowing and warm gentleness was absent. When he was with her he felt that he was in some competition: which of them was cleverer, which one wittier, which one more liberated. He tried to offer her himself polished and refined in order to impress her. And she only revealed to him what was on the surface, brilliant as snow, and just as cold. What was the secret of this woman who was almost 24 years old and was still a second-year student? A woman who talked of her two ex-husbands as if they were cast-off shirts? A woman who wanted freedom for herself, total freedom. Freedom to marry and freedom to divorce; the marriage of poor people and the acceptance of rich men's presents. And she chastely refused even to hold hands, let alone kiss. As for sex, forget it.

One day when they were in 'The Little Nest', she showed him the file of her letters. Here was a letter from Gamal Abdul Nasser: his signature, not a rubber stamp, and thanking her for a contribution of 5,000 pounds during the Suez War. And here was a letter of thanks from Abdul-Halim Hafez for a birthday present. And there was a poem from Kamil Shinawi and another from Saleh Godat, again in his own hand.

Fuad could not suppress astonished rage. 'What's all this? From Gamal Abdul Nasser and Abdul-Halim Hafez. Are you some sort of star fucker?'

'The opposite.'

'Where did you see Abdul-Halim Hafez? Was there anything between you?'

She laughed heartily. 'Why do you think I chose him? Nothing happened between us.'

'And me?'

'What about you?'

'Where do I come in amongst this lot?'

'You're completely different from them. They want me. But I want you.'

'You want me? What are you waiting for?'

'The poem only emerges when it is ripe. It is the same with the wedding night.'

'Wedding night? I have no wish to become your third husband!'

'I think you know what I mean.'

'No, I don't. And I won't be waiting for the time to be ripe. My feelings are not on tap.'

She looked at him for a long time. She came close to him, and whispered, kissing him on the cheek. 'You'll wait, Fuad. And you'll be there.'

# CHAPTER EIGHTEEN

## April 1961

───────────

When Aisha opened the door she found Yacoub beaming before her. She was so stunned that she embraced him then rushed through the apartment whooping. 'Yacoub has come back. See Yacoub is back safely!'

The friends raced in and Yacoub was crushed in embraces.

Fuad was the first to speak. 'What a fabulous surprise. Why didn't you let us know?'

'I was afraid there would be last-minute complications.'

'But what happened?' cut in Qasim. 'We want to hear everything from the time you left Cairo.'

Yacoub told his story. He arrived in Beirut and stayed in a small hotel near Martyrs' Square. A few days later a young Palestinian Ghassan Kanafani contacted him. He was a friend of Majid and that he had heard of the problem from Majid. Ghassan worked on a Lebanese paper with Nasserite leanings and through him Yacoub got to know many Lebanese writers and poets. Ghassan told him that his problem could only be resolved through a personal decision of Nasser. So the search began for a Lebanese leader with a special friendship with Nasser. Eventually Ghassan was of the opinion that the best person to intervene was Kamal Jumblatt. The two young men went to see Kamal Jumblatt in his palace at Mukhtara and Ghassan explained the position. Jumblatt then sent a message to Nasser in which he requested that Yacoub might return to Egypt to complete his studies. One month later the Egyptian Embassy in Beirut contacted Yacoub. He was told that His Excellency the President had agreed to his return to Egypt until graduation, conditional on of his abstention from political activity.

'All the credit,' said Yacoub back home, 'is due to Ghassan Kanafani, and to Majid.' Then, looking over at Fuad, 'Looks like Majid's influence is on the increase, doesn't it?' Fuad agreed.

───────────

Fuad could not tell his friends that Majid had become the delegate in the Movement responsible for the Peninsula and that in this capacity he was in touch with all its leading figures. Nor could he tell his friends that he had decided to join the Movement. The fact was that Fuad did not actually know the motives that had made him overcome all his old reservations. He was aware, however, of some reservations.

He felt that the Nasserite tendency had reached an impasse: its enemies were now no longer from outside the Arab world. Nor were the helpmates of imperialism within the Arab Nation the only source of danger. There was now a violent undercover, opposition to Gamal Abdul Nasser, led by the Ba'ath party. There was an even more overt violent opposition by the Communist Party. Fuad had only to recall the attitude of Suad and Yacoub to Gamal Abdul Nasser to realize the extent to which things had changed. Fuad saw that the cord linking Nasser to the Arab masses was threatened from all quarters.

However, Fuad now saw that socialism was the ideal way to organize economic activity in the coming Arab state and was sure that to abandon it now was wrong. As his knowledge and reading about economics grew, the picture of socialism began to crystallize. He rejected atheistic communism, and he rejected vague Ba'athist socialism and he came to the conclusion that the ideal form of socialism for the Arab nation was what Abdul-Ra'ouf called the socialism of the British Labour Party: ownership by the state of the major means of production and private ownership of everything else, with sliding scale taxes on income. Fuad now hoped that this would be put forward by the Movement.

A third aspect was that Fuad did not feel in the Movement any of that sense of conviction that he had seen in the Ba'ath party. There was no figure as the 'Leader and Founder' whose every word had to be learned by heart. Nor was there that stubborn insistence on commitment and on conscripting literature into the service of the Cause. The Movement was like a large family, except for the special care that Yacoub had received from the Brothers in Beirut, of course.

It was ironic that Fuad should begin his life in the Movement with two clashes with the Ba'ath party. The scene of the first was the League of Bahrain Students where the Ba'athists particularly wanted to control the study body running the League and the ANM were equally determined to keep the Ba'athists out. The confrontation came about as the Ba'athists put up independent students who were sympathizers and the ANM mustered students not known for any party allegiance. Although it really was a trial of strength between the Ba'ath and the ANM the elections seemed to be about the personalities of the candidates. The ANM lost by a very slim margin.

This was educational, so that when the second confrontation came, in the

League of Kuwait Students, for control of the student body, the ANM students were on maximum alert. The apartment of Barrak Al-Nafi was converted into an operations room in which strategy and tactics were decided. The campaign was riddled with Machiavellian tactics, promises, threats and rumours and contrived lies. Victory was by a small margin again, but this time in favour of the ANM.

Fuad emerged from these experiences with mixed feelings about elections and democracy in general. The majority of the Bahrain and Kuwaiti students were uninterested in politics but a well-organized Ba'athist minority was able to impose its candidates on the Bahrain students while the ANM was able to do the same for the Kuwaiti student body. All of this was done in a democratic manner, with elections and a secret ballot. So, was democracy, then, just a clever wrapping for domination by a party minority? If it was possible to delude the élite of well-educated Arab students by rumours about this candidate or that would it not be even easier to influence illiterate Arab masses? Were those who called for the rule of the Enlightened Despot right after all? Fuad decided that democracy had better be postponed for the time being. The same went for socialism... The present phase required massing of all forces behind Gamal Abdul Nasser.

But all this feverish political activity in addition to the intensive study needed for imminent finals could not divert Fuad from his relationship with Laila which was growing more bizarre.

He complained to Abdul-Ra'ouf, 'I swear, sometimes I imagine I'm dealing with an evil spirit, Abdul-Ra'ouf. No human being could be like Laila!'

He was cynical. 'Does she walk through walls? Does she vanish into the ground? Or claim she's the spirit of your dead grandmother?'

'What she does is more amazing than any of that. This woman knows Field Marshal Abdul-Hakim Amir well and once spoke to him on the phone, while I was there. How? By way of her first husband. She's also a close friend of Michel Aflaq. How? By way of the second husband.'

'So, what's strange about all that? It's obvious: Husband No. 1 was a rightist and Husband No. 2 a lefty.'

'But what about the woman herself? How does she stand, right or left? A while back she made a trip to Kuwait and said that she was going to make a contribution to drawing up the draft constitution. Then she came back in a rage because the draft did not contain votes for women. Before that she made a trip to Damascus to call on Michel Aflaq. Last week she spent time with Dr Ahmad Khatib.'

'Maybe she works for Egyptian Intelligence? She could be a spy.'

Fuad ignored his flippant remark and continued grimly.

'And there is not a film star or poet or writer that she has not exchanged letters with. She has a photo from Abdul-Halim Hafez dedicated to "My Arabian Princess".'

'Ah, now I understand. Jealousy. The whole thing is just jealousy.'

'If there was only one man, I'd feel jealous but how can you be jealous of *The Who's Who of the Arab World*? And that's not the end of the mystery: have you ever, in your life, Abdul-Ra'ouf, heard of a millionairess who owns villas but lives in a room in the Kuwaiti women students' dorm?'

'Why not? Rich, but a woman of the people! A woman of talents, my friend! Have you never read what the owners of fine carriages put on the back of their vehicles? "King of Kings if he is the object of bounty ... but don't ask why and how...." '

'Yes, I can see all that but what does she want from me? I'm not a film star, or a big shot in politics, or a celebrity.'

'An investment for the future, my friend ...'

'And in the meantime, every time we meet we have a fight. I vow to finish with her. Once I said to her, "Take your letters and poems and your pictures and go to hell." Two nights later she recited over the phone:

"I long for you and for what is in your eyes ...
And for the yearning for myself, so when will your lips meet mine ...?"

So I said: "OK, right now." And she said, "I'll be right over!" She was there within minutes. She came into my room and kissed me passionately, she'd never kissed me like that before. Then, out of the blue, she screamed, "Stop. He's back!" And she left as suddenly as she'd come.'

'That's not normal.'

'I know she has strange moods, but what concerns me is not her mind, but mine.'

'Fuad, you're in love with her.'

'Yes, and she's going to drive me mad. I feel like a fly in a spider's web: as soon as I struggle free from some strands I'm wrapped around by new ones.'

'Look out for the new literary sensation ...'

Yacoub was still unable to analyse his feelings after being arrested and gaoled. While he was in gaol, in the few moments when he was able to think, bitterness burned in his brain. Where were the oppressed for whom he had been struggling? Where were the proletarian states? Had the USSR intervened to rescue him? Had the Soviet Ambassador protested to Nasser? The peasants co-operated submissively with the feudal masters as usual. The workers in the Iron and Steel Complex submitted to the management. Had a single peasant laid down his tools? Had the Soviet Ambassador declined to attend that cocktail party? The world just went on the way it had done before he had gone into that dark hole where night had been indistinguishable from day.

Bitterness was followed by fierce self-contempt for being so feeble and insipid. Where was the solidity of the combatant? Where was the power and strength of the revolutionary? Just a few weeks in one room and he collapsed. He wept and screamed like a child. He saw ghosts and gallows. And he wanted to confess without anyone even asking him. How fragile were his nerves? What future awaited the toiling masses if the resistance of the leadership collapsed like this?

He had long, furious debates in Beirut with Ghassan Kanafani. Ghassan tried to convince him that the hostility of Marxism to nationalism had no basis. 'You are a writer and poet, Yacoub. Do you relish Polish literature the way you relish Arabic? Is your feeling towards me the same as your feeling towards a Chinese? Don't kid yourself: you are an Arab first, last and always. Is there anywhere in the world that has in your heart the same place as Palestine? Didn't you once volunteer in the cause of Palestine? Are you ready to volunteer for the cause of Hungary? And then again we can choose from Marxist theory what suits our particular circumstances and leave aside the rest. We can make use of Marx's economic theory and ignore his thoughts on nationalism. Nothing forces us to swallow it.'

'Just a minute, Ghassan. We are not in the market, picking a marrow here and choosing a cucumber there. This is a fully integrated theory – either we take it or we reject it. This is a harmonious whole which can't be broken up. If you accept Marx's analysis of capitalism you have to accept his view of nationalism. You can't separate the economic issue from the political. That's just bourgeois trickery.' But Ghassan did pick and choose. He gave half of his time to his homeland and half to his heart and felt no contradiction, cursing Marx in the morning and glorifying him in the evening.

In Beirut Yacoub recognized the schizophrenia. The Nasserite papers talked about workers and peasants while Nasser gaoled those who adopted their causes. His own pardon by Nasser had come via Jumblatt who was the tribal leader. *His* boss, of the Lebanese Socialists, gave lectures on the theory of socialism from his feudal seat at Mukhtara. Yacoub was living in Beirut on money sent to him by Qasim. So he was living on capitalism. What kind of a crazy world was this?

After returning to Apartment Freedom Yacoub decided that the only way for him was to go back to his old friend Abu Nuwas, at least for the time being.

Abu Nuwas said, ' "Pour out the libations until you see me thinking that a cock is a donkey." ' You should know, Yacoub thought, that in this Arab world there is no difference between the cock and the donkey, except in the minds of drunks.

The Isfahan rug reached Apartment Freedom and was received with applause, laughter and joy. It was then taken with due ceremony to Qasim,'s room. It turned out after the pursuit was over that the rug had indeed arrived at Sabtiya Customs but finding it had taken one week, twenty signatures and the payment of thirty pounds. Then thirty more signatures and fifty pounds had been needed. This interim stage, taking a month, was followed by estimating the value which required more sixty signatures and another seventy pounds. Finally the customs charges had to be paid. Those only required ten signatures and 200 pounds.

'Oh God, praise and thanks to you! The money of the capitalists is distributed freely among the junior officials.' Fuad was sarcastic.

'There's the revolution for you. That's the President for you. Thieves and robbers,' exclaimed Qasim.

Abdul-Ra'ouf realized that this appointment at 9 a.m. at the Casinore must be about some highly sensitive matter. An ancient waiter, still rubbing his eyes, peered at the two clients who had arrived hours before lunch.

Abdul-Karim got right down to the subject. 'I want your help in a very important personal matter.'

'I'm at your disposal.'

'I want to join the Muslim Brotherhood!'

Abdul-Ra'ouf went silent. He had been expecting anything but this. He stammered and then became silent again. Abdul-Karim resumed.

'I'm not stupid, Abdul-Ra'ouf. You don't have to let your beard grow luxuriantly and carry photos of Hassan Al-Banna to announce your allegiance. We all know you belong and your stories fool no one.'

Abdul-Ra'ouf's face went red and he spoke slowly. 'I never tried to fool anyone. The organization has been dissolved and anyone caught even sympathizing with the group finishes up in prison and may be tortured.'

'I know that.'

'No, I don't think you do. What you said about growing a beard is no joke. Lots of men have been arrested for just that. Have you noticed that there are no more bearded men in Egypt? In fact people have been arrested on buses because an informer has heard them being called, "Brother".'

'But I want to join the Muslim Brotherhood.'

'There's another thing, Abdul-Ra'ouf, and please don't be angry ... there are no Shia in the Brotherhood.'

'Sunni! Shia! *Et tu, Brute.*'

'I just want to make things clear. It's true that the Sheikh of Al-Azhar put out a proclamation recognizing the Ja'fari School of Jurisprudence, but the opinion of the Sheikh of Al-Azhar is one thing and the opinion of the Brotherhood is another. The fact is I don't know anything about the Shia except for what I've heard from you.'

'Isn't it enough that we are Muslims, believe in the same Lord, in the same Book, and one Prophet?'

'Abdul-Karim! We are in Egypt. As far as I know there is not a single Shia in the country. But the sect is not the main obstacle. So far there is no organization for the group. That means that if you want to join there is nobody for you to join. You won't find members or an office or a newspaper.'

'But there must be some way.'

'The only way is for you to join them in gaol. I don't think that is what you had in mind.'

'I want to join a movement that will abolish the differences between Sunni and Shia, simple as that.'

'The split between them is almost as old as Islam: do you think we can resolve it now?'

'Can't we try?'

'Going to gaol is not the best method. Didn't you see what happened to Yacoub? After just a few weeks he came back a wreck. Do you want that to happen to you?'

'You've let me down. I had been expecting encouragement.' Abdul-Karim was incensed.

'I don't know what your motives are, but I do know that you don't understand. My brother spent three years in gaol just because they found him with a few pamphlets of Hassan El-Banna. Three years' hard labour. And there are thousands who've disappeared because the authorities complained that they were in sympathy with the group. If you are persistent then begin by reading Islamic books, even though that alone is not without risk.'

'I take it that you don't want to help me.'

'How can I help you? Today you can stand up in the Faculty and say in a loud voice, "God have mercy on Hassan Al-Banna!", or, "The Muslim Brothers are oppressed!" and within a few hours you'll find yourself in gaol with them. You don't need my help for that.'

'Abdul-Ra'ouf, I'm serious and you're making fun of me.'

'No. It's the reality. Why not join Fuad and Majid? I don't believe they have differences between Sunni and Shia, or between Muslims and Christians.'

'I want to join an Islamic organization.'

'Start with reading. Fuad often goes to Sheikh Abu-Zahra in his study. Go with him and ask for the names of a few books dealing with the Islamic position.'

'And then?'

'We'll see. I'm not promising anything. Can I ask you a question?'

'Go ahead.'

'Are you sure your decision's not based on an uneasy conscience? Please, Abdul-Ra'ouf. It's enough having one Freud in the Apartment!'

*Lights were blazing in the Imperial Palace for tonight was the night of the monthly wedding and the party of the Virgin Empress, Shana. In the Imperial boudoir the ladies in waiting crowded around Shana helping her to don the wedding dress studded with precious jewels. In a remote corner of the Palace a group of slaves were busy with the bridegroom, Sheen, attempting to make the handsome young peasant with the tattered clothes and rough hands worthy for the Empress.*

*Sheen had never expected this. Everything had happened so fast. A few days before a platoon of the Imperial Guard had surrounded the field where he had been working and had called in all the peasants. He had been chosen. The Guard Commander then told him to present himself at the Palace.*

*Everyone in Sa'bad knew that the man selected to be the husband was cursed. A handsome young peasant working in the fields would be chosen to be the bridegroom. Celebrations would be proclaimed and there would be beating of drums while the capital would be flooded with lights. The Empress would be seated on her silver throne, her new husband beside her. The next morning the husband would join the ranks of the eunuchs charged with keeping clean the Imperial Palaces. Word would get out that the husband had not been up to his duties and that the Empress remained a virgin: preparations would then begin for the next month's wedding feast.*

*Like everyone else Sheen knew perfectly well the truth of what actually happened: the new bridegroom did not go directly to the Imperial bed but was led off to the surgeon. He would be castrated, just as the Imperial horses and dogs were. Then he would be brought to the Imperial bedchamber. The following morning he would join the other eunuchs.*

*Sheen carefully hid his little razor and the preparations proceeded. The Empress smiled as did her bridegroom. The ceremony ended and the Empress disappeared. He went to the surgeon's room and within seconds the razor was plunged into the neck of the doctor and then returned to its hiding place. Sheen emerged and entered the Imperial bedchamber. He saw the Empress in a delicate and diaphanous négligé and could not believe that this woman was over 60 years of age. Everyone in Sa'bad believed that it was witchcraft which was the secret of the eternal youth of the Empress. The Empress summoned him but he did not move. She ordered him to approach and then he leaped upon her. Before the Empress realized what had happened he had slapped her face and fell upon her like a ravening wolf falling upon a ewe. The blood flowed and the Empress screamed, 'You beast! You have taken me by force!'*

*Sheen looked at the Empress who was no longer a virgin and was bewildered by the transformation: the childlike, charming face was ugly and wrinkled.*

*The unmarked complexion was now mottled with boils. Sheen saw the true face of the witch. He plunged his razor into her neck, its veins raised, and she screamed. The guards came from all directions and Sheen laughed.*

'Ah, I see! A new phase. Is this due to Laila?'
'Maybe.'
'Don't tell me you've made it to the Imperial Bedchamber. Don't tell me she's still a virgin after two husbands.'
'No comment.'
'What does "Sa'bad" mean?'
'It means "Stop! He's come back!"'

Did the story really say everything? About everything that had happened? Last Thursday night Laila came to Apartment Freedom and took him off in the red Buick and announced they were going on a journey. They stopped outside a villa in Muhandiseen. As soon as they crossed the threshold Fuad felt that he was moving into a new world. Fabulous furnishings, oil paintings, discreet lighting, and music coming from he knew not where intoxicated him.
'Who lives here?' he asked stupidly.
'I do.'
'But I thought you lived in the girls' dorm.'
'I live there, too.'
'Did you live here with your ex-husband?'
'I lived here with the second one.'
'You mean you lived here with the revolutionary socialist, in this capitalist home?'
'That's enough. He's come back.'
The villa was hardly a palace but neither was it ordinary. What really amazed Fuad was the difference between the outside, which was like that of dozens of other villas nearby, and the inside. The carpets just laughed at Qasim's lone rug: Fuad had no idea how she managed to import so many carpets into Egypt. The blue curtains: so those who talked about the 'velvet society' were not exaggerating! And the photos! A picture of herself with her first husband in a Roman piazza. A picture with her first husband and Anwar Sadat. A picture with her first husband and Farid Al-Atrash. Then a picture of her second husband, the image of Omar Sharif. Next, a picture of them in Feisal's Restaurant in Beirut, followed by a picture of him with Sulaiman Easa. A weird world, one of poets and politicians, revolutionaries and rulers, rich and poor, of materialism and spiritual matters. And she lived in these two worlds as if she was a compound made up of two human beings: the rich capitalist woman who married one of her own kind and the revolutionary socialist who also married one of her own kind. Even after the departure of

the husbands she still lived separate lives. On the one hand the humble room in the women students' dorm, and the humble boyfriend from Bahrain who only had twenty-five pounds a month and had published half a book. And on the other hand the red Buick and this villa of which every square inch spoke of obscene wealth.

For the first time in his life Fuad partook of whisky and cigars and for the first time outside of films he saw a woman drinking whisky and smoke a cigar. From which of her husbands had she acquired these habits? Fuad choked on his cigar and forced himself to swallow the yellow liquid. And then things began to cloud over as suddenly he heard her voice coming from a recording machine, in a whisper:

'Am I your heart or are you mine? You are my desire, my heart's desire, I have given you my spirit, my fate and my body, my eyes and to you I have surrendered my leading strings.'

Hardly had he recovered from the shock than he heard the same words, first in the voice of Abdul-Halim Hafez, followed by the voice of Farid El-Atrash, this time to a lute accompaniment. This could not be real. He could not be here in this palace close to this beautiful woman, listening to poetry which she had composed about him, poetry with his own name in it, sung by Abdul-Halim and Farid. As long as he was in a dream, then he would do just what he wanted.

The events in the dream went by like scenes from a film. The bedroom, the bed, the fragrance of Chanel No. 5. Kiss after kiss. And then, 'Stop! He's come back!' But this time he would not stop. A slap stung his cheek. The dream ended and the nightmare began. He was possessed by a drunken craze. He slaps her hard, first on one cheek, then the other. His hand reaches out and tears the shirt – or was it the blouse? In nightmares, the names are not important. His hand reaches out and removed her trousers. Or was it a skirt? The Muhandiseen part of town departs and the villa disappears. The beautiful Kuwaiti poet, Laila Khazini, the socialist capitalist, fades away. Fuad Tarif, the young Bahraini short-story writer who changed from being a Ba'athist to being an Arab nationalist disappears too. Laila becomes merely an object of Stone Age hunting and Fuad becomes a caveman. The quarry passes in front of the cave with a whiff of Chanel No. 5 and the caveman pursues the fragrance. The caveman feels a pang of hunger. He's not eaten for days. Is his prey a gazelle? Or a wild cow? In nightmares the objects of pursuit are similar. The quarry runs and the caveman pursues. The caveman turns and sees a large number of men chasing his prey. Here is a man with the features of Omar Sharif, and here is another with the features of Farid El-Atrash. And here is Nasser himself. What has brought Gamal Abdul Nasser into the heart of a nightmare? And there's the Professor. They are all chasing the quarry. The caveman is angry: this is his prey. It's his quarry alone. He reaches his prey and hits her on the back of the neck. She falls. He decides to enjoy his prey before the others arrive. He hears the sound of clothes being torn and hears the smack of more blows. The prey groans. Resistance becomes more feeble. From far away he hears the voice of Abdul-Halim Hafez, screaming, 'It is fire, my darling, fire!' Flames lick at the remainder of his clothes and his insides burn. He hears a voice scolding. The prey screams, 'Stop! Stop! You're mad, you're mad!' He could hear words at intervals, interrupted by sobs, 'You've raped me. You filthy beast!' All there was was a writer and a woman poet. Where had the blood come? The red handkerchief? The virgin's blood? Was this a reasonable nightmare? This is ordinary nightmare. It was invented by the Abthists, no the Ba'athists . . . Just a moment. How did you transform me into a filthy beast? How did you make me rape her? Does criminal law punish the crime of rape? We said that 'by force' is redundant . . .' O, respected sir. . . . Did it happen in a dream? Must ask the Dean. The Head of the Department of Criminal Law. The end is soft and milky. . . . You filthy beast you will go to gaol. You may see Zaghloul there. The Imam of the Mosque and a rapist in the same prison. Or maybe they'll put you with Yacoub? That's better . . . the man who raped capitalism with the man who raped a capitalist woman. And what is this broad smile spreading all over her face? There's a certain amount of surrealism in it. Never heard of surrealism, Your Excellency? It's a bit like existentialism, or Jew's Mallow. . . . Are you playing word-games, Your Honour? Sorry, in surrealism, anything can happen and everything. Birds talk and chairs speak and frogs cackle with laughter. A woman can marry twice and stay a virgin. But then she can fix up the hymen again, with needle and thread. The Oriental wants only a virgin. I don't plan to be your third husband! Where have I heard that before? And this wounded and bleeding prey is still smiling. That smile is an existentialist stand. Nightmare, please explain to me, slowly, why I'm here, and what I'm doing, at this time of morning, on this bed with this woman who is bleeding who claims I'm a filthy beast who raped her by force. Speak, nightmare, I kiss your hand!

# CHAPTER NINETEEN

## June 1961

O n the day of the viva examination in Civil Law Fuad stood at the door, surrounded by gloomy faces, long beards and dirty clothes. He alone seemed as if he had just arrived from the barber. He had slept very well after long walks and was confident. His turn came and he went in with two other students. Dr Sulaiman Murqus sat behind a desk with the President of the Court of Appeal, Counsellor Zahir Husni. Dr Sulaiman began and asked each student a question in turn. Then it was the turn of the Counsellor to put questions. Dr Sulaiman then questioned again and for some reason concentrated on Fuad. One question after another came. As far as Fuad could tell it was OK. Then Dr Sulaiman, switched to another subject.

'And what about the sale of real estate by a seller who does not actually own the object?'

Fuad replied, 'In good faith or otherwise, Doctor?'

'In good faith.'

'And what of the purchaser, Doctor? Good faith or otherwise?'

'Who's being examined?' exclaimed Dr Sulaiman, laughing, 'What is meant is good faith on both sides.'

Fuad said, 'The opinion which you mentioned in the book, Doctor, and which is based on the rulings of the Appeal Courts in France and Egypt comes down in favour of protection of the purchaser acting in good faith and compensation for the actual owner with the equivalent consideration. But I disagree with this opinion.'

Had Fuad said, 'I now plan to kill you, Doctor!' it would not have had the same effect as his last words. An awful silence prevailed in the room. The two students shifted uneasily, terrified. The Counsellor turned his gaze towards him as if wondering whether Fuad was in full possession of his faculties. Dr Sulaiman went red in the face as Fuad went on. 'Your opinion, Doctor, is of course based on logic. It is illogical that I should knock down a building even though the person who built it did so on land bought from someone who was not the actual owner. But I look at the matter from the angle of justice which requires the protection of the real owner.'

'Since when did the principles of justice contradict logic?' growled Dr Sulaiman.

The Counsellor added, 'It is clear, Doctor, that he has not fully taken in your opinion.'

'I am sorry, Counsellor. I have fully understood the opinion of the Doctor, I appreciate and respect it. But it is my view that the principles of justice require the protection of the actual owner. Just assume, Doctor, that I own land on which I intend to build a house for my family and I then am absent for a few weeks and return to find someone else has sold the land to another who has built a house on it. Where lies my fault?'

The Doctor was clearly agitated. 'I must remind you that we are talking about a seller in good faith who was unaware that he was selling another's property, and a purchaser in good faith unaware that is buying from other than the owner. What is the fault of the purchaser of the land who is fully confident that he is buying from the real owner and actually builds a house on the land? By what logic can I destroy the house?'

'That,' said Fuad, calmly, 'is the point, Doctor. You say what is the fault of the purchaser and I say what is my fault, the actual owner of the land?'

'But the real owner will be compensated, my son,' cut in the Counsellor. 'He will be compensated.'

Fuad refused to be persuaded. 'But let's suppose he does not wish to sell in the first place and does not want to be compensated. He only wants his land.'

'So,' said Dr Sulaiman in astonishment, 'you want to destroy the house and put the land back to its original state, handing it back to its real owner?'

'That is what justice requires, Doctor.'

'Just suppose the buyer puts up a huge hotel on the land: will you remove the hotel? Or a hospital – will you pull it down?'

'That is what is required by justice.'

'Justice requires that I pull down a building costing 1 million pounds just to protect land whose value is no more than 10,000 pounds?'

The Counsellor intervened to calm things down and addressed Fuad, 'Your opinion, my son, is acceptable from a theoretical point of view but it is quite impracticable. A number of Cairo's quarters were sold and built on before anyone discovered that the seller was not the owner.'

Dr Sulaiman added, 'Do you not remember the story of Heliopolis, Zahir Bey? Half of the area was sold in this way.' He turned to Fuad. 'Where are you from, my son?'

'From Bahrain.'

'Right, off you go.'
Before Fuad reached the door Dr Sulaiman called him back and whispered in his ear, 'Your opinion is completely mistaken but ... bravo! I'll give you full marks. I've never done that before.'

Yacoub turned the pages of *Arab Society* in preparation for his exam. He now had to go all out to cover this semester's work. But the book disgusted him. It was full of hypocrisy with little understanding of the reality of Arab society anywhere: Bahrain was not even mentioned. Yacoub could understand why slogans about unity and Arab resources and the approaching Paradise were repeated in the media but could not understand how it could be presented to students at university as an objective account of the state of Arab society. I wonder, he thought, what would happen if I were to write in my answers just glimpses of Arab society as I have experienced it?

Let's begin with that bastion of Arabism, the Mother of the World, Egypt. You, honoured sir, the examiner, as an Arab national from the Southern Region of the UAR, are aware of conditions in Egypt, far better than I am. But it is dangerous for you to deal with them in your book. So let me speak on your behalf ...

In this Arab society, honoured sir, the Officers of the Revolution own everything. And I mean that literally: the government, the National Assembly, the National Union, the Press, the buildings of the French and the English, the local governorates, young women wanting to get married. Ask Abdul-Karim. They own the centres for solitary confinement. I should know. Have you tried the centres for solitary confinement, honoured sir? No, this is a serious question. There is one in a nice ordinary villa in Abbasiyya, with no sign, and no guard, a lovely, pleasant house. No torture goes on, all that solitary confinement means is that you don't know the difference between night and day. And honoured sir, do you know what that means? Quite simply, it means insanity. When there's no longer any difference between dawn and sunset, between breakfast and dinner, between light and darkness, there's no longer any difference between reason and madness. Believe me, honoured sir. Would I cheat you? Go and ask questions in Abbasiyya. Ask questions there. Go and ask about an ordinary villa with nothing about it to indicate it is a centre for solitary confinement.

What about Arab society in Lebanon, honoured sir? That's a really weird society, like Never-Never Land; it lies beyond Night 700 of *1001 Nights*. On every fragrant hilltop of Lebanon there is an independent empire. Do you remember the Empire of Zifti, honoured sir? Ruled by an independent clan, ruled by a tribal sheikh, who represents it in Parliament. And every sheikh has his army of thugs, there are more of these than there are in the Lebanese Army. You can believe me or not, honoured sir, but the Sheikhs of Lebanon number more than those of the Kingdom of Saudi Arabia, Qatar, Bahrain and Kuwait put together. You didn't know that before? And then, honoured sir, at the top of the heap is the Sheikh of Sheikhs, the President of the Republic, who is in his turn a Prince!

What I really mean, honoured sir, is that you must in the next edition of your book give up all this rubbish about the role of the Arab masses in the unified Nasserite Arab Nation and write instead that the Arab nation is not ruled by the masses but by Kings, Princes and Sheikhs, and who in Egypt are called the Officers, and in Syria called Prince or Bey. You must, honoured sir, in the next edition of your book set it down that your big shot in Egypt, Gamal Abdul Nasser, is no longer content to be a big shot here alone but wants to be the Big Chief in the Arab countries stretching from the Atlantic Ocean to the Persian Gulf. Sorry, honoured sir, I mean the Gulf. When I came to Egypt in the summer of 1956 it used to be called the Persian Gulf but now it's called the Arabian Gulf because the Arabian Big Shot got mad with the Persian Big Shot. The main thing, honoured sir, is that I am with Gamal Abdul Nasser to the death, whatever it is called.

Abdul-Karim muttered to himself as he read *Private International Law*. His illness following Reeri's death had led to his failing in two subjects from the first semester, and for him to fail in any of the second semesters would mean he would have to stay on for an extra academic year instead of just one semester. He pressed on with his studies. This topic really was a strange one: it had two names, 'Private International Law' and 'Conflict of Jurisdictions'. Abdul-Karim preferred the latter name since in the end life was just a collection of 'Conflicts of Jurisdictions'. The laws of Reaction and the laws of Progress; the laws of Wealth and the laws of Poverty; the laws of Love and the laws of Hate; the laws of Woman and the laws of Man; the laws of the Sunnis and the laws of the Shia; the laws of Cowardice and the laws of Courage.

Cowardice and courage. This was the greatest of all conflicts, the basic Dialectic, to use the phrase of Yacoub the former existentialist/communist and now someone with an unknown Ideology. Cowardice and courage: out of their conflict history is made. But is history made by the brave or the cowards? By Hussain or Yazid? At first sight it seems that history is made by the brave but actually the brave usually die. Generally the cowards survive and they then steal history. Brave soldiers are the fodder for battle and cowardly commanders are the heroes. Is this a historical truth? History is like the Thursday market in Bahrain or like the Maqasis Market in Cairo, full of all manner of goods. . . .

Well. . . . better lay aside history and have a look at himself. Hadn't his life been a conflict between cowardice and bravery? Between traditions and rebellion? Between obedience and dissent? How would he categorize himself now that he had reached the age of 23? Maybe he was in a state of Conflict of Jurisdictions. Dr Gaber Gad was talking about laws of personal status and criminal law. But the book did not address the conflict of the laws of courage and cowardice and which of them applied to Abdul-Karim. The door of his room opened and Fuad looked in. 'Farida's on the phone.'

His world clouded over with thick clouds of black fog. He could hardly see or hear. 'Karim, Farida's on the phone! What do I tell her?'

Abdul-Karim opened his mouth but the words would not come out. Fuad noticed him shiver. 'I'll take her number and tell her you'll call her later.'

Fuad went away but the shivers did not. He automatically assumed she was calling because her marriage was over. Farida! After all this? What would she say to him? 'Sorry . . .' 'Don't be cross with me . . .' And what would he say to her, 'It's nothing . . .' 'Hope everything is OK . . .' 'It's only a wedding, nobody died . . .' Except Reeri . . . And what happened to His Excellency, the Officer? Had he fallen in battle? Or had he died of depression? Should he talk to Farida or not? Conflict of laws. Laws of courage and cowardice . . . Did the law of courage require him to speak to her or to ignore her? Was cowardice here turning away or rushing forward? A very tricky question. Not to be resolved by Dr Gaber Gad's book. Nor by any book in all the Faculties of Law. Was he just a coward dressing up as a brave man? Or a brave man who sometimes wore the mask of cowardice? To speak to her or not to speak, that was the question.

*From the moment Magdi's eyes fell on those of Safa he had been in love with both her and her eyes. She lived in an apartment on the third floor of the building where he had a small room on the roof. At the time she was aged 13, in intermediate school, while he was 15 at the beginning of secondary school. He waited a whole year before he had the courage to say, 'Good morning!' to her. She only smiled. For months smiles were the only communication between them and then they exchanged a few words, a sentence or two, when they met on the stairs or the roof when she put out the washing.*

*Safa's father was an official in the Governorate offices in Giza, almost a Chief Clerk. He was eager that Safa should marry an official like himself and not waste her future on a poor student. He warned her against talking to Magdi and threatened to get him thrown out of the building if he found her talking to him. But still the words and smiles continued and love grew in Magdi's heart.*

*How was she so beautiful while her father was so ugly and evil-tempered and her mother was so short and fat? She was like a flower in a desert. She had rosy cheeks and was slender, while her large eyes were rimmed with kohl and her hair gloriously unruly.*

*When Magdi came from Cairo he found his cousin Rashad in this little room so he moved in with him. As Magdi was beginning in the Faculty of Arts his cousin was graduating as an agricultural engineer and found a job at Fayyoum. His place in the room was taken by another relative. It was an unending cycle. One relative graduates, his bed becomes vacant and then along comes another relative.*

*Rashad, on a surprise visit from Fayyoum, said to him happily, 'You'd better congratulate me, Magdi! I'm engaged to Safa. Her father has given his approval. We sign the contract next week.'*

*It was like a dagger-thrust to Magdi's heart: Safa, who, he had imagined, loved him as he loved her was now going to marry Rashad. The contract was signed and then came the wedding feast with Magdi present on both occasions. Safa went off with Rashad to Fayyoum. Since he had heard the news from Rashad he had only been face to face with her once, on the stairs. They looked at each other and neither spoke. Then two large tears rolled down her face and as she passed by him she whispered 'It is fate, destiny, See Magdi.'*

*She disappeared. The days passed and he decided that she had forgotten him. Two years went by and he believed that he had been fooling himself about her. Three years went by and he convinced himself that he had never known her and that she had not known him.*

*Then Safa appeared on the stairs. Nothing had changed. The same wondrous beauty, the same brilliant smile. She whispered – she seemed only to speak in whispers – that Rashad had divorced her. Magdi asked why and there came the same whisper as he had heard the last time they had met on these stairs, 'It is fate, destiny, See Magdi!'*

*Would her father now accept his divorced daughter marrying a postgraduate student in the Faculty? Would he accept that rank as being worthy of the daughter of a Chief Clerk? The answer to that is known only to fate and destiny.*

'Do I say "Congratulations!" now?', asked Fuad.

'Better wait! Till I graduate and get the appointment,' said Abdul-Ra'ouf.

'A thousand congrats. In advance. How did you live the last few years?'

'Who said I lived? I was just floating on the surface of life.'

'I've noticed a terrific change in you these last few weeks. I can see happiness all over your face. I thought maybe I was imagining things.'

'No, you weren't, Fuad. I did not know life till she returned.'

'May God complete your happiness.'

The voice of Fatima – the Duck! – came to him on the phone, broken by sobs, 'Fuad? I have to see you. Can you come over right away!'

'What's happened?' he asked anxiously. 'Is Mr Shareef all right? Are the children all right?'

At Mr Shareef's apartment Fuad was met by a scene of mourning. All were in tears: his wife Fatima; Muhammad, the eldest son; the youngest son, Arif, and all the domestic help. Fuad was bewildered. 'I saw Mr Shareef a couple of days ago, he was in great shape. How did he die?'

'I wish he had died!' wailed his wife.

'Well, what happened then?'

She gave him the piece of paper and he turned it over and read it several times before he realized that it was an announcement of divorce, just a coupon with lots of official stamps.

Fatima sobbed, 'Just imagine that! An old man like him! He's marrying a young woman from the Ministry no older than his daughter. Then he divorces me. They told me he had made a contract to marry that bitch but I didn't believe it. They told me he'd rented an apartment in Zamalek and I didn't believe it. Where did he get the money from? He puts me and the children in this little place and sets her up in Zamalek. I couldn't believe it! I said it's just rumours. Then he began to stay away. And to tell lies. Some assignment in Alexandria. Another one in Ismailia. And now I get this bit of paper. The lying old sod! Abandoning me after all these years.'

Fuad spoke to the others at the apartment. 'Is there any way we can intervene? Is it any use having a word with Mr Shareef?'

'But he's 55 years old!' retorted Qasim. 'How can *we* advise him?'

'Remember Freud,' was Yacoub's comment. 'Mr Shareef couldn't find the sexual satisfaction in the old wife so he married someone else. That's all there is to it.'

'That's all there is to it? After all these years? What about the children?' Abdul-Karim snapped back.

'You're the lawyers!' said Yacoub laughing. 'The children will get their due. I advise you not to interfere. Sex drive is stronger than all the advice in the world.'

Fuad sighed. 'Just suppose we were to speak to him. What would we say?'

'We would ask him to take her back under his protection,' said Abdul-Karim.

'That's really smart,' said Yacoub. 'If he intended to do that why would he divorce her? We can do nothing,' finished Yacoub. 'Just remember that it is Mr Shareef who is looking after you, not the other way round!'

On the Friday morning Mr Shareef came at his usual time and began talking to Fuad, 'I should have told you before she told you. I'll not try to explain. You wouldn't understand what I was talking about. You're twenty with your whole life ahead of you but I'm approaching sixty. I only have a few years left. At my age opportunities are not repeated. You'll not understand now, Fuad, but you will when you reach fifty.'

'If I reach fifty,' Fuad replied coldly.

To F.

Shall I apologize to you? Or you to me? Or was what happened pre-destined? That's not important now. The main thing is I love you, as I've never loved anyone, as I can never love anyone else in the future. I beg you to believe me this time. I beg you to give me another opportunity, the last one.

L.

Fuad glimpsed the red Buick standing on the other side of Durri Street. He pulled the sheet of blue notepaper from his pocket and tore it up into small pieces which he tossed into the air. They flew up and Fuad smiled as he saw one piece get caught on the windscreen of the Buick.

Fuad looked imploringly at Majid, 'Please, Majid, let me get on with my studies. This is a very funny month, some are getting married, others are getting divorced, and some are coming back from unknown parts. And you're talking about a conference! Can't it wait?'

'The conference is next month and I've got to send in your name now. You absolutely must attend. Remember this may be your last chance to attend the General Assembly of the ANM. Who knows when you'll have another opportunity?'

Fuad decided that this month would be called the month of last chances. Laila is asking him for a last chance. Mr Shareef has seized his last chance. Farida has come back hoping for another, last chance. Abdul-Ra'ouf has seized upon his. And now here he was facing the last chance to attend the General Assembly of the ANM, held in Bhamdoun next month.

'Just suppose I don't attend. What will happen?'

'You've just got to. You've got a big role in America and it's essential you get to know the leading figures in the ANM. They pin great hopes on you.'

'On me? Since when have I become a party boss?'

'The ANM needs leaders. In America the members are disorganized. You've got excellent experience and now you can organize the Movement there. You must get to know the country delegates. You can't help the Movement over there if you haven't mixed with these officials.'

'I'll leave it in God's hands. I'll attend.'

# CHAPTER TWENTY

## August 1961

Fuad now wished that he had not gone to the three day conference even though it had been one of the most fruitful and exciting experiences of his life and he had had face to face meetings with all the leading figures. Even though he had been involved in noisy and interesting discussions and had learned a great deal about the organization of pan-Arab conferences still he emerged from the proceedings with not only a bitter taste in his mouth but with bitterness in his heart. It had become clear that the differences between the ANM and the Ba'ath were much slighter than he had wished. The ANM was just as much a party as any other with the same internal conflicts and squabbling factions, conspiracies large and small. The collective leadership which the ANM boasted of existed only in the minds of its followers. At the end of the day it was 'The Doctor', George Habash, who took all the main decisions. The democratic spirit of which the Movement sang was nonexistent and everything happened not by election but by nomination. Every time that a member objected to some resolution he was told that the principle was 'Act first discuss afterwards'.

Throughout the conference Fuad was troubled as to whether the ANM was a Palestinian movement that included some other Arabs or an Arab movement that included some Palestinians? Despite his belief in the importance of the Palestinian cause he could not understand how the great majority in a pan-Arab movement should come from just one country. Majid refused to discuss the subject, considering that raising it would betray a tendency to regionalism.

It also became clear to Fuad that for all its clearly Nasserite impetus the ANM had its own priorities that sooner or later would clash with those of Gamal Abdul Nasser. If the ANM achieved power in harmony with Nasserism well and good but, if not, then power would be given priority over loyalty to Nasserism. Nobody actually said this but it was implied in the discussions.

What if our movement differed from Our Leader? Priority would be given to our movement just as priority went to the Ba'ath when its objectives differed from those of Gamal Abdul Nasser.

Another thing which astonished Fuad was how much was heard during the conference of Marxist-Leninism. 'According to Marxist analysis...' 'From a Leninist standpoint...' Majid justified this on the basis that there was in the ANM a small minority which borrowed its concepts from Marxist thought, but he added that it was an unimportant minority. But this minority imposed its terminology on the conference proceedings nonetheless. What about Islam? Marxist phraseology resounded throughout every session and Islam was not mentioned once. Fuad tried to link Arab nationalism with Islam but his attempts were received coolly or with violent hostility. 'This is not a conference for the Muslim Brotherhood.' What was the point of abandoning the Ba'ath for the ANM if he was just moving from one intellectual gaol to another?

A few hours before the conference broke up Majid told him that Dr George Habash wanted to have a private meeting with Fuad. It took place in the 'Operations Room', Habash's room at the Rabiya Hotel.

'Majid tells me you are about to leave for New York.'

'Yes, I am going to study Comparative Law at NYU.'

'I wish you every success. I hope you'll keep up your activities there. The Movement is always in need of new blood.'

Habash gave him a piece of paper. 'These are the members of the ANM in the States with names and addresses. As you can see there are hardly 100. They're scattered all over the country and up to now there has never been an ANM conference over there. We're relying on you to hold the first one,' he said, staring closely at Fuad. 'And of course you will be responsible for the Movement.' Without a word Fuad took the paper.

Responsible for the Movement in the States. And Majid was in charge for the Peninsula. Power. Actually Majid had already begun to act like a party boss and had begun to speak in the plural: 'in our state...'; 'in our programme...'; 'in our organization...'. Fuad felt deep anxiety: he had joined the ANM to use all his might to add impetus to Nasserism. But he hid his apprehension and returned to Bahrain with many sad questions in his mind.

As he had expected Fuad's father, after long hesitation, approved of his leaving for the States, but he was still puzzled. 'Why do you want to travel there? Haven't you got your degree?'

My dear father, how can I explain to you that the degree has nothing to do with real knowledge? You cannot know people unless you get immersed in them? You can't know cities unless you wander freely in their narrow streets? Can you believe, my dear sir, that after five years of study in Cairo I'm leaving with more questions than I came with? I've reached the age of 22 and I still find myself puzzled by economic questions. It is not, sir, justice that the good things of society should be kept by a small minority while the majority become professionals experienced in hunger, begging, thieving or prostitution. But then, father, it is no justice that I should transfer my wealth to be disposed of by party officials. Capitalism is not the answer, nor is Communism. You will tell me, sir, as did Abdul-Ra'ouf, that the solution is alms-giving, and I know that you are charitable. But how many of your wealthy friends are similar? You will say that alms should then be taken by force but who would have confidence in any government that did that? Where would the funds go after being taken? When you taught me to go with you to the mosque before I was six, and had me finish the Koran before I was ten, you did not warn me that I would, some day, face the problem of reconciling Islam with Arab nationalism. The theory of nationalism, wide-spread in the Arab world today, was developed by members of non-Muslim minorities. That is the truth. How can I explain to you that I am going to America to plunge into another sea of troubles and complications?

His father sighed. 'And Khalil has gone, too. He left the shop and began new work. Furnishing apartments and letting them. I ask you, Fuad, is this fit work for a man? Why did he leave home? Why did he go to live in one of his furnished apartments?'

Fuad thought his answer but did not verbalize it. Oh, my dear father! The world is changing with terrible speed. This little house in a remote area of the Fadil quarter is no longer a fit place to live for a new generation business-man. Khalil's work now requires him to give a party from time to time and how could he do that here?

Oh, my dear father! How can I explain to you, without hurting your feelings, that the Bahrain you know and love is no longer here. The wife now wants to live with her husband without her in-laws. And this kitchen, stained with smoke, is no longer fit for use in the age of steak and frozen chicken. And, father, there is not another man in Bahrain who has your means and yet lives without air-conditioning. Even your old friend Sheikh Salman who hates air-conditioners as much as you do has recently agreed to install them. My dear father, can you not see what is going on around you? Can't you hear? Oh, my dear father, you, with your smiling and amiable face, have not changed. You get up before dawn and pray in the mosque, then go on to have your coffee with Hajji Hassan and then go back home. You have your little rest and then have breakfast. You then go to the same shop as you always have, and your same old friends visit you there and you drink the same mint tea.

After that you go home for lunch, always the same lunch. Shilani bread and fish. Then you have your siesta, after which you say the Asr prayers on your way to the shop. There you have a visit from Uncle Abdullah and together you go to the mosque for the sunset prayer. On the way you call in on Hajji Mansour for coffee and then you go home. You have the same evening meal: nukhakh and dabl. Then you say the Isha prayers after which you listen to the BBC Arabic Service. Then you go to bed. It's thirty years, or maybe more, since you changed your daily routine. And you yourself have not changed. But in these years, father, many new things have happened to Bahrain. Women have begun to drive cars, sir. Sunnis have begun to marry Shias. In Bahrain, my dear father, there are now Ba'athist cells and cells of the ANM and if it had not been for the arrest of Yacoub there would even be Communist cells. And the Gymkhana Club has begun, father, to allow the admission of Bahrainis. And the BAPCO cinema has stopped requiring you be a member before being allowed in. And, father, your son Khalil goes from one girlfriend to the next. Ah, father! How can I explain to you that the world you see around you is fooling you when it says that nothing has changed. It puts on the familiar old mask when you pass by both morning and evening. But after you have heard the BBC and gone to bed the world reveals its new face, its true face. There is a roaring trade in beer in the homes of the Indians. And the youths of Bahrain gather together in their tight trousers and open neck shirts with their girlfriends at parties. You, father, are the prisoner of the old world, the prisoner of these cushions that I am embarrassed to have around in front of my friends and the prisoner of this low table that I have found it difficult to sit at. Did you know, father, that in the Na'im Hospital there are now four Bahraini doctors? Did you know that there is a big military base built by the British at Hamla? Did you know that this base has been a stimulus to the Bahrain economy and especially to merchants who are Nasserites? But don't be surprised, father: we shout slogans for Gamal Abdul Nasser by day and let out furnished apartments to the soldiers of Imperialism by night. As Qasim says, 'Business is business!' And you, father, are still sleeping on the roof and wake drenched in sweat or dew. You have never known the taste of steak and you've never seen the new jewels that have started to arrive from Italy: a ring in the form of a fish, a necklace like a snake, a watch that shows it works. It's better that way, father, better that you live your way and leave Bahrain to its destiny. It's better for you to stay securely in this old, safe house and to leave your youngest son to his fate. He may become a big shot in politics, or a famous novelist, or he may come back to let furnished apartments to the soldiers of Imperialism. Who knows, my dear father, what will happen to your son, who goes from one political party to another, and does not settle; who loves one woman after another and still is not happy? It's better for you, father, and sir, to do what my mother does. Consider me as Fuad-o who just goes from one school to a bigger school but still remains a schoolboy. It's better for you that Bahrain should remain as you knew it in the days of your youth.

The exam results came out with no great surprises. Nash'at and Fuad got grades of 'Very Good' while Qasim got 'Good'. Abdul-Ra'ouf got a grade of 'Excellent' as everyone had expected, but with the distinction of 'First Honours Grade'. Abdul-Karim and Yacoub would have to stay on an extra semester to finish the remaining subjects while Fuad and Qasim completed their travel arrangements, deciding to stop off in Cairo on their way to New York.

# CHAPTER TWENTY ONE

## September – October 1961

What a difference a short time makes ... Nash'at, now a senior official in the Council of State, met Qasim and Fuad at the foot of the aircraft steps. The office manager made all the necessary arrangements so that the airport procedures were over in minutes. And waiting at the Arrivals entrance were both Yacoub and Abdul-Karim: Abdul-Karim got into the famous little old car Ba'kooka with Fuad and Nash'at while Qasim and Yacoub got into the VW and the cortège set off. Fuad recalled the day he arrived in Cairo more than five years before and burst into laughter. Nash'at turned to him in surprise.

'I was just remembering my first day here. I was just a clumsy boy, I really was. I'd still be at the airport if God had not pressed into service for me first a porter who rescued me and then old Mahgoob the taxi-driver who thought Bahrain was in the Hejaz.'

Nash'at said. 'Maybe he was a Ba'athist or one of the ANM. Oh, and by the way, Majid is sorry he couldn't be here. He's on duty at the Hospital – he's one of the top doctors now.'

The friends gathered together in the main room of Apartment Freedom and as soon as Aisha had got over her screams of joy they settled down to exchanging news. Yacoub insisted he'd had no harassment since he returned to Cairo and that he was thinking of staying on for a higher degree. Fuad could see in Abdul-Karim's face a ruddy glow he had not seen before, a glow of happiness. He could also see something new about Nash'at's appearance but could not put his finger on what it was. Questions poured out between the friends and the Abdul-Karim turned to Nash'at. 'There's no need to put it off any more. Tell them what happened.'

'No, you tell them!' said Nash'at, clearly embarrassed.

'Oh, get on with it. Both of you tell,' yelled Qasim.

'OK,' said Yacoub, cutting in. 'I'll tell you. Abdul-Karim has married Farida and Hash'at is engaged to Iman.'

This announcement was followed by a stunned silence broken by Fuad. 'Iman, the actress?'

'Iman is my cousin on my mother's side. It's a long story,' said Nash'at.

Qasim turned to Abdul-Karim and said sharply. 'Sure, it's a surprise he's engaged to his cousin, but it's a nice surprise. But what about you? What's the story of your getting married?'

'It's a common-law marriage.'

'Oh, come on. We're not in the Law Faculty. Marriage is marriage. Why did you marry her?'

Fuad interrupted. 'Why don't we go and have lunch at the Kasr El Nil Casino and hear everything in detail?' At the familiar table close to the river Nash'at resumed.

'It's a story like a film plot: I knew Iman from the time we were children but we were separated when she was 6 and I was 10. She went abroad with her father who was working in the Egyptian Embassy in Washington and then with the World Bank. This summer we met again – the young girl had become a lovely young woman with all the qualities of the ideal wife. I fell in love at first sight and I think it was the same with her. Then things moved like lightning: we got engaged and we'll marry next year when she's finished her secondary schooling in Washington.'

Qasim smiled and said nothing but Nash'at knew what he was going through his mind. 'That's it then! No Swiss girls and no girls from Upper Egypt!'

'What about you?' Fuad asked Abdul-Karim. 'We want to know the secrets of the love that returned.'

'Destiny has made up to me and to her for everything,' smiled Abdul-Karim. 'Praise be to God. The poor girl suffered a lot more than I did. She got married to a beast disguised as a man. As soon as the honeymoon was over he started treating her like a concubine and beating her up. He wouldn't even give her housekeeping money. Her life became unbearable. She took refuge with her family and brought a case against him, and when the judge heard the details he ordered the married to be ended.'

'Isn't that what they call "khal" that we studied in the Sharia?' asked Fuad.

'Exactly. There was a divorce on the basis of a court order. Our friend recovered all he had paid out, the bride-price, the trousseau, everything. Even the bottles of perfume he'd bought her on honeymoon he insisted on getting those back, too. She had to buy new ones and give them to him.'

'Yes – well, I can see all that,' said Qasim. 'But how did you agree to going back to her? When we left Cairo you weren't even going to talk to her.'

Abdul-Karim looked over to Nash'at, who laughed and explained, 'I'm responsible for that. I brought her with me to Apartment Freedom and we gave Abdul-Karim a shock. As soon as he saw her he forgot everything and forgave everything.' Abdul-Karim nodded his head in agreement.

'Love came back just as it had been, in fact stronger. Just as if nothing had happened. We decided to waste no more time and so we had a common-law marriage with Nash'at and Yacoub as witnesses. And nothing will ever put us apart.'

Qasim could not overcome his curiosity. 'But how are you managing to live?'

'For the time being she's living with her family.'

'Yeah,' yelled Yacoub. 'She spends 99 per cent of her time in Apartment Freedom with us and 1 per cent of her time with her family.'

Abdul-Karim added. 'It's just until the formal wedding takes place. I don't know when that will be but the only thing that matters is that we are the two happiest people on earth.'

Qasim got up and embraced Abdul-Karim. 'The time for giving advice is over. A thousand congratulations, Abdul-Karim!'

Fuad also embraced him, asking. 'And what about children in the future?'

'Shia, of course! What else do you expect from the grandchildren of a Sheikh?'

It was after midnight when Fuad went back to his old room but he could not sleep. He thought of the courage of Abdul-Karim which no one had expected of him. He'd married Farida and that was that. People could like it or lump it. One thing was for sure, that was a truly heroic existentialist position to take. His thoughts then turned to Nash'at because his decision, too, was brave, brave to the point of madness. He was abandoning his life to link his destiny to that of a young woman he had not seen since she was a child. He was going to abandon his rowdy ways, adventures and liaisons, and live the rest of his days with an adolescent who had not finished secondary school. And Yacoub? Fuad knew from endless hours of discussion he had had with him that Yacoub had got over the ordeal of his solitary confinement and expulsion and had emerged stronger than before. Fuad was certain that Yacoub would never abandon his Marxist principles.

And what about you, Fuad? Are you the only one of the group who is a coward? Qasim had decided years before that he would work to achieve two objectives: money and girls. He took his decision, stuck to it, and proceeded on his way. And Majid had now become one of the leading figures in the ANM. But what about you, Fuad? You've failed in love and failed in politics. Paralysis in both heart and mind. You're neither a Ba'athist nor in the ANM. Neither a capitalist nor a socialist. Just going along with the Nasserites. And what will you do when you get to the States? Will you get to work on organizing the first ANM conference over there? Or will you get absorbed in writing a story with an American girl as heroine?

*Khalaf did not get a wink of sleep all night. Tomorrow he would be going into class, a teacher for the first time. The transition from being a university student to being a secondary school teacher without any preparation. No sooner had the Head of the Al-Ahram Private School for Boys seen his degree certificate in Arabic with a grade of 'Excellent' than he appointed him on the spot. Tomorrow he had a date with his students. The graduation class, the top class. He could imagine himself standing in front of a class of ruffians. Private school students were normally those who had failed in government schools and there would be bound to be a number of troublemakers. How would he conduct his first lesson? Khalaf realized from his long experience with schools that the first impression was the longest-lasting one. When students sense weakness in the teacher they exploit it and have the upper hand ever afterwards. And on the contrary when the teacher imposes respect in the first confrontation respect for him remains until the end of the year. If any student were to be allowed to laugh or sneer or make comments then the class would slip out of his control. But the biggest problem was the students' age: what would he do with some student who was as tall as he was? He could not smack or insult him. But determination was called for. Sending someone out of the class would be the least he could do.*

*Morning came and Khalaf gathered up his courage and strode into class with a serious expression. He opened his book on Eloquence and ordered the students to do likewise. He could hear a disruptive voice at the back of the class. He identified a very large student with a vacuous face. 'Yes, what is it?'*

*'I haven't got a book.'*

*'Why not?'*

*'Well, as a matter of fact, I haven't written one.'*

*The class exploded in laughter. Khalaf lost his temper, 'Outside. Go straight to the Head.'*

*The boy went quite happily to the door but before leaving the class he turned to Khalaf and cheekily asked, 'While I'm there can I get you anything from Papa?' The class once more exploded in laughter. Khalaf went red. 'What's all this about?'*

*A student in the front row answered. 'Well, sir, he is the Head's son!'*

Fuad cackled with laughter. 'So have you started teaching?'

'Yes,' was Abdul-Ra'ouf's reply. 'I gave my first lecture last week. As you know assistants like me only teach in the Discussion period.'

'And you had the Dean's son in your class?'

'The story was just an expression of how nervous I was about the experience. But I found the students very well behaved and responsive.'

'And what about Safa?'

'Her father gave his approval finally.'

'Congratulations! Is the marriage contract to be signed soon?'

'We are delaying it a while.'

'What for?'

Abdul-Ra'ouf replied in embarrassment, 'It's the problem of the bride-price.'

Fuad presented Mr Shareef with a Rolex watch and his new wife with a gold ring with two large pearls decorating it. He whispered, 'A little present from my father.'

Mr Shareef thanked him warmly. Fuad was astonished at the change in his appearance: Mr Shareef's white hair had disappeared totally through both dyeing and cutting; his face had softened and he had shed a good deal of weight. The new young wife was clearly pregnant.

'You have done us proud, Fuad, coming in the first ten. This is just the beginning. You'll finish up as a Minister.'

'We don't have Ministers in Bahrain, sir!' said Fuad, laughing. 'We only have heads of departments.'

'OK, so you'll be the head of a department.'

His wife cut in, 'Forget about government jobs. Open your own office and make some real money.'

Mr Shareef now surprised him again. 'Have you heard, my first wife plans to remarry. A woman of her age! An old wreck like her, getting married again, abandoning her children.' He seemed oblivious to the irony or hypocrisy of his remarks.

'May God bring prosperity to all!' was Fuad's reply.

Shaikh Muhammad Abu-Zahra rose to embrace Fuad. 'Congratulations, Fuad, my son! "Very Good" and then "Excellent" in Sharia. And how is Bahrain?'

'Still not three seas, sir!' said Fuad, anticipating the Shaikh's usual joke on Bahrain's name.

The Shaikh laughed and said, 'I heard you're leaving for America. Look out for the machinations of that criminal Schacht.'

Fuad did not know what was meant since the only Schacht he had ever heard of was Economy Minister to Hitler. Seeing he was puzzled the Shaikh continued. 'Schacht is an orientalist who is a real son of a bitch. He causes people to doubt the Sunna of the Prophet. He's spent his life teaching the Sunna with the sole object of raising doubts about it. He says that all the Hadiths of the Prophet are forgeries.'

'Did no one answer back?'

'Many did and I was one of them. But I don't know any foreign language. This is your assignment, now, Fuad. You must explain Islam to them over there, in language and with logic they understand.'

'I'll do my best, reverend sir.'

'Many are the suspicions aroused by the enemies of Islam but they are as insubstantial as the threads of a spider's web. They'll raise the subject of slavery: tell them it is now at an end. All religions dealt with it, Judaism and Christianity before Islam, but it was Islam which handled it with the greatest justice. They'll raise the subject of polygamy. Tell them that polygamy is better than having lots of lovers. Their own statistics prove that every husband in the West has one or more lovers. Don't attempt to apologize for anything in the Sharia. Through the grace of God, our Sharia is perfect and contains nothing we have to apologize for.'

'I understand, reverend sir.'

'And they'll raise the topic of physical punishments. They are interested in this in the West to the point of hysteria. Say to them, "Yes, in the Sharia, there are injunctions to flogging and cutting off hands." Tell them that cutting off one hand is better than having defective security in 1,000 houses. Tell them that flogging one person is better than having terror invade the hearts of 1,000 women.'

'I'll do my best, reverend sir.'

Shaikh Radwan invited Fuad and Abul-Ra'ouf back to his apartment after Friday prayers. As he was handing them tea he addressed Fuad. 'Congratulations. I heard from Abdul-Ra'ouf that you graduated with fantastic grades and you are going to America. Don't let your studies take up all your time. Set aside some time for spreading the call to God.'

'Shaikh Radwan, if you knew the sins I've committed against God.'

'No, my son. The Prophet (peace be upon him) has said "All my nation are protected except for those who proclaim aloud. These are people who do something at night but in the morning God has protected them. But they then say, 'Yesterday I did such – and such" Do not reveal God's protection of you, my son.'

'But if only you knew, O Shaikh ...' Fuad murmured.

'Youth can go astray,' said the Shaikh, 'but the door of repentance is open. I expect a lot of good from you. In the last few years you have not missed one Friday prayer, and I call upon God to give guidance to you and to me.'

As they left Fuad turned to Abdul-Ra'ouf. 'Shaikh Abu-Zahra wants me to explain Islam in America. And Shaikh Radwan wants me to give some time to the call to God. What's going on here? And Dr George Habash wants me to be the leader of the ANM over there.'

'They've all got you wrong.'

'What about you? What do you think?'

'What I think is that you won't listen to Shaikh Abu-Zahra or to George Habash, either. You'll concentrate on your writing.'

'You've got me wrong, too.'

Nash'at offered to pay Qasim his proportion of the office's capital in cash but Qasim refused.

'Keep it with you, for Yacoub to use. No one knows what will happen to him. I left the car with him and asked him to agree with you about it before leaving Cairo.'

'Don't worry about Yacoub. Or Abdul-Karim,' said Nash'at. 'As soon as Abdul-Karim graduates I'll fix him up with a job in the office. I don't think he can go back to Bahrain the way things are just now.'

'But how can he work here? Isn't that against the law?'

'Have you forgotten?' said Nash'at, laughing. 'The Council of State has some of the finest legal brains in Egypt. One phone call even from a junior official like me works miracles.'

'I don't know how to thank you, Nash'at!'

'There's no need for thanks, between us two!'

'Why did you choose this strange name, the "Victories" Office? Anyone who doesn't know would imagine it's a reference to the victories of Gamal Abdul Nasser.'

'Work it out for yourself!'

Fuad woke up to the sound of someone knocking and when he opened the door he found Abdul-Karim standing there with a copy of *Al-Ahram* in his hand 'What's up, Abdul-Karim? What time is it?'

'Nine thirty.'

'I don't have any lectures, why did you wake me?'

Abdul-Karim pointed to the huge advertisement that took up a quarter of a page for a concert to be given that night at the Opera for the benefit of the Artists' Union. Her name leaped out at him: Shahenaz Shakir. 'Is there any way to get a ticket?'

'I've got two, one for each of us, front row!'

'How did you manage that?'

'Just leave it to "The Victories Office".'

The various acts of the concert went by with Fuad in a fever of anticipation, unable to follow anything, and unheeding of Abdul-Karim's comments. There was one song after another, male singers and female singers, but he was miles away. Then the MC announced: 'That brilliant singing talent, Shahenaz Shakir.' It seemed to Fuad that his heart had stopped for two or three beats. As the curtain rose his eyes fell on the enchantress, dressed in a long pink dress, her blonde hair hanging quite loose, every part of her shining brilliantly, her smile, her eyes, her dress, and her jewels. She bowed to her applause and the orchestra struck up. And then... her eyes fell upon him, for the longest moment. She smiled and made a slight bow in his direction. She retraced her steps and had a word with the leader of the orchestra. The music stopped and then the orchestra started on another piece as the audience applauded again. Her voice came from the depths of time.

'Where did your heart go? I have not found it.
And I did not even have two days of his love.'

She repeated '... go?' twice, five times, ten times, in a different tone each time. The audience went wild. Fuad felt an iron grip of sorrow crushing his chest, reminding him of what had been and what never was.

When they went back to the apartment he went straight to his room. Abdul-Karim followed him. 'Are you all right? What's this tragic look? You should be rejoicing. She remembered you, laughed in your direction and sang your favourite song. What more do you want?'

'Did you see her jewellery?' Fuad spoke slowly. 'Did you see the diamond necklace on her neck? The diamond rings on her fingers? The diamond brace-let on her wrist? Do you have any idea what all that cost?'

'My father's not the jewel merchant. He's a man of religion. What's the problem? All the female artistes wear jewellery.'

'I had always been afraid of this. And what I'd been frightened of has actually happened.' He choked.

'I don't know what you're on about. Anyway I've had my fair share of catastrophes. Good night.'

Fuad yelled at the top of his voice in Majid's face, 'Why doesn't he move? What's he waiting for?'

'Don't talk about Gamal Abdul Nasser like that! Are you out of your mind?' yelled Majid.

'He's the one who's mad, not me! If the coup had happened in Alexandria would he have just looked on as he's doing now?'

'He's not just looking on. He's sent paratroopers and naval units.'

'Yes, then he ordered them back again. Why?'

'Do you want a war to start between Egypt and Syria?'

'I want to stamp out the secession movement. No one has the right to break up the union.'

'Union can't be achieved by force. Isn't that what we have always said?'

'The union didn't come about by force: it is the secession that is happening by force. Why doesn't Gamal Abdul Nasser answer violence with violence? Why doesn't he make a move?'

'I told you: don't talk about Gamal Abdul Nasser like that.'

'You know I love Gamal Abdul Nasser a thousand times more than I love you but I just can't understand his position now. He's put an end to the union. He's killed it.'

'Gamal Abdul Nasser's killed the union?'

'Yes. He just let a handful of officers destroy the greatest achievement of the Arabs.'

'If it had just been a handful of officers the thing would have been settled in minutes. But there is an international conspiracy against the union. An imperialist conspiracy with the Zionists and reactionaries and all the Arab elements with regional outlooks.'

'Excuse me, Majid. What I can see is military men emerging from their barracks in tanks to arrest that genius of a Field Marshal and occupy the radio station. If Gamal Abdul Nasser had hit back at them it would have been all over.'

'I don't know what's got into you, Fuad. Do you want to inflame hatred between one Arab people in Egypt and another in Syria? Do you want civil war?'

'A short civil war is better than a permanent secession. A brief battle is better than the death of the union.'

'Who told you the union is dead? The secession will be over in a matter of weeks. Our Movement will resist.'

'Our Movement, or rather your Movement, does not have tanks or aircraft. It only has rhetoric and pamphlets. Only iron can dent iron.'

'In Nasser's place what would you have done?'

'I'd have sent aircraft to knock out the military HQ, the radio station and all the strongpoints of the secessionists.'

'And do you think that all that would have gone on without any resistance?'

'I've already asked you: if the coup had happened in Alexandria would he not have crushed it by force?'

'The situation is different. It would have meant fighting between Syrians and Egyptians.'

'I can't accept that. Typical regionalist thinking. From the constitutional point of view this was a state of union and it is the constitutional right of the President, his duty, to crush any illegal uprising whether in this region or that.'

'You're talking just like a law student. It's not a matter of constitutional forms. It's a matter of the future of the Arab Nation. Massacre today will impede the return of union tomorrow.'

'Union has been murdered and is in the grave. From today onwards there will not be a union. Some officers have challenged Gamal Abdul Nasser and have shown he is impotent. There will be echoes of this in all parts of the Arab nation. This week the era of the unionists has ended and the era of the secessionist has begun.'

'Fuad! You really have gone out of your mind. What are you talking about? Why this despair? Look, this is just a temporary setback. In a few weeks unity will be restored. I'm prepared to put money on it.'

'Forget it – not within weeks nor within months. Or even years. Union is finished.'

'Calm down. Don't be so negative and worked up.'

'I am worked up but I know what I'm saying. I'm saying that 30 tanks defeated Gamal Abdul Nasser and showed him up to be a feeble pygmy to the masses that had thought he was a giant.'

'Don't talk about Gamal Abdul Nasser in this way . . .'

'OK, sorry. Long live Gamal Abdul Nasser.'

The sad features of Nasser looked out from the TV screen. His sombre tones indicated that he would not stand in the way of recognition of Syria and would not allow Arab weapons to shed Arab blood. He proclaimed that the UAR would keep its name and its flag. The sad features then disappeared, the republican national anthem was played and then Nagat Al-Saghira sang those lines of Kamil Shinawi:

'I heard him the way I always love to hear him,
With his voice he carries me away to higher regions
I saw him fighting the enemies in the heat of the battle
He overcame them and they did not take anything from him not even a
    finger
Our beloved! Our commander! Our leader! How wonderful he is!
And how magnificent his stand! God and the people are with him!!'

As he switched off the TV at the apartment Fuad muttered ' "Not even a finger" . . . Words! Words!'

The trip back to Cairo had been a tragedy from beginning to end. When he had left in the summer he had been one of the city's sons but when he came back in the autumn he was a visitor. There was a world of difference between the owner of a house and a guest in it no matter how warm the welcome. Everything had changed. The daily pattern had changed: he was no longer a student who had to get up early to attend lectures; Aisha now called him 'Mister Fuad', instead of 'See Fuad'; old Zakaria the concierge greeted him with exaggerated respect. Even the Faculty, though it had not changed externally, was completely different inside. Shaikh Abu-Zahra did not now talk to him the way he talked to students and the waiters now treated him like a member of the teaching staff. As he moved around the corridors Fuad felt like a spy who had been sent by hostile agencies to carry out surveillance. He was linked to the Faculty now by nothing but memories. A spy? No, just a tourist, inspecting the ruins. Here, in this lecture-hall he had sat with Suad. Over there in the cafeteria the gang used to meet every day. What is the difference between modern history and ancient history? The past is the past and the present is the present.

How the gang had changed. Nash'at was simply revolving in the orbit of an adolescent girl called Iman. Does marriage wipe us out and cancel out all that is exciting, rebellious and interesting in our personalities? Abdul-Karim? The union had crashed in ruins and he was just cackling away, like one stoned on hashish 'It's enough that I am at one with Farida.' Does the loved one become more dear to you than your homeland? Abdul-Ra'ouf had now become 'The Assistant Bey' and had started to wear a tie and give lectures in normal conversation. Majid had become transformed into a creature of the Movement who had lost the capacity even to get agitated. If the ANM had said, 'Strike at the secessionists!' Majid would have yelled, 'Strike at the secessionists!' But if the ANM had said, 'It is not right to use force!' he would have obeyed that order too. He had renounced the right to think, to criticize and to protest. And Yacoub? Well, he could not conceal his gloating at the death of the union. Bourgeois exploiters had risen in revolt against bourgeois exploiters. Stones were breaking other stones. Every one had changed except for Qasim, who was as steady as a rock. Money and girls were all that mattered. Kings were kings and postmen were postmen. The rich were rich and the poor poor. Everyone was after money and girls. Qasim's world was ship-shape and harmonious and worked on the basis of laws which never changed.

And what about you, See Fuad formerly and now become the lawyer Mr Fuad? Have you not changed? Have you not insulted Gamal Abdul Nasser? You have called him a dumb idol and a coward? The man for whom you were nearly expelled from secondary school. The man for whom you joined the ANM and for whom you came to hate that same ANM. He's now proclaiming that Arab weapons can not spill Arab blood. What does that mean, Mr President? You who opened the door of freedom! Or as some of his malicious fellow students in the Faculty would say 'You who opened the door of Sha'riyya' (referring in a pun to a quarter of old Cairo). Didn't Arab blood flow because of Arab weapons in Baghdad, Mosul, Amman and Beirut? Hasn't The Voice of the Arabs been calling every night for Arab blood to be spilled, the blood of Arab hirelings, traitors and reactionaries? What does that mean now? You abandon the Arab masses. And the union. I am the Nasserite youth, blindly devoted. The youngster who kissed you on the forehead and saw the cut on your chin from shaving. Who cheered and applauded you as you stood smiling in your open car in Cairo while the bombs were falling on the city. And now you are in retreat, abandoning the union. And you are content to keep just the name and the flag and the anthem. Damascus Radio has restored 'Peace be upon the defenders of the homeland' and has announced that the first Arab citizen has been freed from the obligation of the covenant of unity. It has also announced that the Ba'ath Party has welcomed the secession. And what about Suad? She's bound to be with Michel Aflaq now.

Suad, the blonde who was so committed. And the others! Shahenaz! The one who was in love only with her own future. The one whom you left the last time you saw her a poor student and whom, a few nights ago, you saw weighted with diamonds. The way of obedience is long, as Yacoub said. And Madiha! The young woman with Arpège! The brunette from the penthouse. And Laila!! The woman who was a puzzle in herself. The eternally renewed virgin. The mother of palm branches and fibres. Why don't you write their stories? Why not write a novel about Cairo?

Some day the time would come for writing but right now was the time for farewell. This city which clutched me to its bosom. The city that gave me a degree in Law with a grade of 'Very Good' – and I would have had a place of honour if it had not been for that teacher of French who would lead anyone astray! The city that gave me my first collection of short stories, or rather half a collection! The city that led me to my first night of love. Cairo, choking with its millions of people. This young man who left some part of his life on Bus No. 6 and in Tahrir Square in the revered Mugamma' and in Sa'eediyya. And a great deal in Apartment Freedom. This young man is saying farewell now. He opened his spirit and stored there as much as he can of Cairo: the faces, the smells, the cafés, the delicious Kushari and the bread rusks and the boiled eggs.... The moon is on the gate.... It is you alone who are my beloved.... The Ezbekiyya wall. The Island of Tea. Recite the Fatiha to the Sultan. Shoe shine, Your Excellency? 'Rose El-Yousuf'; 'Sabah Al-Khair'; *Al-Ahram*. The pickpockets. Will you remember this young man who will be taking all these things with him to New York? And when the skyscrapers crowd in upon him and the cowboys assault him he will stand up, challenging, chewing seeds and spitting them out, and yelling at the Yanks, 'Hey, you lot! What an evil lot! That's the truth!'

My Cairo! Cairo of the capitalists and socialists and sometimes of the Marxists. Cairo of the oppressors and the oppressed. The deprivers and the deprived. The rulers and the ruled. O Mother of the World. Will I ever see you again? And what if I should see you? Would we meet as strangers? ... I know the answer. I've become a stranger in fact, myself, after an absence of only four months. Written on my forehead at the airport in invisible ink was the word 'Tourist'. The word has remained. Welcome to His Excellency the

Tourist! Mr Fuad Bey Tarif, the lawyer. I'm just Fuad. Your old friend. The student. Students are students and tourists are tourists. But I'm not a tourist. I did not come to shout for Gamal Abdul Nasser by day and spend the night with the Girls, as so many of our Nasserite brethren do. I only came to say goodbye. To cast a last glance over my life here. To see Cairo, to see Apartment Freedom. May God have mercy on Freedom! Unity! Revenge! And Socialism too.

Qasim shook him. 'Fuad. Have you been asleep?'

Fuad looked out of the window at Cairo which is sinking below the horizon. Tears pour from his eyes.

'Fuad, why are you crying?'

Slowly Fuad pulled out from his pocket the piece of paper with the names of the ANM members in America and tore it up, putting the pieces in the ashtray.

'Fuad, what are you doing? Why are you crying?'

Fuad looks towards the city which has now disappeared completely and makes no response.